KIERKEGAARD'S CONCEPTS

TOME I: ABSOLUTE TO CHURCH

Kierkegaard Research: Sources, Reception and Resources
Volume 15, Tome I

Kierkegaard Research: Sources, Reception and Resources
is a publication of the Søren Kierkegaard Research Centre

Kierkegaard's Concepts
Tome I: Absolute to Church

Edited by
STEVEN M. EMMANUEL, WILLIAM McDONALD
AND JON STEWART

ASHGATE

Published by
Ashgate Publishing Limited
Wey Court East
Union Road
Farnham
Surrey, GU9 7PT
England

Ashgate Publishing Company
110 Cherry Street
Suite 3-1
Burlington, VT 05401-3818
USA

www.ashgate.com

British Library Cataloguing in Publication Data
A catalogue record for this book is available from the British Library

The Library of Congress has cataloged the printed edition as follows:
Library of Congress Control Number: 2013943923

ISBN 9781472417497 (hbk)

Cover design by Katalin Nun

MIX
Paper from
responsible sources
FSC
www.fsc.org   FSC® C013985

Printed in the United Kingdom by Henry Ling Limited, at the Dorset Press, Dorchester, DT1 1HD

Contents

List of Contributors

Christopher B. Barnett, Villanova University, Department of Theology and Religious Studies, Saint Augustine Center 203, 800 Lancaster Avenue, Villanova, PA 19085, USA.

Lee C. Barrett, Lancaster Theological Seminary, 555 W. James St., Lancaster, PA 17603, USA.

Sara Carvalhais de Oliveira, Unidade I&D Linguagem, Interpretação e Filosofia, Universidade de Coimbra, Faculdade de Letras, Praça da Porta Férrea, 3004-530 Coimbra, Portugal.

David Coe, Concordia Seminary, 801 Seminary Place, St. Louis, MO 63105, USA.

Claudine Davidshofer, Emory University, Philosophy Department, 516 South Kilgo Circle, Atlanta, GA 30322, USA.

Steven M. Emmanuel, Department of Philosophy, Virginia Wesleyan College, Norfolk, VA 23502, USA.

Peter Fenves, 2-375 Kresge Hall, Department of German, Northwestern University, Evanston, IL 60208, USA.

Henrike Fürstenberg, Universität Kiel, Institut für Skandinavistik, Frisistik und Allgemeine Sprachwissenschaft (ISFAS), Christian-Albrecht-Platz 4, 24098 Kiel, Germany.

Diego Giordano, Dipartimento di Scienze Economico-Quantitative e Filosofico-Educative, Università di Chieti, Campus Universitario, Via Pescara, 66013 Chieti scalo, Italy.

Nathaniel Kramer, Brigham Young University, Department of Humanities, Classics, Comparative Literature, 3008 JFSB, Provo, UT 84602, USA.

Esben Lindemann, Professionshøjskolen UCC, Pædagoguddannelsen Frøbel, Grundtvigsvej 11, 1864 Frederiksberg C, Denmark.

William McDonald, School of Humanities, University of New England, Armidale, NSW, 2351, Australia.

J.D. Mininger, Department of Social and Political Theory, Faculty of Political Science and Diplomacy, Vytautas Magnus University, Gedimino 44, Kaunas, 44211, Lithuania.

Shannon M. Nason, Department of Philosophy, University Hall, Suite 3600, Loyola Marymount University, One LMU Drive, Los Angeles, CA 90045, USA.

Guadalupe Pardi, Universidad de Buenos Aires, Facultad de Filosofiá y Letras, Puán 480, 1406 Ciudad de Buenos Aires, Argentina.

Robert B. Puchniak, St Paul's High School, 2200 Grant Ave, Winnipeg, Manitoba, R3P 0P8, Canada.

Leo Stan, Department of Humanities, York University, 262 Vanier College, 4700 Keele St., Toronto ON, M3J 1P3, Canada.

Curtis L. Thompson, Thiel College, 75 College Avenue, Greenville, PA 16125, USA.

Gerhard Thonhauser, Institut für Philosophie, Universität Wien, Universitätsstraße 7, 1010 Vienna, Austria.

J. Michael Tilley, Hong Kierkegaard Library, St. Olaf College, 1510 St. Olaf Ave., Northfield, MN 55056, USA.

Sean Anthony Turchin, c/o Søren Kierkegaard Research Centre, University of Copenhagen, Farvergade 27 D, 1463 Copenhagen K, Denmark.

Joseph Westfall, Department of Social Sciences, University of Houston-Downtown, One Main Street, Houston, TX 77002, USA.

Jacobo Zabalo, Universidad Pompeu Fabra, Ramón Trías Fargas, 25-27, 08005, Barcelona, Spain.

Preface

Søren Kierkegaard knew that the religious relationship calls the human being into a twofold process involving language. On the one hand, human beings are called to name and describe in language the reality being experienced; yet, on the other hand, they are called to negate the naming and the discursive, linguistic descriptions because such naming and descriptions always fall short of giving proper expression to the reality being named. Kierkegaard's potency as a religious and philosophical thinker resided in his singular capacity for carrying out both sides of this calling. He could engage in naming with the best of them, but he was also unrelenting in his engagement in the activity of negating. A rationality of the deepest sort is at play more obviously in naming but also less obviously in negating, and Kierkegaard's dialectical gifts served him well in the two arenas.

One element of language that plays an important role in both naming and negating is the concept. Some concepts come to be very important for a thinker because they are terms that express in a word a whole set of claims being affirmed. To gain an understanding of these central concepts can facilitate the inquirer's grasping the viewpoint of the thinker employing them. This surely is the case with Kierkegaard: learning the meaning of his central concepts is the key into his world of thought.

Kierkegaard was not an academic philosopher, and he was critical of and ironically mocked the convoluted, technical language of, for example, the German Idealists. He rejected the use of neologisms and esoteric terms. By contrast, he drew his vocabulary from everyday language, which he then used in his own special context with his own special shades of meaning. Famous Kierkegaardian terms such as "the moment" or "repetition" can be heard in daily speech, but in his conceptual universe they are invested with a rich meaning that must be established, often painstakingly, by the reader.

The present volume offers students and scholars a comprehensive survey of key concepts and categories that inform Kierkegaard's writings. Each article is a substantial, original piece of scholarship, which aims to give a thorough conceptual analysis of relevant terms across Kierkegaard's *corpus*. Concepts have been selected on the basis of their importance for Kierkegaard's contributions to philosophy, theology, the social sciences, literature, and aesthetics. They extend from those most frequently discussed in the secondary literature to those that are often overlooked. Many have been included for the sake of limning a sphere of inquiry in Kierkegaard's conceptual world, in the way that Judaism, Mohammedanism, Catholicism, Protestantism, and paganism do for Kierkegaard's typology of religion. Others have been included because they are central to Kierkegaard's project as an author (for example, authority, indirect communication, and life-view) or because they are pivotal to understanding Kierkegaard's engagement with his contemporaries (for example, Romanticism, aesthetics, irony, and *Bildungsroman*). Yet others have been included because they inform Kierkegaard's philosophical, moral, and religious psychology; these include a wide range of familiar Kierkegaardian concepts, such as anxiety, despair, guilt, faith, and hope, as well as many lesser known themes, such as care, courage, defiance, patience, and pride. Often concepts are fully intelligible only when they stand in contrasting pairs, such as objectivity/subjectivity and immanence/transcendence, while others form complementary sets, such as time/temporality/eternity.

Authors have been instructed to give the etymology and lexical meaning of each concept, to identify their distribution and concentration in Kierkegaard's *corpus*, to describe Kierkegaard's idiosyncratic usage, to explicate the development of the concept across the pseudonymous, signed, published, and unpublished writings. The articles also show how each key term functions in the wider context of his thought. References to secondary literature have been kept to a minimum, in favor of focusing on an analysis of the concepts themselves. Accounts of the sources of the concept in the work of other authors have also been minimized since that is the focus of the "Sources" section of the present series.

The richness and complexity of Kierkegaard's concepts has made it necessary to enlist the help of a large number of scholars from different disciplines and research traditions. *Kierkegaard's Concepts* assigns specific concepts to specific authors, who are especially qualified for the relevant conceptual field. However, the volume is not artificially constrained by assigning the concepts to a specific field or discipline ahead of time. In this way the concepts can be illuminated from a philosophical, theological, psychological, or literary point of view as the material itself dictates, with no prior disciplinary constraints or prejudices.

While the first part of the present series is dedicated to source-work research, and the second to the history of reception, the present volume from the third part of the series introduces a new methodology: conceptual analysis. This typically involves breaking down the target concept into its constituent parts and then rationally reconstructing the whole in order to highlight its sense. It also typically involves showing how the constituent elements of the concept relate to other concepts in Kierkegaard's writings. To facilitate the reader's apprehension of conceptual constellations, each article ends with a list of cross-referenced terms.

Kierkegaard's Concepts fills a gap in the existing resources in the field of Kierkegaard studies. It expands on the project begun by Niels Thulstrup and Marie Mikulová Thulstrup in some of the volumes in the series *Bibliotheca Kierkegaardiana*.[1] It also complements Julia Watkin's *Historical Dictionary of Kierkegaard's Philosophy*, Gregor Malantschuk's *Nøglebegreber i Søren Kierkegaards tænkning*, and Frederick

---

[1]   *Bibliotheca Kierkegaardiana*, vols. 1–16, ed. by Niels Thulstrup and Marie Mikulová Thulstrup, Copenhagen: C.A. Reitzel 1978–88. This series contains several volumes devoted to conceptual studies: vol. 3, *Concepts and Alternatives in Kierkegaard* (1980); vol. 5, *Theological Concepts in Kierkegaard* (1980); and vol. 16, *Some of Kierkegaard's Main Categories* (1988).

Sontag's *A Kierkegaard Handbook*.[2] *Kierkegaard's Concepts* analyzes a much more extensive range of concepts than these works. It also draws on a wider international pool of scholars. It is neutral with respect to the question of what Kierkegaard (as opposed to his pseudonyms) actually thought, and it reveals the astonishing consistency in the way that many key terms, concepts and categories are deployed across the pseudonymous and non-pseudonymous works.

Kierkegaard's Concepts complements the other sections of the present series both conceptually and methodologically. It thereby contributes to the aim of *Kierkegaard Research: Sources, Reception and Resources* to cover systematically the different areas and methodologies represented in Kierkegaard studies today. It provides ready access to compendious information on a wide range of concepts. It is neither a dictionary nor a thematically limited anthology of articles, but a substantial body of scholarship, which, it is hoped, will constitute the first reference point for anybody seeking lucid analyses of the key terms in Kierkegaard's authorship.

Steven M. Emmanuel, William McDonald, and Jon Stewart

---

[2]   Julia Watkin, *Historical Dictionary of Kierkegaard's Philosophy*, Lanham and London: Scarecrow Press 2000. Gregor Malantschuk, *Nøglebegreber i Søren Kierkegaards tænkning*, ed. by Grethe Kjær and Paul Müller, Copenhagen: C.A. Reitzel 1993. Frederick Sontag, *A Kierkegaard Handbook*, Atlanta: John Knox Press 1979.

Acknowledgments

The present volume represents the collaborative work of a large group of international Kierkegaard scholars. We would like to gratefully acknowledge the help of María J. Binetti, Heiko Schulz, and Curtis L. Thompson for their useful suggestions and criticisms concerning the Preface. We are grateful to Finn Gredal Jensen and Philip Hillyer for doing the proof-reading for this volume. We are especially thankful to Finn for his generous help with the etymologies and the Greek words and phrases that appear here. We greatly appreciate the efforts of Richard Purkarthofer who originally suggested a volume dedicated to Kierkegaard's concepts in this series and developed the general idea and conception behind it. Finally, we would also like to acknowledge the pioneering work and mentoring spirit of Julia Watkin, which inspired some of the entries in this work.

List of Abbreviations

BA   *The Book on Adler*, trans. by Howard V. Hong and Edna H. Hong, Princeton: Princeton University Press 1998.

C   *The Crisis and a Crisis in the Life of an Actress*, trans. by Howard V. Hong and Edna H. Hong, Princeton: Princeton University Press 1997.

CA   *The Concept of Anxiety*, trans. by Reidar Thomte in collaboration with Albert B. Anderson, Princeton: Princeton University Press 1980.

CD   *Christian Discourses*, trans. by Howard V. Hong and Edna H. Hong, Princeton: Princeton University Press 1997.

CI   *The Concept of Irony*, trans. by Howard V. Hong and Edna H. Hong, Princeton: Princeton University Press 1989.

CIC   *The Concept of Irony*, trans. with an Introduction and Notes by Lee M. Capel, London: Collins 1966.

COR   *The Corsair Affair; Articles Related to the Writings*, trans. by Howard V. Hong and Edna H. Hong, Princeton: Princeton University Press 1982.

CUP1   *Concluding Unscientific Postscript*, vol. 1, trans. by Howard V. Hong and Edna H. Hong, Princeton: Princeton University Press 1982.

CUP2   *Concluding Unscientific Postscript*, vol. 2, trans. by Howard V. Hong and Edna H. Hong, Princeton: Princeton University Press 1982.

CUPH   *Concluding Unscientific Postscript*, trans. by Alastair Hannay, Cambridge and New York: Cambridge University Press 2009.

EO1   *Either/Or*, Part I, trans. by Howard V. Hong and Edna H. Hong, Princeton: Princeton University Press 1987.

EO2   *Either/Or*, Part II, trans. by Howard V. Hong and Edna H. Hong, Princeton: Princeton University Press 1987.

EOP   *Either/Or*, trans. by Alastair Hannay, Harmondsworth: Penguin Books 1992.

EPW   *Early Polemical Writings*, among others: *From the Papers of One Still Living*; *Articles from Student Days*; *The Battle Between the Old and the New Soap-Cellars*, trans. by Julia Watkin, Princeton: Princeton University Press 1990.

EUD   *Eighteen Upbuilding Discourses*, trans. by Howard V. Hong and Edna H. Hong, Princeton: Princeton University Press 1990.

FSE   *For Self-Examination*, trans. by Howard V. Hong and Edna H. Hong, Princeton: Princeton University Press 1990.

FT   *Fear and Trembling*, trans. by Howard V. Hong and Edna H. Hong, Princeton: Princeton University Press 1983.

FTP   *Fear and Trembling*, trans. by Alastair Hannay, Harmondsworth: Penguin Books 1985.

JC   *Johannes Climacus, or De omnibus dubitandum est*, trans. by Howard V. Hong and Edna H. Hong, Princeton: Princeton University Press 1985.

JFY   *Judge for Yourself!*, trans. by Howard V. Hong and Edna H. Hong, Princeton: Princeton University Press 1990.

JP   *Søren Kierkegaard's Journals and Papers*, vols. 1–6, ed. and trans. by Howard V. Hong and Edna H. Hong, assisted by Gregor Malantschuk (vol. 7, Index and Composite Collation), Bloomington and London: Indiana University Press 1967–78.

KAC   *Kierkegaard's Attack upon "Christendom," 1854–1855*, trans. by Walter Lowrie, Princeton: Princeton University Press 1944.

KJN   *Kierkegaard's Journals and Notebooks*, vols. 1–11, ed. by Niels Jørgen Cappelørn, Alastair Hannay, David Kangas, Bruce H. Kirmmse, George Pattison, Vanessa Rumble, and K. Brian Söderquist, Princeton and Oxford: Princeton University Press 2007ff.

LD   *Letters and Documents*, trans. by Henrik Rosenmeier, Princeton: Princeton University Press 1978.

LR   *A Literary Review*, trans. by Alastair Hannay, Harmondsworth: Penguin Books 2001.

M   *The Moment and Late Writings*, trans. by Howard V. Hong and Edna H. Hong, Princeton: Princeton University Press 1998.

P   *Prefaces / Writing Sampler*, trans. by Todd W. Nichol, Princeton: Princeton University Press 1997.

PC   *Practice in Christianity*, trans. by Howard V. Hong and Edna H. Hong, Princeton: Princeton University Press 1991.

PF   *Philosophical Fragments*, trans. by Howard V. Hong and Edna H. Hong, Princeton: Princeton University Press 1985.

PJ   *Papers and Journals: A Selection*, trans. by Alastair Hannay, Harmonds-
          worth: Penguin Books 1996.

PLR   *Prefaces: Light Reading for Certain Classes as the Occasion May Require*,
          trans. by William McDonald, Tallahassee: Florida State University Press
          1989.

PLS   *Concluding Unscientific Postscript*, trans. by David F. Swenson and Walter
          Lowrie, Princeton: Princeton University Press 1941.

PV   *The Point of View* including *On My Work as an Author*, *The Point of View
          for My Work as an Author*, and *Armed Neutrality*, trans. by Howard V.
          Hong and Edna H. Hong, Princeton: Princeton University Press 1998.

PVL   *The Point of View for My Work as an Author* including *On My Work as an
          Author*, trans. by Walter Lowrie, New York and London: Oxford University
          Press 1939.

R   *Repetition*, trans. by Howard V. Hong and Edna H. Hong, Princeton:
          Princeton University Press 1983.

SBL   *Notes of Schelling's Berlin Lectures*, trans. by Howard V. Hong and Edna
          H. Hong, Princeton: Princeton University Press 1989.

SLW   *Stages on Life's Way*, trans. by Howard V. Hong and Edna H. Hong,
          Princeton: Princeton University Press 1988.

SUD   *The Sickness unto Death*, trans. by Howard V. Hong and Edna H. Hong,
          Princeton: Princeton University Press 1980.

SUDP   *The Sickness unto Death*, trans. by Alastair Hannay, London and New York:
          Penguin Books 1989.

TA   *Two Ages: The Age of Revolution and the Present Age. A Literary Review*,
          trans. by Howard V. Hong and Edna H. Hong, Princeton: Princeton
          University Press 1978.

TD   *Three Discourses on Imagined Occasions*, trans. by Howard V. Hong and
          Edna H. Hong, Princeton: Princeton University Press 1993.

UD   *Upbuilding Discourses in Various Spirits*, trans. by Howard V. Hong and
          Edna H. Hong, Princeton: Princeton University Press 1993.

WA   *Without Authority* including *The Lily in the Field and the Bird of the Air,
          Two Ethical-Religious Essays, Three Discourses at the Communion on
          Fridays, An Upbuilding Discourse, Two Discourses at the Communion*

on Fridays, trans. by Howard V. Hong and Edna H. Hong, Princeton: Princeton University Press 1997.

WL   *Works of Love*, trans. by Howard V. Hong and Edna H. Hong, Princeton: Princeton University Press 1995.

WS   *Writing Sampler*, trans. by Todd W. Nichol, Princeton: Princeton University Press 1997.

Absolute

Steven M. Emmanuel

Absolute (*det Absolute*—noun; *absolut*—adjective)

The Latin term *absolutus* is the past participle of *absolvere* (to loosen or detach from, to absolve or acquit), signifying of a thing that it is perfect, self-contained, unconditioned, or complete in itself.[1] The term does not appear in Christian Molbech's 1833 Danish lexicon, but it was already well established in the philosophical vocabulary of the modern period. Immanuel Kant, for example, defined the absolute as that which is valid in all respects and without limitation, while Fichte, Schelling, and Hegel used the term substantively (*das Absolute*) to refer to the ultimate, unconditioned reality.

Throughout the authorship, Kierkegaard and his pseudonyms frequently use the term *absolut* adjectivally and adverbially for emphasis, as in the expressions "absolute validity" (*absolut Gyldighed*) and "absolutely adequate" (*absolut adæquat*). However, the term takes on added significance when it is used to modify other key terms for the purpose of drawing important conceptual distinctions, as in the "absolute difference [*absolut Forskjellighed*] between God and man." In some instances, an entirely new concept is formed in this way, as is the case with "the absolute paradox" (*det absolute Paradox*). The term is also used substantively (*det Absolute*) in various contexts, often as an expression for Christianity or as a way of highlighting the particular difficulties of being a Christian. In this context, "absolute" generally refers to the unconditional quality of Christian faith. The life of the believer must not only express that there is an absolute, but the believer must will to be related to it absolutely.

In *The Concept of Irony*, Kierkegaard observes that the distinguishing mark of the ironist is his total disregard for the absolute: "The ironist, however, is obviously very casual even with the idea; he is completely free under it, for the absolute to him is nothing."[2] Later he notes that Socrates appears to represent an advance, in so far as he "continually let being-in-and-for-itself become visible." However, because he "had being-in-and-for-itself only as the infinitely abstract, he had the absolute in the form of nothing. By way of the absolute, reality became nothing, but in turn the absolute was nothing."[3]

---

[1]   *Ordbog over det danske Sprog*, vols. 1–28, published by the Society for Danish Language and Literature, Copenhagen: Gyldendal 1918–56, vol. 1, columns 90–1.
[2]   *SKS* 1, 196 / *CI*, 145–6.
[3]   *SKS* 1, 277 / *CI*, 236.

Judge William takes issue with the Hegelian understanding of the absolute in relation to ethical choice. Speculatively viewed, "my thinking is an element in the absolute, and therein lies the necessity of my thinking, therein lies the necessity with which I think it."[4] The absolute is not merely a totality of which the individual is a part. Rather, the individual stands before the absolute and must make a conscious ethical decision to be related to it: "It is otherwise with the good. The good is because I will it, and otherwise it is not at all."[5] This point is elaborated further in the discussion of the absolute difference between good and evil, where Judge William argues that to be an ethical individual requires an absolutely decisive personal commitment. As he says, "only when I have absolutely chosen myself have I posited an absolute difference [*en absolut Differents*]: namely, the difference between good and evil."[6]

In *Fear and Trembling*, Johannes de silentio observes that the single individual in faith "stands in an absolute relation to the absolute."[7] Reflecting on Luke 14:26, which is presented here as a biblical teaching on absolute versus relative ends, de silentio explains how Abraham reconciles his absolute duty (*absolute Pligt*) to God with his duties as a father: "The absolute duty can lead one to do what ethics would forbid, but it can never lead the knight of faith to stop loving."[8] Abraham's silence reflects his understanding of the paradoxical nature of his situation, namely: that his dilemma is not due to his "wanting to place himself as the single individual in an absolute relation to the *universal* but to his having been placed as the single individual in an absolute relation to the *absolute*."[9] The concept of the absolute functions in this context to distinguish between the moral law, understood as the universal, and the higher law that God represents.

A central concept in Johannes Climacus' writings is the absolute difference (*den absolute Forskjellighed*) between God and human beings: "if a human being is to come truly to know something about the unknown (the god), he must first come to know that it is different from him, absolutely different from him."[10] This difference is identified as sin: "What, then, is the difference? Indeed, what else but sin, since the difference, the absolute difference, must have been caused by the individual himself."[11] This discussion is preliminary to the formal definition of the absolute paradox (*det absolute Paradox*). For though the god-man is absolutely different from us, he reveals himself in a form that is nevertheless indistinguishable from other human beings: "Thus the paradox becomes even more terrible, or the same paradox has the duplexity by which it manifests itself as the absolute—negatively, by bringing into prominence the absolute difference of sin and, positively, by wanting to annul this absolute difference in the absolute equality."[12]

---

4   *SKS* 2, 214 / *EO2*, 224.
5   Ibid.
6   Ibid.
7   *SKS* 4, 150 / *FT*, 56.
8   *SKS* 4, 165 / *FT*, 74.
9   *SKS* 4, 183 / *FT*, 93.
10   *SKS* 4, 251 / *PF*, 46.
11   *SKS* 4, 251 / *PF*, 47.
12   *SKS* 4, 252 / *PF*, 47.

In the *Concluding Unscientific Postscript*, Climacus again makes use of the absolute paradox and related concepts in an extended polemic against Hegelian philosophy. The absolute cannot be mediated in thought: "If Christianity is the opposite of speculation, then it is also the opposite of mediation, since mediation is speculation's idea….But what is the opposite of mediation? It is the absolute paradox."[13] This opposition is further reinforced by a series of observations that stress the unique and unconditional quality of Christian faith. Climacus argues that the absolute telos (*det absolute* τέλος) of the existing individual is an eternal happiness,[14] which he then identifies as the absolute good (*den absolute Gode*). To choose this good requires that an absolute decision (*en absolut Afgjørelse*) be made. This cannot be done speculatively since mediation "is not actually aware of any relation to an absolute τέλος, because mediation exhausts itself in the relative."[15]

The task of faith is complicated, however, by the fact that the existing individual must be related to the absolute τέλος in time. The believer must therefore reconcile all worldly pursuits with the absolute and unconditional demands of faith. The believer's task is "to relate himself simultaneously to his absolute τέλος and to the relative—not by mediating them but by relating himself absolutely to his absolute τέλος and relatively to the relative."[16]

William Afham, in "In Vino Veritas," recounts Constantin Constantius' use of the concept of the absolute to draw a fundamental distinction between the sexes: "She is properly construed only under the category of jest. It is the man's function to be absolute, to act absolutely, to express the absolute; the woman consists in the relational. Between two such different entities no real interaction can take place."[17]

In the first of two essays published under the title "Two Ethical-Religious Essays," the pseudonym H.H. considers whether or not a person has the right to allow himself to be martyred for the truth. The answer to this question turns on a correct understanding of how human beings relate to each other with respect to the truth of Christianity.[18] The author contends that martyrdom is permissible only in the event that the individual stands in an absolute relation to the truth with respect to others. This must be the case, since to allow oneself to be put to death for the truth means that others must assume the guilt of putting one to death. There is no doubt that Christ could do this, since "he was *the Truth*."[19] The difference between Christ and human beings is thus the absolute difference between truth and untruth. This difference not only justifies Christ's sacrifice (which, technically speaking, is not an act of martyrdom but of atonement), but it also justifies the sacrifices of the apostles who became martyrs of the early church. For in that context, the martyrs were bearing witness to the truth of Christianity before non-Christians. Within Christianity, however, there can be only relative differences among individual

---

13   *SKS* 7, 345 / *CUP1*, 379.
14   *SKS* 7, 366 / *CUP1*, 402.
15   *SKS* 7, 370 / *CUP1*, 407.
16   Ibid.
17   *SKS* 6, 50 / *SLW*, 48.
18   *SKS* 11, 87 / *WA*, 83.
19   *SKS* 11, 77 / *WA*, 73.

human beings, and hence "no individual Christian dares to think he is in absolute possession of the truth: ergo, does not dare to let others become guilty by putting him to death for the truth."[20]

As humanity grows increasingly apathetic and the absolute "goes more and more out of use," it might seem that the need for renewed spiritual awakening would justify the appearance of a martyr. Indeed, the author notes that there is an "*absolute* difference" between this manifest lack of spirit in Christendom and authentic religious zeal.[21] However, the phrase "*absolute* difference" is clearly used here in an attenuated sense, since the author distinguishes this from the absolute difference that separates Christianity from paganism. The act of self-sacrifice can be justified only by the need to introduce the truth where it does not already exist.

In *Practice in Christianity*, Anti-Climacus uses "the absolute" as an expression for Christianity and, more specifically, for the person of Christ:

> Christianity came into the world as the absolute, not, humanly speaking, for comfort; on the contrary, it continually speaks about how the Christian must suffer or about how a person in order to become and remain a Christian must endure sufferings that he consequently can avoid simply by refraining from becoming a Christian.[22]

Being the absolute, there is no way to be related to Christ except in the present moment: "In relation to the absolute, there is only one time, the present; for the person who is not contemporary with the absolute, it does not exist at all. And since Christ is the absolute it is easy to see that in relation to him there is only one situation, the situation of contemporaneity…for who he is is revealed only to faith."[23]

Finally, a rare but noteworthy form of our term appears in the expression *status absolutus*. The expression derives from a convention in Hebrew grammar governing the genitive construction. In the phrase "the identity of the author," for example, "the author" occupies the *status absolutus* position, while "the identity" is in *status constructus*. In Hebrew, the term in *status absolutus* is always the normal form of the noun, while the term in *status constructus* must undergo a change to reflect the possessive construction. In *Philosophical Fragments*, Climacus invokes this grammatical concept to reinforce the idea that every individual stands in the same position with respect to the absolute fact of the Incarnation. This fact, though not itself a *casus*, is "declinable in all the *casibus* of life" and remains continually the same.[24] As the object of faith, the absolute fact of the god's historical existence is the *status absolutus* with respect to all people at all times; and it functions as the necessary condition for the spiritual transformation (conversion) of every individual who seeks to be related to it.

See also Authority; Decision/Resolve; Faith; God; Paradox; Qualitative Difference; Revelation; Teleological Suspension of the Ethical; Truth.

---

[20]   *SKS* 11, 92 / *WA*, 88.
[21]   *SKS* 11, 88–9 / *WA*, 84–5.
[22]   *SKS* 12, 75 / *PC*, 63.
[23]   Ibid.
[24]   *SKS* 4, 297 / *PF*, 262.

Absurd

Sean Anthony Turchin

Absurd (*det Absurde*—noun; *absurd*—adjective)

From the Latin, *absurdus*, its lexical meaning in Danish is that which is unreasonable or contrary to the senses.[1] The concept *absurd* occurs most frequently in the *Concluding Unscientific Postscript to Philosophical Fragments*, *Philosophical Fragments*, and *Fear and Trembling*. After this, it is seen a couple of times in *The Sickness unto Death* and also throughout the journals and papers. That which is designated absurd is beyond human comprehension.[2] But more than this, the concept of the absurd expresses the degree to which human understanding is offended when presented with something it cannot possibly grasp.[3]

Being unable to comprehend something does not necessarily imply that it is absurd.[4] Rather, the absurd is something that boggles comprehension and offends our understanding. It is closely related to the notion of paradox. In the three works where the absurd is predominantly found, there also one will find human understanding confronted with a paradox.[5] As will be noted later when distinguishing the difference in nuance in the meaning of the absurd in *Fear and Trembling* and the *Postscript*, to be characterized as absurd depends on the level of the paradox. Nevertheless, the category of the absurd in the hands of Kierkegaard's pseudonyms, Johannes de silentio and Johannes Climacus, manifests a sense of that which is beyond the capacity of reason to comprehend. As such, the offense to reason occasioned by the absurd can only be appeased by faith.

The category of the absurd becomes decisive when one seeks to distinguish the act of faith from ethical judgment. To highlight this distinction de silentio focuses on the Old Testament patriarch, Abraham, who is lauded as the paradigm of faith in Judaism, Christianity and Islam. The crucial test of Abraham's faith occurs when God commands him to sacrifice his son Isaac, a command whose execution entails the violation of normal ethical duties. But we know how the story goes: as Abraham raised his knife to kill his son, God stopped him and commended him for his faith.[6] Thus we praise Abraham as an example of one who exercised complete obedience to

---

[1] *Ordbog over det danske Sprog*, vols. 1–28, published by the Society for Danish Language and Literature, Copenhagen: Gyldendal 1918–56, vol. 1, column 1919.
[2] *SKS* 4, 128 / *FT*, 33.
[3] *SKS* 4, 129 / *FT*, 33.
[4] *SKS* 23, 23, NB15:25 / *JP* 1, 7.
[5] Ibid.
[6] Genesis 22:11–12.

God. But Abraham's act of faith presents a problem for de silentio. He can understand Hegelian philosophy and thinks himself quite astute in its teachings, but Abraham he cannot understand.[7] That Abraham was willing to murder his son Isaac places him beyond the realm of public reason.[8] What is also beyond human comprehension is that Abraham believed that, after the horrific event of killing his son, God would restore Isaac to him.

From a religious point of view, Abraham's act is conceived in terms of sacrifice, and thus he is heralded as a man of faith. But from the ethical point of view he is a murderer.[9] One could imagine that if in our day and age a parent killed their child in the name of the divine, it would be deemed an act of monstrous insanity or criminality. Furthermore, to believe that God would command such thing is absurd. And yet it is written in the Holy Scripture that God commanded this of Abraham and that Abraham proceeded to obey. Thus for de silentio, he cannot think along with this hero of faith: "[he] cannot make the movement of faith, [he] cannot shut [his] eyes and plunge confidently into the absurd."[10] In light of this example, it appears that de silentio thinks faith not merely a category that exists in close proximity to the absurd, but also the only means to grasp and overcome the absurd. "When an individual has faith, "the absurd is not the absurd—faith transforms it."[11] By faith Abraham is transformed from a murderer to a knight of faith.[12] In sum, Abraham, *by virtue of the absurd*, believes God and receives Isaac.[13]

The importance of having faith by virtue of what is absurd is not merely isolated to such unfathomable situations as Abraham's. In order to account for the extent of its reach in relation to the rest of us, de silentio offers another example, which further clarifies the nature of the absurd. There are two figures in this example: the knight of infinite resignation and the knight of faith. Both subjects affirm the impossibility of what they desire, viz. as commoners to be joined with a princess they love. The knight of infinite resignation, aware of the impossibility in seeking to be with her, finds peace and rest in his infinite resignation.[14] What has kept this individual from seeking to attain the impossible was the absurdity inherent in the idea that a common man could be with a princess.

On the other hand, the knight of faith ventures to believe that the impossible is possible; he believes by virtue of the absurd that he can have her. He does not believe the absurd is merely improbable or unexpected, but fully acknowledges its impossibility. The knight of infinite resignation, too, realizes the impossibility—and therein lies his consolation. There is nothing he can do about it except resign himself and thereby retain his commitment to the understanding. The knight of faith, by contrast, believes the absurd *against* the understanding.[15] In sum, the absurd is not

7   *SKS* 4, 128–9 / *FT*, 33.
8   *SKS* 4, 126 / *FT*, 30.
9   Ibid.
10   *SKS* 4, 129 / *FT*, 34.
11   *SKS* 4, 131 / *FT*, 35; *Pap.* X–6 B 79 / *JP* 1, 10.
12   *SKS* 4, 150 / *FT*, 56.
13   *SKS* 4, 150–1 / *FT*, 56–7.
14   *SKS* 4, 137–40 / *FT*, 42–5.
15   *SKS* 4, 140–1 / *FT*, 46–7.

a calculation of the understanding within degrees of certainty. Rather, according to human calculation, the absurd denies human understanding and action. Both the knights of infinite resignation and of faith are faced with the absurd and commence in resignation. But where the former stops, the latter continues and exhibits faith.[16]

In 1850 Kierkegaard writes, "the concept of the absurd is precisely to grasp the fact that it cannot and must not be grasped. This is a negatively determined concept but is just as dialectical as any positive one."[17] While reason tries to rationalize it as nonsense, the power of the absurd is only lost if faith is abolished: "it is a symbol, a riddle, a compounded riddle about which reason must say: I cannot solve it, it cannot be understood, but it does not follow thereby that it is nonsense."[18] The importance of the absurd, then, lies in its dialectical function as the ungraspable foil to reason. It points beyond the limits of reason to the possibilities of faith—as does the paradox.

The somewhat difficult interrelation between the absurd and the paradox is played out between the *Fragments* and the *Postscript*. They work together to maximize the sense of absurdity that results from the paradox. This is achieved partly by distinguishing between believing "by virtue of the absurd (the formula only of the passion of faith) and to believe the absurd. The first expression is used by Johannes de silentio and the second by Johannes Climacus."[19] For Abraham, to believe by virtue of the absurd was to believe that he would receive his son back despite the absurdity that he must kill him first. On the other hand, to believe the absurd, as posed in the *Fragments* and the *Postscript*, is to believe that the eternal God had become temporal in Christ. In the *Postscript*, Climacus asks, "What, then, is the absurd?" and answers, "The absurd is that the eternal truth has come into existence in time, that God has come into existence in time."[20] The centrality of this conception of the absurd to Christianity is illustrated by contrast with Socrates' faith:

> When Socrates believed that God is, he held fast the objective uncertainty with the entire passion of inwardness, and faith is precisely in this contradiction, in this risk. Now it is otherwise. Instead of the objective uncertainty, there is here the certainty that, viewed objectively, it is the absurd, and this absurdity, held fast in the passion of inwardness, is faith.[21]

The absurd, in the *Fragments* and the *Postscript*, is the ungraspable claim that "the eternal truth has come into existence in time, that God has come into existence, has been born, has grown up, etc., has come into existence exactly as an individual human being."[22] This is indeed absurd according to human understanding. And yet, Christianity demands that one believe the absurd, believe what is deemed impossible by human understanding. The absurd doctrine of the Incarnation functions to displace the hegemonic claims of reason and make room for faith. Only by means

---

[16]   *SKS* 4, 141–2 / *FT*, 47.
[17]   *SKS* 23, 23–4, NB15:25 / *JP* 1, 7.
[18]   Ibid.
[19]   *Pap.* X–6 B 80 / *JP* 1, 11.
[20]   *SKS* 7, 193 / *CUP1*, 210.
[21]   *SKS* 7, 192–3 / *CUP1*, 210.
[22]   Ibid.

of its "objective repulsion" of reason does the absurd become "the dynamometer of faith in inwardness."[23]

However, this nuance in the *Concluding Unscientific Postscript* of "believing the absurd" does not contradict how *Fear and Trembling* employs the concept of the absurd.[24] When the New Testament calls Abraham the father of faith, this is "the formal definition of faith. So it is also with the absurd."[25] In Abraham's case and with respect to the Incarnation, faith takes the impossible to be possible (for God). Both de silentio and Climacus maintain that only faith overcomes the absurd, by displacing human understanding and propelling the individual into inwardness.

In the *Fragments*, the paradox manifests itself when the understanding realizes that it seeks to know that which it cannot.[26] This unknowable, with which the understanding is constantly colliding, is revealed as God.[27] But God does not remain unknown. Rather, he becomes incarnate in Jesus Christ. In sum, the eternal has entered time.

The historical "is dialectical with respect to time."[28] That is, since the past has at some time come into existence it is not necessary. Yet the unchangeableness of the past suggests it might be necessary rather than contingent. But it is still potentially changeable with respect to *how* we appropriate it and interpret it—as, for example, repentance can change how we relate to the past by seeking "to nullify a certain actuality."[29] But God is said to be necessary in a different sense: "only the eternal has absolutely no history."[30] So when Climacus affirms that the "historical is that the god *has come into existence* (for the contemporary), that he has been one present *by having come into existence* (for one coming later),"[31] we are confronted with a contradiction. Either God is eternal and thereby is excluded from history, or God comes into existence and is therefore neither eternal nor necessary. The absurd claim that God entered time at a particular historical point, as an individual human being, challenges us to set aside the question of truth and instead to assent (or to maintain our offense).[32]

At times the *Postscript* uses the concept of the absurd interchangeably with the concept of the paradox.[33] Even more, these concepts are used interchangeably to describe the nature of the Incarnation in relation to human reason. Christ is "the absolute paradox, the absurd, the incomprehensible."[34] And yet, although these terms appear synonymous, the concept of the absurd again is used to describe the ultimate

23   *SKS* 7, 194 / *CUP1*, 210–11.
24   *Pap.* X–6 B 81 / *JP* 1, 12.
25   Ibid.
26   *SKS* 4, 244 / *PF*, 39; *SKS* 4, 249 / *PF*, 44.
27   *SKS* 4, 244 / *PF*, 39.
28   *SKS* 4, 275–6 / *PF*, 75–7.
29   Ibid.
30   Ibid.
31   *SKS* 4, 286 / *PF*, 87.
32   Ibid.
33   *SKS* 7, 507 / *CUP1*, 558.
34   *SKS* 7, 511 / *CUP1*, 561.

incomprehensibility of the Incarnation by means of human reason.[35] It is because Christ is the absolute paradox that he is the absurd. The absurdity arises when we reflect upon the contradiction when a man claims to be other than a man. God and man are infinitely qualitatively distinct.[36] The absurdity reveals itself in light of what contradicts our senses or our understanding.[37]

In that the understanding is unable to reconcile the two opposing categories of God and man, which are said to be reconciled in Christ, the absurdity arising from the God-man is an offense to rationalism and historicism.[38] It is not the case that faith makes sense of the paradox, since the absurdity must be maintained as "the expression for the passion of faith"[39] and to effect "a break with all thinking."[40] Even Christ's disciples, who were contemporary with the God-man, are in the same position as those who later become contemporary with Christ through faith. The absurd paradox offends reason and arouses the passion of faith, which is the only antidote to despair.

Climacus reminds the reader that the absolute paradox "is an offense to the Jews, foolishness to the Greeks, and the absurd to the understanding."[41] But the understanding itself does not understand the relationship between the paradox and the absurd: "The understanding declares that the paradox is the absurd, but this is only a caricaturing, for the paradox is indeed the paradox, *quia absurdum* [because of the absurd]."[42] The paradox needs to be appropriated with passionate inwardness, not to be understood from the point of view of reason. The absurd catapults the individual into offense, which is an affective reaction and therefore the relevant modality for faith.

In conclusion, confrontation with the absurd precipitates an affective reaction, which defies rational mediation. This is its dialectical import with respect to reason, since it has the potential to change the individual's orientation from objective understanding to existential pathos. Only when the individual appropriates Christian doctrine inwardly and with passion, rather than with disinterested objectivity, can there be a possibility of the essential change involved in becoming a self, in which the self becomes new in Christ.

See also Appropriation; Certainty; Decision/Resolve; Faith; God; History; Immanence/Transcendence; Individual; Irrational; Offense; Paradox; Passion/Pathos; Qualitative Difference; Reason.

---

[35]   Ibid.
[36]   *SKS* 11, 237 / *SUD*, 126.
[37]   *SKS* 25, 456, NB30:86.
[38]   *SKS* 7, 555 / *CUP1*, 611.
[39]   *SKS* 7, 390 / *CUP1*, 429.
[40]   *SKS* 7, 527 / *CUP1*, 579. Cf. *SKS* 7, 194 / *CUP1*, 212.
[41]   *SKS* 7, 199 / *CUP1*, 219; *SKS* 7, 195 / *CUP1*, 213.
[42]   *SKS* 4, 256 / *PF*, 52.

Actuality

Steven M. Emmanuel

Actuality (*Virkelighed*—noun; *det Virkelige*—noun; *virkelig*—adjective)

The Danish *Virkelighed* is a loan word from the German *Wirklichkeit*. In its primary sense the word denotes the existence of something as a concrete reality, as opposed to something that exists merely in thought or as a theoretical possibility.[1] Kierkegaard's usage is philosophically informed by the account presented by Aristotle and glossed in the commentaries of Wilhelm Gottlieb Tennemann and Friedrich Adolf Trendelenburg.[2] In Aristotle's writings, actuality is understood in relation to the concept of potentiality. Generally speaking, potentiality (δύναμις) refers to the possibility a thing has to become something, while actuality (ἐντελέχεια or ἐνέργεια) is the activity or change that represents the realization of that possibility.

Kierkegaard contrasts the term "actuality" with "possibility" (*Mulighed*), and in some instances with "ideality" (*Idealitet*). The term is employed chiefly to describe the process of moral and religious development leading to authentic selfhood. For this reason, discussions of actuality occur in many places in Kierkegaard's writings. However, the most extensive treatment of it is found in the philosophical pseudonym, Johannes Climacus. In *The Concept of Irony*, Kierkegaard explains that the term refers primarily to "historical actuality—that is, the given actuality at a certain time and in a certain situation." He adds that the term is used in two ways in metaphysical discussions: on the one hand, it refers to the concretion of an idea, while on the other it refers to "the historically actualized idea."[3]

In the context of Kierkegaard's analysis of irony, actuality refers to the concrete circumstances of an individual's life and to ways of thinking about life that lead to the concrete choices and actions that define an individual's personality. In terms of what a particular person has the ability to do or become, actuality distinguishes real possibilities from merely abstract or theoretical possibilities. To become an authentic self requires that one recognize the absolute validity of actuality.

---

[1]   *Ordbog over det danske Sprog*, vols. 1–28, published by the Society for Danish Language and Literature, Copenhagen: Gyldendal 1918–56, vol. 27, columns 189–90. Christian Molbech explicitly contrasts "actuality" with "possibility" in his 1833 Danish lexicon. See his *Dansk Ordbog*, vols. 1–2, Copenhagen: Den Gyldendalske Boghandlings Forlag 1833, vol. 1, p. 667.

[2]   See Wilhelm Gottlieb Tennemann, *Geschichte der Philosophie*, vols. 1–11, Leipzig: Johann Ambrosius Barth 1798–1819, vol. 3, pp. 17–330, and Friedrich Adolf Trendelenburg, *Logische Untersuchungen*, vols. 1–2, Berlin: G. Bethge 1840.

[3]   *SKS* 1, 297 / *CI*, 259.

The natural tendency of the Romantic ironist is to want to resist the limitations of the concrete historical situation. Longing for freedom, he refuses to acknowledge the absolute validity of actuality, preferring instead to take pleasure in the infinite possibilities afforded by the poetic imagination. Believing that everything is possible, he becomes free, but only in a negative sense. Detached from the actuality of existence, the ironist lacks the necessary conditions for achieving an integrated personality, and hence risks losing himself.

Socratic ignorance represents a special case of irony. As an ironist, Socrates did not set out to negate actuality in general, but rather the actuality of the prevailing Greek culture. Yet, to the extent that he uncompromisingly maintained the ironic stance of ignorance, his position was "infinite absolute negativity,"[4] and hence the liberation his ignorance afforded him was merely a negative freedom. Viewed from a world-historical perspective, however, Socrates was justified, in that his irony was in fact demanding the actuality of subjectivity in his interlocutors.[5] In this way, Socratic irony signaled the beginning of subjectivity and the movement toward moral and religious development.

In the concluding section of the dissertation, Kierkegaard points out that "no genuinely human life is possible without irony."[6] Learning to master irony is therefore part of the healthy development of every individual. But the mastery of irony occurs only when a person is able to use it as a "controlled element."

In the soul of every human being there is a longing for "something higher and more perfect."[7] But there is also a danger that this longing can "hollow out actuality,"[8] as is the case with the Romantic longing for freedom mentioned above. Irony as a controlled element is the conscious recognition of the validity of actuality. In this way, the content of one's life becomes "a genuine and meaningful element in the higher actuality whose fullness the soul craves,"[9] and longing is transformed into "a sound and healthy love."[10] The controlled use of irony marks the "absolute beginning of personal life."[11]

In the case of the poet, Kierkegaard points out that it is the mastery of irony in his own existence that allows him to stand in a conscious and inward relation to his work. This mastery depends on the development of a "totality-view" of the world, in which the poet understands himself in relation to the concrete historical circumstances of his life. Goethe was exemplary in this regard: "The reason Goethe's poet-existence was so great was that he was able to make his poet-life congruous with his actuality."[12] To the extent that a poet is grounded in actuality, his poems will have their own center of gravity. The master of irony is thus able to effect the proper

---

4   *SKS* 1, 307 / *CI*, 271.
5   *SKS* 1, 308 / *CI*, 271.
6   *SKS* 1, 355 / *CI*, 326.
7   *SKS* 1, 356 / *CI*, 327.
8   *SKS* 1, 357 / *CI*, 328.
9   Ibid.
10   *SKS* 1, 357 / *CI*, 329.
11   *SKS* 1, 355 / *CI*, 326.
12   *SKS* 1, 353 / *CI*, 325.

distance between himself and his literary productions. The controlled use of irony allows both the poem and the poet to be free.[13]

The concept of actuality figures prominently in the writings of Johannes Climacus. In the "Interlude" section of *Philosophical Fragments*, he explicitly affirms the Aristotelian analysis of change as a transition from possibility to actuality. Climacus stresses, however, that this process of coming into existence is not governed by necessity. What is necessary cannot suffer the change of coming into existence, because what is necessary simply *is*.[14] Coming into existence is not a change in essence (*Væsen*), but a transition from non-being to being (*Væren*), where "non-being" represents a possibility that is made actual in coming to be.[15] This transition always occurs, therefore, in freedom.[16]

Climacus employs the concept of actuality in an extended critique of Hegelian philosophy, which assumes that all historical change proceeds by necessity, and that freedom is simply the rational understanding of that necessity. According to the speculative view, thoughts and ideas are immanent in actuality. Climacus rejects this view on the grounds that it not only conflates thought and existence, but radically undermines the freedom associated with all ethical-religious development: "If what is thought were actuality, then what is thought out as perfectly as possible, when I as yet have not acted, would be the action. In this way there would be no action whatever, but the intellectual swallows the ethical."[17] For Climacus, thought represents the medium of possibility, and hence as soon as one begins to think about existence, the actuality of existence is reduced to an abstraction: "To conclude existence from thinking is, then, a contradiction. Because thinking does just the opposite and takes existence away from the actual and thinks it by annulling it, by transposing it into possibility."[18]

Climacus acknowledges that objective thinking nevertheless has some kind of reality for the thinker. However, this "thought-reality" (*Tanke-Realitet*), as he calls it, must not be confused with the historically actualized idea, since it is merely possibility.[19] The same point is made earlier in the book, where Climacus points out that objective thinking represents a misunderstanding in relation to subjectivity: "Even if a man his whole life through occupies himself exclusively with logic, he still does not become logic; he himself therefore exists in other categories."[20]

---

[13]   Kierkegaard makes a parallel point, without any reference to irony, in his review of Hans Christian Andersen's 1837 novel, *Only a Fiddler*. Because Andersen lacks a "life-view," he is unable to create any distance between himself and his characters. As Kierkegaard puts it, "his own actuality, his own person, volatilizes itself into fiction, so that one is actually tempted to believe that Andersen is a character who has run away from an as yet unfinished group composed by a poet." See *SKS* 1, 31 / *EPW*, 75.

[14]   *SKS* 4, 274 / *PF*, 74.

[15]   *SKS* 4, 273 / *PF*, 73.

[16]   *SKS* 4, 275 / *PF*, 75.

[17]   *SKS* 7, 309 / *CUP1*, 338.

[18]   *SKS* 7, 289 / *CUP1*, 317. Cf. *SKS* 7, 314–15 / *CUP1*, 286–7.

[19]   *SKS* 7, 299 / *CUP1*, 328.

[20]   *SKS* 7, 92 / *CUP1*, 93.

Metaphysical and ethical points are intertwined in Climacus' discussion. The change of coming into existence describes the process whereby an individual moves from the *idea* of being a certain kind of person to the existential embodiment of that idea in action. Both ethically and religiously understood, actuality is therefore always superior to possibility.[21]

To these metaphysical and ethical observations Climacus adds an epistemological point regarding the limits of what we can know about our own or another individual's actuality. Because knowledge always involves translating the reality of its object into the abstract medium of thought (language), the knower is incapable of grasping actuality directly: "All knowledge about actuality is possibility. The only actuality concerning which an existing person has more than knowledge about is his own actuality, that he exists, and this actuality is his absolute interest."[22] Even someone who has resolved to change his or her life, to bring it into conformity with that person's understanding of an ethical ideal, has merely arrived at a new kind of potential that must constantly be realized in the form of ethical action. In this situation, the ethical individual always risks backsliding into ideality: "When I think something I want to do but as yet have not done it, then what I have thought, however precise it is, however much it may be called a *thought-actuality*, is a possibility."[23] The difference between the possible and the actual is not a matter of what one knows, but rather the individual's infinite interest in realizing the ideal in every moment. For the ethical individual, "his interestedness is existing in his actuality."[24] According to Climacus, actuality is not an object for knowledge, but rather "an *inter-esse* [between-being] between thinking and being in the hypothetical unity of abstraction."[25]

With respect to the actuality of another person, it follows that one can know this only by thinking about it, that is, as a possibility.[26] As Climacus succinctly puts the point: "ethically there is no direct relation between subject and subject."[27] Just as it is a mistake to inquire aesthetically and intellectually about one's own actuality, so too is it a mistake to inquire ethically about another person's actuality.[28]

Climacus explains that the situation of the religious believer is "different from an ethicist in being infinitely interested in the actuality of another."[29] More specifically, the object of faith is "the god's actuality in the sense of existence."[30] Climacus emphasizes that this object is neither a doctrine, nor a person with a doctrine, for then faith would be reduced to a mere abstraction, a possibility for thought.[31] Rather, actuality refers to "an interiority in which the individual annuls

---

21   *SKS* 7, 291 / *CUP1*, 320.
22   *SKS* 7, 288 / *CUP1*, 316.
23   *SKS* 7, 292 / *CUP1*, 321.
24   *SKS* 7, 286 / *CUP1*, 314.
25   Ibid.
26   *SKS* 7, 289 / *CUP1*, 317.
27   *SKS* 7, 293 / *CUP1*, 321.
28   *SKS* 7, 295 / *CUP1*, 323.
29   *SKS* 7, 295 / *CUP1*, 324.
30   *SKS* 7, 299 / *CUP1*, 326.
31   *SKS* 7, 298 / *CUP1*, 326.

possibility and identifies himself with what is thought in order to exist in it."[32] Just as the ethical individual strives to embody an ethical ideal, so the Christian believer, in the inwardness of subjectivity, strives to bring his or her life into conformity with the example of the Teacher.

The relationship between the believer and the object of faith is explored further by Anti-Climacus in *Practice in Christianity*. Picking up on a theme in *Philosophical Fragments*, he explains the meaning of contemporaneity in terms of the concept of actuality:

> But that which has actually happened (the past) is still not, except in a certain sense (namely, in contrast to poetry), the actual. The qualification that is lacking—which is the qualification of truth (as inwardness) and of all religiousness is—for you. The past is not actuality—for me. Only the contemporary is actuality—for me. That with which you are living simultaneously is actuality—for you.[33]

The concept of contemporaneity is further developed by Anti-Climacus in light of the distinction between an "admirer" and an "imitator" of Christ. This distinction is brought out most clearly in relation to what he calls "the danger of actuality"[34] implicit in the Christian requirement to die to the world. The imitator is one who strives to be related to the actuality of Christ by living in accordance with the highest ethical requirements of the faith, while the admirer merely pays lip service to them. As Anti-Climacus puts it, "the imitator has his life in these dangers and the admirer personally remains detached although they both are nevertheless united in acknowledging in words the truth of Christianity."[35]

In *The Sickness unto Death*, Anti-Climacus explores the concepts of actuality and possibility in connection with his analysis of sin and the role of despair in the Christian understanding of selfhood. Whereas in Climacus' writings actuality represents the annihilation of possibility, Anti-Climacus suggests that in relation to sin actuality is "the consummated, the active possibility" of despair.[36] To eliminate the possibility of despair is to remove the very condition for repentance and faith. "The earnestness of sin," he says, "is its actuality in the single individual."[37]

These considerations lead Anti-Climacus to a sharper formulation of the concept of actuality: "What the self now lacks is indeed actuality....However, closer scrutiny reveals that what he actually lacks is necessity."[38] In other words, the self must not only fully acknowledge the fact that he exists in sin, but that what is missing "is essentially the power to obey, to submit to the necessity in one's life, to what may be called one's limitations."[39]

---

[32]   *SKS* 7, 310 / *CUP1*, 339.
[33]   *SKS* 12, 76 / *PC*, 64.
[34]   *SKS* 12, 244 / *PC*, 252.
[35]   Ibid.
[36]   *SKS* 11, 131 / *SUD*, 15.
[37]   *SKS* 11, 231 / *SUD*, 120.
[38]   *SKS* 11, 152 / *SUD*, 36.
[39]   Ibid.

We note that there is also a single use of the Latinate form *Actualitet* in *The Sickness unto Death*, where Anti-Climacus uses the term to characterize spirit: "In the life of the spirit there is no standing still [*Stilstand*] (really no state [*Tilstand*], either; everything is actuation [*Actualitet*])."[40]

See also Being/Becoming; Contemporaneity; Philosophy.

---

[40]   *SKS* 11, 206 / *SUD*, 94.

Admiration

Guadalupe Pardi

Admiration (*Beundring*—noun; *beundre*—verb)

The Danish verb *beundre* is derived from *undre*, which in turn is derived from the Old Danish and Old Norse *undra*. These correspond to the German *wundern* and the English *wonder*.[1] The lexical meaning of *Beundring* in Danish is a feeling of wonder combined with recognition, awe, and excitement. In its colloquial connotation it can mean an astounding veneration of a person, creature, object, or God. According to *Ordbog over det danske Sprog*, the Danish word *Forundring* can also be rendered in English as *admiration*. Both *Beundring* and *Forundring* contain the root *undring*, while their corresponding English terms, derived from Latin, are *admiration* and *astonishment*, *surprise*, *wonder* respectively.[2] Though the two Danish words can be found in Kierkegaard's works, he particularly uses *Beundring* when writing about admiration.

The most frequent occurrence of "admiration" is in *Practice in Christianity*, published under the pseudonym Anti-Climacus. This is followed by *Four Upbuilding Discourses*, published under the name Søren Kierkegaard in 1843, and then by "The Crisis and a Crisis in the Life of an Actress," published under the pseudonym Inter et Inter. But the most precise developments of the concept of admiration occur in tandem with his writings on imitation (*Efterligning*), since Kierkegaard often sets in opposition the attitude of the admirer (*Beundrer*) to that of the imitator (*Efterfølger*). These two terms are found in publications both under Kierkegaard's own name and his pseudonyms—for example, in *The Sickness unto Death* published under the pseudonym Anti-Climacus and *Works of Love* published under Kierkegaard's own name.

Throughout his work Kierkegaard's concept of admiration is applied fairly consistently, albeit with slight nuances basically in line with the different figures that might be admired. The greatest distinction in application is between (1) admiration of Christ and (2) admiration of a particular (merely) human being.

I. Admiration of Christ

According to Kierkegaard, admiration of Christ is inappropriate since he did not come to the world to be served, worshipped or admired, but to be a prototype for

---

[1]   Niels Åge Nielsen, *Dansk etymologisk Ordbog*, Copenhagen: Gyldendal 1966, p. 29, p. 442.

[2]   *Ordbog over det danske Sprog*, vols. 1–28, published by the Society for Danish Language and Literature, Copenhagen: Gyldendal 1918–56, vol. 2, columns 574–5.

the way of life that ought to be imitated by all human beings.[3] Correspondingly, one's life itself ought to express what one understands from reading the Scripture and from learning about the life and works of Christ. In order to do this, one must relate to Christ earnestly and inwardly. One must learn to be alone with the word of God and to see oneself in the mirror of the word of God, reiterating constantly, "*It is I to whom it is speaking; it is I about whom it is speaking.*"[4] In this way I enter a personal relationship with God. Otherwise, God's word becomes impersonal, a doctrine, and one relates to it objectively, without being able to experience it subjectively and act accordingly.[5] Likewise, sermons and religious discourses should invoke imitation rather than admiration of Christ. However, sermons are often merely "observations" on contemporary life, and are taken to be on a par with other cultural artifacts, which purport to be objective.[6] Religious discourse having become objective, and so expressing the opposite of what it means to preach, moves away from the truly Christian—that is to say, the personal, the inward—in order "to observe" and thereby keeps infinitely distant from individual subjectivity. In sermons and religious discourses, then, both the speaker and the listener personally maintain an objective distance and, with this, fail to experience their subjectivity. In its true sense, Christianity cannot become the subject of mere "observations" because it requires a task: to become oneself, to be authentic. For the preacher, then, this requires that he *lives* what he preaches or strives to be. Instead, Kierkegaard thinks that the personality of the preacher is in danger of becoming objectified in the form of the observation, and with this the subjectivity of the listener is cut off as well. This objectification is also expressed in the church and in established Christendom when the *imitators* of Christ are replaced by his *admirers*.[7]

From a Christian point of view, Christ is the only way to salvation, and it is a demanding way from the beginning to the end.[8] Those who choose of their own free will and do not hesitate to abandon everything in order to follow Christ bear the mark of true imitation, as witnesses to the truth. This is the real test of the Christian: the imitator is not distracted by any doubts or caveats of reason, but chooses to strive in the direction of suffering, towards the death of merely earthly desires.[9] Admiration, by contrast, implies that one is "personally detached" and "does not discover that what is admired involves a claim upon him, or at least to strive to be what is admired."[10]

Christ was not a teacher of doctrine who expected his followers to accept such a doctrine and to continue living as if nothing was required from them. On the contrary, he was the living exemplar, and his followers were to be imitators of his life. Living in humiliation and lowliness, Christ, as the prototype, was behind everyone "in order to propel forward those who are to be formed according to it [the prototype]."[11]

---

[3]   Cf. *SKS* 12, 232 / *PC*, 238–9.
[4]   *SKS* 13, 62 / *FSE*, 35.
[5]   Cf. *SKS* 13, 63 / *FSE*, 36.
[6]   *SKS* 13, 65–6 / *FSE*, 38–9.
[7]   Cf. *SKS* 12, 227–8 / *PC*, 233–4.
[8]   Cf. *SKS* 13, 80–1 / *FSE*, 57–8.
[9]   *SKS* 13, 89–91 / *FSE*, 67–9.
[10]   *SKS* 12, 234 / *PC*, 241.
[11]   *SKS* 12, 233 / *PC*, 239.

In the confusion of Christendom, however, people admire Christ instead of imitating him. Had Christ lived in majesty and enjoyed all worldly and temporal benefits, he would not have been the prototype; he would have become an object of admiration and the duty to imitate him would have been annulled. The ordinary human being, lacking earthly advantages and benefits, finds it ridiculous and impossible to aspire to the majesty of God and is content to admire. Had Christ appeared in pomp and majesty, "this would have given rise to the greatest possible lie. Instead of becoming the prototype for the whole human race and every individual in the human race, he would have become a general excuse and escape for the whole human race and every individual in the human race."[12]

Even if Christ is consistently admired in his majesty, Kierkegaard says, people are ungrateful to no one as much as to God. People become lazy in their habit of admiration simply because they remain in the idea that they can always have God.[13] "O human admiration, what sheer vanity you are, and not least when you think you are being constant!"[14]

II. Admiration of a Particular Human Being

From the Christian point of view, admiring a particular human being is fraught with the dangers of delusion, laziness, and self-love. Christianity has not taught that the neighbor should be an object of admiration, but a subject of love—where this love is one of self-denial.[15] But when the poet says that in erotic love, "the beloved must admire the beloved," Kierkegaard notes that "if one is to be loved by the one and only admired one," admiration becomes a form of self-love.[16]

In order to escape the narcissism implicit in mutual admiration, we need to heed (a) the asymmetry between oneself and the object of one's admiration, and (b) the ethical imperative to love the neighbor as other. According to Anti-Climacus, if "the object of my admiration actually does not and cannot involve any claim upon me to resemble it, then it is indeed altogether proper for me to limit myself to admiring it."[17] This leaves open as potential objects of admiration "beauty, wealth, extraordinary talents, remarkable achievements, masterpieces, good fortune, etc., because in all this no claim upon me is involved."[18] Admiration is, on this ideal Christian view, no more than an aesthetic attitude.

The ethical stage, on the other hand, makes a very heavy claim upon me—to live according to the universal demands of duty. The categorical imperative of duty applies to everyone equally, thereby excluding the asymmetry of admiration. As ethically committed individuals, we cannot admire someone for doing their duty and not feel obliged to do the same in the same circumstances. "Here admiration

---

12   *SKS* 12, 233 / *PC*, 239–40.
13   Cf. *SKS* 14, 103 / *CD*, 318.
14   Ibid.
15   *SKS* 9, 61 / *WL*, 55.
16   *SKS* 9, 61 / *WL*, 54.
17   *SKS* 12, 234 / *PC*, 241.
18   Ibid.

is totally inappropriate and ordinarily is deceit, a cunning that seeks evasion and excuse," for ethics demands that "I am to resemble him [the ethical individual] and immediately begin my effort to resemble him."[19]

All human admiration involves comparing oneself to others.[20] In doing so, one can compare one's own love, beauty, wealth or talent, and the like, and discover that someone else exhibits a unique fortune in any of these aspects, as does the talented young actress in "The Crisis and A Crisis in the Life of an Actress." This fortunate person receives admiration and is lucky enough not to become the target of envy. Nevertheless, "as an inevitable result of human weakness,"[21] some kind of discomfort on the part of the admiration—which, however, is still not envy—results in wanting to measure this talent and see how long it will last. In other words, "the object of incessantly continuing appreciative admiration"[22] might become an object of suspicion.[23] In calculating one forgets about true beauty, true wealth, true talent and, what is more important, true love. Furthermore, in admiring something that should be their duty, people lose themselves in admiration.[24]

The Sickness unto Death, published under the pseudonym Anti-Climacus, regards offense as "unhappy admiration."[25] This unhappy admiration is in turn related to envy, since "[e]nvy is secret admiration. An admirer who feels that he cannot become happy by abandoning himself to it chooses to be envious of that which he admires....Admiration is happy self-surrender; envy is unhappy self-assertion."[26] Anti-Climacus then draws a parallel between admiration/envy in human-to-human relations, on the one hand, and adoration/offense in the relationship between human beings and God on the other hand.[27] While admiration of God is inappropriately effete, adoration has the requisite passion and represents "happy self-surrender." Whereas envy asserts itself by coveting the attributes that would otherwise be admired, offense asserts itself in relation to God by refusing to humble itself "in adoration under the extraordinary."[28] Both envy and offense, then, are forms of the despair of "willing to be oneself" and are failures to acknowledge the creative and sustaining role of God in one's attainment of selfhood.[29]

In true admiration, the admirer "keeps himself personally detached; he forgets himself, forgets that what he admires in the other person is denied to him, and precisely this is what is beautiful, that he forgets himself in this way in order to admire."[30] In inauthentic admiration, on the other hand, "I promptly begin to think

---

[19]   *SKS* 12, 235 / *PC*, 242.
[20]   Cf. *SKS* 9, 184–6 / *WL*, 183–5.
[21]   *SKS* 14, 100 / *CD*, 314.
[22]   *SKS* 14, 93 / *CD*, 303.
[23]   *SKS* 14, 100 / *CD*, 314.
[24]   *SKS* 12, 236 / *PC*, 243–4.
[25]   *SKS* 11, 200 / *SUD*, 86–7.
[26]   *SKS* 11, 200 / *SUD*, 86.
[27]   Ibid.
[28]   Ibid.
[29]   Cf. *SKS* 11, 181 / *SUD*, 67.
[30]   *SKS* 12, 235 / *PC*, 242.

about myself, simply and solely to think about myself."[31] In this way, egotism transforms admiration into envy, or even hatred, insofar as I fail to assimilate the other to myself.[32]

According to Kierkegaard, then, in relation to Christ's life—the way, the truth—imitation should prevail over admiration, while in relation to other human beings admiration is usually so sentimental and egotistical as to be tantamount to self-love. In the event of danger or the disappointment of great expectations, admiration easily flips into its opposite: jealousy, hatred or betrayal. These dangers of the real world—not necessarily linked to the confession of Christ—can reveal how far one is just an admirer, whereas in Christendom it is very difficult to distinguish between an admirer and an imitator or mere fellow traveler.[33] Where someone asserts vociferously, through speech and gestures, that he fervently accepts a doctrine, but does not allow it to influence one's life, then "the more he is only making a fool of himself [and] informs on himself as being either a fool or a deceiver."[34] Although at first glance there is no essential difference between an admirer and an imitator other than the enthusiastic speech of the former, there is, however, an infinite difference, since the latter "*is* or strives *to be* what he admires" while the former personally remains outside.[35]

Throughout his work Kierkegaard emphasizes the fundamental differences among the various existential stages. In religious terms, the imitator is the true Christian, inasmuch as Christ did not come into the world to be admired or to cause offense. In ethical terms, the admirer, by being indifferent and fickle, is living a lie. Unable to resemble that which he admires, the admirer seeks diversion in his objective "observations," which can turn at any moment into foolish or malicious curiosity or the negative feelings of hatred and envy. The true admirer recognizes the asymmetry between himself and the one admired, while the untrue admirer uses the other as an occasion to mire himself in egotism. In the absolute difference between human beings and God, adoration is more appropriate than admiration, and in the relation between human beings and the God-man Christ, admiration is an impediment to the true goal of imitation.

See also Being/Becoming; Choice; Christ; Duty; Envy; Ethics; Experience; Imitation; Objectivity/Subjectivity; Offense; Personality; Self; Suffering.

---

[31]   Ibid.
[32]   Cf. *SKS* 12, 235–6 / *PC*, 242–3.
[33]   Cf. *SKS* 12, 238 / *PC*, 245.
[34]   *SKS* 12, 241 / *PC*, 249.
[35]   *SKS* 12, 234 / *PC*, 241.

Aesthetic/Aesthetics

William McDonald

Aesthetic/Aesthetics (*Æsthetik*—noun; *æsthetisk*—adjective)

The Danish and English words are derived from the Greek αἰσθητά, which means "that which can be sensed." The first modern usage of the word is in the work of the German philosopher Alexander Baumgarten, who in his book *Aesthetica* (1750–58) defined the beautiful as the sensuous representation of the perfect. Subsequently, aesthetics became the discipline that deals with the beautiful in art and nature. This in turn gave rise to the notion of the aesthete, as a person who to an extreme degree pursues beauty in everything.[1]

"The aesthetic" in Kierkegaard's work designates (a) the artistic apprehension of beauty and (b) an existential sphere. "Aesthetics" designates critical reflection on art. By far the most frequent usage of the term by Kierkegaard is in the sense of an existential sphere, though the three senses are interrelated.

I. Aesthetics

Kierkegaard borrows his aesthetics strategically from German Idealism and Romanticism, though this is partly motivated by his interest in Greek concepts that had been incorporated into eighteenth-century German aesthetics. While he criticizes the German Romantic model of aesthetics explicitly in *The Concept of Irony* and implicitly in *Either/Or*, he retains some of the central assumptions of idealist aesthetics in his critique of "the aesthetic" as an existential sphere. The primary idealist assumption retained by Kierkegaard is that art mediates between the idea and the sensuous. This notion goes back to Aristotle, who understands imagination as the mediator between αἴσθησις (perception—of particulars) and νόησις (thought—of universals).[2] In Kant's *Critique of Judgment* this is transformed into the claim that imagination provides a bridge between the intuitions of our sensuous experience of deterministic nature and the freedom inherent in our concepts of practical reason. Aesthetic judgment engages the imagination in a free play between the faculties of the mind, thereby opening the mind to the feeling of freedom. In judgments of beauty,

---

[1]   *Ordbog over det danske Sprog*, vols. 1–28, published by the Society for Danish Language and Literature, Copenhagen: Gyldendal 1918–56, vol. 27, column 1401.

[2]   Cf. Göran Sörbom, "Aristotle on Music as Representation," in *Musical Worlds: New Directions in the Philosophy of Music*, ed. by Philip Alperson, University Park, Pennsylvania: Pennsylvania State University Press 1998, pp. 37–8.

this freedom is expressed through harmony and continuity within a shared community of taste; in judgments of the sublime, this freedom is felt as the moment of excess when the categories of understanding and even imagination are overwhelmed in the direction of the unlimited. Kierkegaard recasts this mediation by imagination as the *interesse* (being-between, interest, concern) of consciousness—between thought and being or between the ideal and the real.[3] The mediation is achieved by imagination in the modality of possibility. This is its infinitizing aspect. As such, imagination for Kierkegaard is the capacity *instar omnium* (for all capacities).[4] Kierkegaard's concept of anxiety corresponds to the Kantian sublime, as the pivot between nature and freedom that problematizes representation. Anxiety is "*a sympathetic antipathy and an antipathetic sympathy*,"[5] neither free nor determined, both desired and repelled, which opens through the narrow pass of decision onto a field of possibilities.

For Kant the imagination is crucial to apprehension, recognition, and reproduction of experience by synthesizing concepts with intuitions. But imagination also has a productive synthesizing role in art. Aesthetic intuition perceives disparate phenomena as wholes, while artistic imagination projects this perception onto the sensuous world. The transient, finite, external, and fragmentary elements of the world are thereby transfigured by their integration with the eternal, the infinite, and inwardness in the artistic vision of the whole. Aesthetic experience has a timeless quality due to the perceived congruence of form and content in the "classical" work of art. In *Either/Or*, for example, the aesthete argues that we can discern Mozart's "true immortal greatness"[6] as an artist in *Don Giovanni*, since it manifests "the absolute relation between idea, form, subject matter, and medium."[7] This perfect synthesis distinguishes Mozart's work, but also renders it merely a work of art. It is "classical" by conforming to "that happy Greek view of the world that calls the world a κόσμος [cosmos]"[8]—a limited and harmonious whole found only in ideals. Kierkegaard contrasts this with "romantic" art, which "flows beyond all limits" like Kant's sublime.[9] The aesthetic simplifies, or introduces a *deus ex machina,* to accommodate form to content and is therefore strictly inadequate to a full existential engagement with the complexities of actuality. Ethical-religious consciousness ultimately despairs of finding perfect congruence in actuality. This opens the way for faith as the cure for despair, by acknowledging absolute dependence on God for reconciliation of life's complexities and contradictions.

Kant introduces two other important concepts in his analysis of aesthetic judgments: (1) that they are disinterested; and (2) that art can be classified by analogy with the modes of human communication: (1) speech (rhetoric, poetry), (2) gesture (plastic arts), and (3) tone (music, color). Kierkegaard's aesthete implicitly rejects Kant's notion that aesthetic judgments are disinterested and instead insists with

---

3   Cf. *SKS* 15, 57–8 / *JC*, 150–2; *SKS* 7, 286–7 / *CUP1*, 314–15.
4   *SKS* 11, 147 / *SUD*, 30–1.
5   *SKS* 4, 348 / *CA*, 42.
6   *SKS* 2, 80 / *EO1*, 74.
7   *SKS* 2, 78 / *EO1*, 72.
8   Cf. *SKS* 2, 55 / *EO1*, 47.
9   *SKS* 27, 162, Papir 219 / *JP* 3, 3796.

the German Romantics that the proper object of aesthetic judgment in modernity is not beauty but the *interesting*.[10] Kierkegaard retains the Kantian typology of art, although these types are understood in ways inflected by G.E. Lessing and G.W.F. Hegel. Lessing departs from Kant in understanding the typology of art not by analogy with various modes of communication but along the dimensions of spatiality and temporality. Poetry and music are primarily temporal arts, since their performance unfolds in time, while the plastic arts are primarily spatial, since they are extended in space and their forms are temporally fixed once they have been completed.[11] Kierkegaard initially follows Hegel in attributing to poetry the maximum potential for articulating spirit, since poetry is temporal, conceptual, and sensuous, and therefore an appropriate vehicle for the dialectical unfolding of spirit over time in its relation to sensory experience.

Hegel brings history to bear on his analysis of aesthetics. In addition to the dialectic of ideal aesthetic forms, he considers the evolution of actual aesthetic forms in order to arrive at the conclusion that poetry is the most spiritually and historically advanced of the arts. Kierkegaard's understanding of the dialectic of aesthetic forms takes as its starting point Hegel's lectures on aesthetics, together with modifications to Hegel's position by Johan Ludvig Heiberg. The main difference between Hegel and Heiberg is in their historical-dialectical ordering of poetic genres. Whereas Hegel argued that the development is in the order epic, lyric, dramatic, Heiberg claimed that the correct order is lyric, epic, dramatic.[12] Kierkegaard sides with Heiberg about the order of poetic genres, but also differs from him by seeing in this order not only the historical evolution of poetic genres but also stages in the personal development of the individual. The lyric represents immersion in immediacy and mood. It lacks the capacity of the epic to develop personality and subjectivity by directing narrative, and life, towards a single goal by means of reflection. The lyric and the epic as poetic genres correspond, respectively, to Kierkegaard's existential spheres of the aesthetic and the ethical. For Heiberg and Hegel, irony is used as a means of detaching the poet from the immediacy of the lyric—as a propaedeutic to epic reflection. This corresponds in Kierkegaard's work to the status of irony as a *confinium* (border region) between the aesthetic and ethical stages. For Kierkegaard, however, the transition from the aesthetic to the ethical stages of life requires *pathos* rather than dialectic, in order to usher in a qualitatively different dialectic.[13]

Hegel and Heiberg concur in regarding dramatic poetry as a synthesis of the lyric and epic. Kierkegaard does not explicitly follow Hegel and Heiberg in this, but his literary practice resonates with it. His method of indirect communication, which uses the dramatic device of pseudonyms and multiple narrative points of view, is tantamount to what Hegel and Heiberg mean by dramatic poetry and corresponds to Kierkegaard's representation of the religious existential sphere within his (first)

---

[10]   Cf. *SKS* 22, 23, NB11:27 / *JP* 6, 6396; *SKS* 27, 460, Papir 387 / *JP* 2, 2105; *SKS* 18, 195, JJ:172 / *KJN* 2, 180–1; *SKS* 21, 261, NB10:10 / *JP* 6, 6330; *SKS* 2, 112, 329, 334–5, 341–2, 357, 424–5 / *EO1*, 109, 339, 345–6, 351–2, 368, 437–8.
[11]   Cf. *SKS* 2, 167 / *EO1*, 169.
[12]   *SKS* 27, 143, Papir 172 / *JP* 2, 1565.
[13]   *SKS* 19, 375, Not12:4 / *KJN* 3, 373.

pseudonymous authorship. The religious is supposed to recuperate both aesthetic and ethical elements in a higher unity—though not through Hegelian mediation and dialectical synthesis. The principal poles of the dramatic are tragedy and comedy. Both of these are defined by Johannes Climacus in terms of contradiction.[14] They are reconciled in humor. Humor, according to Climacus, is the highest existential sphere attainable by human beings under their own powers, and is the *confinium* to the religious sphere.[15] To get beyond human immanence requires a leap of faith and a relationship with the transcendent God. Like his mentor Poul Martin Møller, Kierkegaard argues (against Hegel) that philosophy cannot account for existence in its totality. Art, on the other hand, contains an intuition of unified totality (exemplified in Goethe's *Wilhelm Meister*),[16] which enables the aesthetic transfiguration of the mundane. While this aesthetic transfiguration is still within the domain of immanence, it serves as an adumbration of religious transfiguration through faith.

Kierkegaard also draws on Møller's concepts of life-view and the grounding of personality in the communal life of Christianity to blend the notions of aesthetics as critical reflection on art with the aesthetic as an existential sphere. The aesthetic as artistic apprehension of beauty is incorporated into each of the existential spheres. The aesthete Johannes the Seducer, for example, finds in beauty an occasion for self-titillation, while the ethicist Judge William finds aesthetic beauty in marriage, and Kierkegaard, writing under his own name in *The Concept of Irony* and *Works of Love*, finds beauty in simplicity. Art is distinguished as aesthetic, ethical or religious by its purpose and by its mode of communication: *Either/Or*'s "Diapsalmata" are egotistical expressions of bored aestheticism (addressed *ad se ipsum*—to himself); Judge William's letters are addressed to another in an attempt to communicate the value of civic virtue; while the poetical dwelling with biblical figures and images in the upbuilding discourses aims at building up the love-of-other presupposed in the reader. The upbuilding discourses might be said to express a "second aesthetics" by analogy with the "second ethics" found in the religious sphere and expressed in the "second authorship."[17] Aesthetic poetry has its reality in its ideality and recognizes this by presenting itself as a hypothetical statement in the subjunctive mood,[18] whereas religious poetry is an invitation to make the possible actual in one's own life through acts of faith. The religious effect of this "second aesthetics" involves an inversion of the privileging of word over image. The religious symbolic image has the power, even when presented in words, of showing contradictions without nullifying meaning, but remaining a *sign*. These signs can be turned into truth by regarding them through faith, as the image of the woman who was a sinner, for example, can be regarded as a sign of the forgiveness of sins.[19]

---

[14]   *SKS* 7, 465–6 / *CUP1*, 514–15.
[15]   Cf. *SKS* 7, 273 / *CUP1*, 300.
[16]   *SKS* 19, 102, Not3:5 / *KJN* 3, 100.
[17]   Cf. Ettore Rocca, "Kierkegaard's Second Aesthetics," *Kierkegaard Studies Yearbook*, 1999, pp. 278–92.
[18]   *SKS* 1, 155 / *CI*, 101.
[19]   *SKS* 12, 249–58 / *WA*, 135–44.

II. The Aesthetic as Existential Sphere

The aesthete as an existential type can only be understood in the context of the notions of life-view and life-development. Kierkegaard gives a Hegelian account of psychological development, starting with the infant's immersion in immediate sense experience and ending with mutual respectful recognition of the other and by the other as a mature spirit. Life-development requires a protracted stage of self-alienation, which begins with the awakening of desire. Desire is conceived as a lack (one can only desire that which one does not have, according to Plato).[20] This lack disturbs immediacy's sense of plenitude, and opens a gap between the subject and object of experience, thereby allowing anxiety to arise as an objectless ambivalence on the brink of freedom. Kierkegaard traces the various stages of desire in "The Immediate Erotic Stages" of *Either/Or* through Mozart's figures of the Page (*Figaro*), Papageno (*The Magic Flute*), and Don Giovanni.

The ultimate *telos* of life-development is the attainment of freedom. But Kierkegaard presents a case that the freedom pursued by the aesthete is a false freedom. The first intimation of freedom occurs with the anxiety that accompanies sexual awakening. Here the goal of freedom is taken to be happiness, and the realization of freedom is taken to be subject to luck, chance, and fate. Time is reduced to the moment—the fleeting instant of enjoyment or satisfaction. There is no possibility of life-development conceived through reflection on one's history. Nor is there an understanding of eternity, except as the perfect coincidence of form and content in the work of art—or in intimations of one's immortality through the expansive feeling of romantic love. The aesthetic is discontinuous, as opposed to the continuity of the ethical with others in the community, and of the religious with one's neighbor. The religious also aspires to be continuous with God through faith in the God-Man.

The prime positive motivation for the aesthete as an existential type is desire for *the interesting*; the prime negative motivation is flight from *boredom*. This transformation of the object of aesthetics from beauty to the interesting is characteristic of German Romanticism, which is the principal target of Kierkegaard's critique of the aesthetic as an existential sphere. In pursuit of the interesting the aesthete immerses himself in mood, so that personality is only dimly present as the subject of enjoyment. But mood changes from moment to moment, which exposes the aesthete to the vicissitudes of fate. Escape from this circumstantial determination for the aesthete is only possible by choosing himself in his absolute validity, as a perduring character responsible before God. But that is to choose the ethical. Otherwise the aesthete is limited to choosing to adapt himself to fate through the prudential rotation of moods, or by embracing the arbitrary. This leads to the paradox of finding his greatest happiness in his unhappiness—in the self-alienation of melancholy.[21]

For Judge William there is a spiritual progression in the aesthetic from spatial arts to temporal arts. On this account, painting is more spiritually evolved than sculpture, music more evolved than painting, and poetry more evolved than music. But even

---

20   Cf. Plato, *Symposium*, 200a–200b.
21   *SKS* 2, 211–23 / *EO1*, 217–30.

poetry is limited in its ability to represent temporal sequence. Only *life* is adequate to the aesthetic representation of temporal sequence, by dramatic embodiment in character.[22] But what counts as character is different for the aesthete, the ethicist and the person of faith. The aesthete focuses on difference, especially that embodied in talent and genius, as the root of character. The aesthete is drawn to the hidden and secret, for their role in the libidinal economy of moods. The ethical, on the other hand, champions the universal (the same for all), the open (transparent), and vocation (open to all in different ways), so that character amounts to choosing oneself in these universal aspects. The religious reconciles the aesthetic and ethical notions of character by reprising the aesthetic beyond the (merely) ethical. It transfigures aesthetic difference into the unique individual, the hidden into inwardness, and talent into faith, and presents character in terms of personal repetition before God.

In preparation for his construction of the aesthetic sphere, Kierkegaard traces the development of three great medieval aesthetic figures, all of whom fall short of the ethical-religious: Don Juan, Faust, and Ahasverus (the Wandering Jew). Don Juan is presented as a force of nature, immersed in his erotic immediacy; Faust is a figure of doubt (*Tvivl*) driven by reflective desire; and Ahasverus is a figure of despair (*Fortvivlelse*). These represent stages in the internal dialectic of the aesthetic sphere. The aesthete can be immersed in immediacy, as is Don Juan, or can be a creature of reflection, as are Faust, Ahasverus, and Johannes the Seducer. Judge William defines the aesthetic as that in a person by which he is immediately what he is, while the ethical is that in a person by which he becomes what he becomes.[23] It is not immediacy as such that characterizes the aesthete, but that static element which blocks becoming—like Don Juan's compulsive desire, which gives only a numerical value to his serial seductions ("1003 in Spain").[24] It is not absence of reflection as such that characterizes the aesthete, but absence of *ethical* reflection (or choice)—like Johannes the Seducer's selective reflections of himself in Cordelia for the sake of manipulating her feelings. It is not absence of religious categories that characterizes the aesthete, but despair of their realization in the world—like Constantine Constantius' projection of religious categories onto a poetical fiction of his own invention ("the young man") rather than attempting to embrace them in his own life practices.

The aesthetic as an existential sphere is both divided from and joined to the ethical sphere by the *confinium* of irony. This conjunction with irony has several aspects: (1) Judge William, for example, points out to "A" that his position is ironic, since his manner of pursuit of freedom enslaves him to necessity. In single-mindedly pursuing the interesting by means of arbitrariness and chance, and by seeking to live exclusively in the modality of possibility, the aesthete neglects actuality and necessity, and thereby becomes determined by them; (2) although the aesthete exercises irony, it is not "irony as a mastered moment"—in which irony is subordinated to a higher (ethical or religious) purpose. Rather, the aesthete uses irony to find the interesting on the underside of the boring; (3) the aesthete sometimes uses irony as "midwife at

---

22   *SKS* 3, 135–7 / *EO2*, 137–9.
23   *SKS* 3, 215 / *EO2*, 225.
24   Cf. *SKS* 2, 99 / *EO1*, 92.

the birth of subjectivity," but not in the way Socrates did. For example, Johannes the Seducer manipulates Cordelia with irony (and other devices) in order to engender reflective consciousness in her. But this is for Johannes' own delectation. His use of irony is not under the dictates of a divine imperative, as Socrates' use of elenctic irony was. Nor is it a selfless or self-sacrificing activity for Johannes, as it ultimately was for Socrates—in the service of truth.

Finally, the three existential spheres are distinguished by their aesthetics of love. The aesthete finds love interesting, either in immediate immersion in the infatuation of first love or in the second-order titillations of reflection on love as a game. In either case, it is love in the character of *eros* not in the character of *agape* that preoccupies the aesthete. That is to say, love is felt as *desire* and is principally a form of self-love. For the ethicist, love has an erotic dimension, but this should be subordinated to the (universal) civic duty to love, should the two forms of love be in conflict. This in turn is distinguished from (paradoxical) religious love, which is apprehended as a duty in the form of self-sacrifice for the sake of the other. In the most extreme case of this, even civic duty might be teleologically suspended for the sake of God, as when Abraham was commanded to sacrifice his son Isaac. Aesthetic love fails to relate to the other as other, and thereby fails to open the aesthete dynamically to himself through another, while ethical and religious love both crucially entail openness to the other.

See also Anxiety; Art; Classicism; Comic/Comedy; Demonic; Desire, Epic; Ethics; Freedom; Humor; Imagination; Immediacy/Reflection; Interesting; Irony; Love; Lyric; Melancholy; Mood/Emotion/Feeling; Music; Novel/*Bildungsroman*; Poetry; Religious/Religiousness; Romanticism; Stages; Tragic/Tragedy.

Allegory

J.D. Mininger

Allegory (*Allegori*—noun; *allegorisk*—adjective)

For all practical purposes, the Danish term *Allegori* is identical in meaning to the English word "allegory."[1] Derived from the Greek ἀλληγορεῖν, allegory suggests the act of speaking figuratively—that is, of speaking otherwise than one seems to speak. Literally, it means speaking otherwise, other speaking, or speaking to the other. An allegory offers the opportunity to speak, indicate, or represent one thing, yet mean another thing—in effect signifying two things at once. Used often in medieval and Renaissance literature, many traditional allegories proceed by way of emblems and personification, creating a representation of an abstract idea or theme through material forms. Authors such as Dante, Spenser, and Chaucer belong to the pantheon of allegorists, and Bunyan's *The Pilgrim's Progress* (1678) is arguably the most famous canonical work of allegorical literature as such. In some modern camps of literary criticism, such as deconstruction, allegory has seen a rejuvenation of interest, if not also a radical reinterpretation. The most dramatic reinterpretation of the form has resulted in the notion that all writing is allegorical—that is, no text is free from the possibility that its intended meaning is not, cannot be, transparent and secure. This argument proceeds from the basic premise of structural linguistics, namely, that the relationship between signifier and signified is always an arbitrary one.

Given Kierkegaard's predilection for indirect communication, most readers likely assume Kierkegaard readily employed, or perhaps even privileged allegory within his arsenal of literary forms and devices. However, if essential usage is any indicator, these assumptions are strikingly ill-founded. Kierkegaard very rarely uses the term "allegory." The word *Allegori* (including its variations, such as *allegorisk*) appears only eight times in the entirety of the published works of Kierkegaard and further surfaces eighteen times in Kierkegaard's journals, notebooks, and papers. The use of allegory is not particularly salient in any of these instances.

In the *Concluding Unscientific Postscript*, in Chapter II, "Subjective Truth, Inwardness; Truth Is Subjectivity," Kierkegaard brandishes the term "allegorizing" (*allegoriserende*) twice in four sentences.[2] Tellingly, in both instances the word follows the initial modifier "mythical." Kierkegaard connects allegory so closely

---

[1]   *Ordbog over det danske Sprog*, vols. 1–28, published by the Society for Danish Language and Literature, Copenhagen: Gyldendal 1918–56, vol. 1, column 449.
[2]   *SKS* 7, 199 / *CUP1*, 218.

with myth here that the second instance of the term is literally bonded to the modifier "mythical" with a hyphen: "*mythisk-allegoriserende*" (mythical allegorizing). At least in this instance, allegory is nothing more than metaphorical naming that allows something abstract, conceptual, inward, or mythical (in the sense of fantastical) to be figured outwardly in language. The manner of usage suggests that allegory simplifies, perhaps even cheapens, the otherwise vital, supple nature of the concept, phenomenon, or movement at stake.

Numerous other examples of usage follow suit. For example, later in the *Postscript*, buried in a footnote in which Kierkegaard is chiding sermonizers for taking the faith of the individual members of the congregation for granted, he suggests that in these sermons faith becomes *et Slags allegorisk Figur* (a kind of allegorical figure).[3] His point here is that, via personification, allegory simplifies and trivializes the otherwise complex, existential movement of faith. In *The Concept of Irony*, in the section called "Irony after Fichte,"[4] Kierkegaard twice uses the term *Allegori* in his discussion of Tieck. In both cases the usage is identical, suggesting that the ideal posed by Tieck specifically, and by Romantic poets in general, is effectively a sham since, according to Kierkegaard, Romantic irony is not ordered in a poetic totality. Thus, he writes *ethvert Ideal er i samme Øieblik dog blot en Allegori* (every ideal is instantly nothing but an allegory), which hides a new and higher ideal, *ad infinitum*.[5] Here allegory is simply a linguistic form in which one signifier shelters (somewhat disingenuously, it would seem) a covert meaning. In other words, a Romantic ideal (endeavor) is never genuine, since it proceeds in the infinite regress of poetic freedom, and therefore becomes an ersatz, bogus ideal—a mere allegory of an ideal—which is no ideal at all.

References to allegory in the journals, notebooks, and papers mirror the appearances in the published texts in that they also demonstrate Kierkegaard's essential lack of interest in, and perhaps even mild disdain, for allegory. For instance, in one entry on the topic of "the moment,"[6] Kierkegaard discusses the point that the moment, viewed from a spiritual perspective, can be so ecstatic, and take on such poetic, distended form, that even the most materially oriented workers could catch a bit of the infinite and its truth in a kind of allegorical form. But while there is spiritual reality in that, it is nevertheless the case that they have this reality only insofar as it is an allegory. Another journal entry names allegory as a literary device used in the Bible to protect biblical truth from heretics, since only those of faith would see through the allegorical code.[7] In a list of rough notes on creation, Kierkegaard notes that writers seem always to read the creation story as an allegory.[8] Other points in the journals note similar interpretive trends, in particular beginning in the seventeenth century, towards reading every word, every letter of Scripture, as allegorical.[9] In

3   *SKS* 7, 380 / *CUP1*, 418.
4   *SKS* 1, 338–9 / *CI*, 306.
5   *SKS* 1, 338 / *CI*, 306.
6   *SKS* 18, 45, EE:119 / *JP* 2, 1579.
7   *SKS* 23, 433, NB20:70 / *JP* 3, 2877.
8   *SKS* 19, 79, Not1:9 / *JP* 1, 36.
9   See *SKS* 23, 148, NB16:78 / *JP* 4, 4781.

several cases of the appearance of "allegory" and its variations in the journals and notebooks, Kierkegaard includes "allegory" simply as a term belonging to historical, and especially to mythical interpretation.[10]

Despite all of the tactics of indirect communication performed in the published texts and self-reflectively explained in particular publications, but especially in the private journals, Kierkegaard very rarely used the term "allegory" and its variations. If he had grasped his own intellectual (or religious) project as essentially allegorical in its interpretive slant, or if he had valued his own writing techniques as specifically allegorical, then surely he would have identified himself and his textual strategies by this description somewhere in his massive textual output.

The most illuminating answer (though surely not the only plausible explanation) as to why Kierkegaard so rarely uses the term arises from the historical context. With the advent of Romanticism and its critiques of and responses to Enlightenment rationalism came a historical shift in poetic discourse, which more often than not saw symbolism win greater favor and emphasis at the expense of allegory.[11] Therefore, despite never being one to shy away from breaking with intellectual trendiness, Kierkegaard inherited a culturally and historically received understanding of allegory as associated with wooden, unsubtle, rationalist traditions, whereas, at the very least, the appeal of symbolism as a privileged technique for rendering metaphor surely fits many Kierkegaardian foci, including, the single individual; existence as incommensurable through conventional signification; the renewal of spirituality; and the rather literary nature of life and identity. However, the point here is not that Kierkegaard is a symbolist, but rather that the received notions comprising his historical context would suggest a predisposition for understanding allegory in a very limited way. It is most likely for these reasons that he uses the term "allegory" so rarely, even if some of his textual operations at times look similar to allegory.

Despite his indifference to the term "allegory," there are three techniques and/or concepts wielded over and again in Kierkegaard's writings that nevertheless make a discussion of Kierkegaard and allegory appropriate: analogy, parable, and irony. But this must be taken with an important caveat: that Kierkegaard did not understand himself to be an allegorist, at least in any traditional sense.

The first notable comparison between literary techniques frequently used by Kierkegaard and traditional models of allegory involves analogy as form. At the micro-levels of sentence and paragraph, Kierkegaard so frequently employs analogies that to track them all down would be a rather tedious exercise. At the macro-levels of (among others) the philosophical construction of concepts and the performativity of form in his texts, analogy is an important device in Kierkegaard's

---

[10]   See *SKS* 19, 83, Not1:9 / *JP* 1, 36; *SKS* 19, 34, Not1:6 / *KJN* 3, 29; *SKS* 23, 148, NB16:78 / *JP* 4, 4781.

[11]   Unlike allegory, a symbol, similarly to synecdoche, supposedly maintains an inherent connection between the sensible representation and the insensible meaning it represents. What allegory signifies by means of convention, the symbol represents as a natural link between sign and meaning. This Romantic reaction against allegory, in favor of symbolism, was not an unchallenged pattern: many Romantic writers thought many different ways about allegory. For more on this, see, for instance, Tzvetan Todorov, *Theories of the Symbol*, trans. by Catherine Porter, Ithaca, New York: Cornell University Press 1982.

intellectual production. This is exemplified, for instance, in the narrator's return trip to Berlin in *Repetition* (which is at least a twofold analogy, if one also reads it biographically), or as the form of the individual chapters of *Prefaces* relate analogously to the overall theme(s) of the book—or one step further, how *Prefaces* analogically comments on *The Concept of Anxiety*, which was published on the same day, though under a different pseudonym. These examples possess the appearance of allegorical commentary, because they highlight how one sign comments on another in a somewhat indirect manner. Despite the fact that both allegory and analogy show a kind of metaphorical relationship of meaning, their divergence is crucial: analogy is about establishing similarity of object or situation, whereas allegory does not, in fact, demand similarity at all. Allegory simply despotically attaches one topos to another via (typically extended) metaphorical signification, and in the traditional model of allegory this attachment of the sign to its meaning was highly conventional.

In the matter of the second element of Kierkegaard's literary toolbox that resembles allegory in some critical ways—the parable form—one need look no further than a book published in 1978 by Thomas C. Oden entitled *Parables of Kierkegaard*, which collects in English translation eighty-six parables from across Kierkegaard's body of work.[12] This volume is at once an excellent resource for those wishing to examine the extent to which Kierkegaard's knack for storytelling bends in an allegorical direction and a cogent defense-by-example of why Kierkegaard is not a traditional allegorist, but rather a parabolist—and surely one belonging to the pantheon of the Western tradition of parabolists, which might include, among others, Plato, Jesus, Nietzsche, Kafka, and Gide. In terms of the relationship between allegory and parable, both storytelling models employ metaphorical operations (whether of writing or of reading); but parables are defined specifically in reference to their didactic goal, which is most often a moralistic message of some sort.[13] A parable might employ a few allegorical principles, but its structure is more particular than allegory.

The third literary operation in Kierkegaard's work that is discrete yet similar to allegory is irony. If Kierkegaard largely ignores allegory as a term and practice, then perhaps it is due to the enormous emphasis placed on irony in his work. Like irony, allegory traffics in concealed meanings, even if traditional allegory often depended upon well-established conventional agreement as to what meaning a given sign signified. Irony fulfills its etymological roots (dissimulation) when an ironist says less (or differently) than what is thought or intended. In this way traditional allegory may agree with irony, in that it signifies beyond itself, saying one thing but meaning another. If there were ever a logical place for Kierkegaard to address allegory, it would be in *The Concept of Irony*. But traditional allegory does not match Kierkegaard's definition of Romantic irony, which negates the totality of existence in

---

[12]   Søren Kierkegaard, *Parables of Kierkegaard*, ed. by Thomas C. Oden, Princeton: Princeton University Press 1978.

[13]   In the Introduction to his volume, Oden gives what he calls a "classical" definition of a parable: "a brief story of spare characterization and surprising reversal, with the underlying intent of moral or spiritual illumination." Oden, "Introduction," in *Parables of Kierkegaard*, p. x.

its indiscriminate ironic posture. For Kierkegaard, Romantic irony has no goal, and strives for nothing other than self-entertainment. Traditional allegory might signify beyond itself, but its rationalist and conventional nature secure its termination in meaning. For Kierkegaard, what is at stake in irony is precisely the ability to control the intended leap of meaning from literal to the ironic/figural level. Thus, if allegory were to have been an important modification of irony for Kierkegaard, then the final section of *The Concept of Irony*, on "Irony as a Controlled Element," would have been the most obvious place to address allegory's notable potential in this regard. Despite the book's appearance at the beginning of the authorship, Kierkegaard never returned to the topic of irony with the same intense focus, and therefore never again created the textual potential to explore the relationship between irony and allegory.

Beyond these three similar operations, there still remains the possibility that, *avant la lettre*, Kierkegaard indeed employs and perhaps even provides theorizations of some version(s) of allegory, though perhaps by another name. For example, new research might conceivably pick up on several clues left by Theodor Adorno in *Kierkegaard: Construction of the Aesthetic*,[14] which suggest the possibility that at some points when Kierkegaard spoke of myth, he meant something very similar to certain modern understandings of allegory. Myth has a peculiar dialectical truth: myth's truth is that it is untruth. In *The Concept of Anxiety* Kierkegaard states very clearly what function myth's dialectically riddled truth has: "myth allows something that is inward to take place outwardly."[15] Despite the fact that modern allegory constantly serves as a reminder that allegorical relations might be merely outward— pure surface and nothing more—many of Kierkegaard's literary techniques endeavor to indicate by means of language what are ineffable, unrepresentable, "inward" truths. The continued study of allegory in Kierkegaard could potentially contribute to a better understanding of his essential literary task: rendering silence with words.

See also Irony; Myth; Story-Telling.

---

[14]   Theodor W. Adorno, *Kierkegaard: Construction of the Aesthetic*, trans. by Robert Hullot-Kentor, Minneapolis: University of Minnesota Press 1989.
[15]   *SKS* 4, 352 / *CA*, 47.

Ambiguity

Jacobo Zabalo

Ambiguity/Equivocalness (*Tvetydighed*—noun; *tvetydig*—adjective)

The Danish term *Tvetydighed*, when applied to a word or expression, indicates that there is more than one possible meaning, and hence more than one possible interpretation. But it may also be used in a more general sense to indicate that something is unclear or lacking in precision in a way that settles doubt.[1]

Kierkegaard's references to the concept of ambiguity (*Tvetydighed*), a term also translated as "equivocalness," are present both in his pseudonymous writings (*Either/Or*, *The Concept of Anxiety*, and *Stages on Life's Way*) and in his signed ones (including his journals and published works such as *The Concept of Irony* and *The Moment*). The use of the adjective "ambiguous" (*tvetydig*) is also common in these texts, but like the noun it is not systematically applied, appearing rather randomly and with different purposes. There arises, therefore, a question about whether ambiguity can be understood as a central concept in Kierkegaard's thought, as is the case with concepts such as irony and anxiety. This question is hard to answer, though it seems reasonable to consider the concept of ambiguity as one among many characteristic Kierkegaardian *contra-concepts*: just like ironic equivocation or ineffable anxiety, ambiguity is characterized by its indeterminacy of meaning. It communicates a difficulty related to the final, complete elucidation of the issue concerned.

I. Literary Duplicity and Participation

One of the most prominent examples of ambiguity in Kierkegaard's writings—where the concept seems to have a structural and illustrative depth—can be found in the posthumously published work *The Point of View for My Work as an Author*. The title of the first section (A) of Part One states the problematic issue: "The Equivocalness [*Tvetydigheden*] or Duplexity in the Whole Authorship, Whether the Author is an Aesthetic or a Religious Author."[2] The answer to this question is clearly laid out in the following section (B), "The Explanation: That the Author is and was a Religious Author."[3] Kierkegaard most unambiguously affirms in this *Direct Communication, Report to History*—the subtitle of *The Point of View*—the

---

[1]   *Ordbog over det danske Sprog*, vols. 1–28, published by the Society for Danish Language and Literature, Copenhagen: Gyldendal 1918–56, vol. 24, columns 1147–50.
[2]   *SKS* 16, 15 / *PV*, 29.
[3]   *SKS* 16, 18 / *PV*, 33.

separation between his religious and aesthetic writings, the latter being merely the medium to promote indirectly a sincere spirituality. According to this explanation, ambiguity characterizes only the literary device, the strategy of pseudonymity; and thus the confession of duplicity puts an end to equivocation. This was already made explicit in the 1851 text *On My Work as an Author*, where Kierkegaard advanced the main ideas concerning his activity: it "began maieutically with esthetical production, and all the pseudonymous writings are *maieutic* in nature."[4]

Together with the posthumous distinction between aesthetic and religious writings, it is clear—as Kierkegaard sometimes acknowledges—that the pseudonymous authors may be equivocal without being either false or opposed to his *authentic* position. An early journal entry anticipates and therefore inversely complements the retrospective understanding of his position as an author: "I think that if I ever do become an earnest Christian, my deepest shame will be that I did not become one before, that I first wanted to try everything else."[5] Even the incipient author of authors was forced to admit that, in spite of the poetical flair and fictional maneuvers of the pseudonymous books, he himself was involved in a dialectical enterprise: a redoubling that also helped construct his own self. By the end of *On My Work as an Author* he clearly questions the *Postscript*'s final explanation: "This is how I *now* understand the whole. From the beginning I could not quite see what has indeed also been my own development."[6]

Fiction—together with the various poetical devices that Kierkegaard employs— is only opposed to *truthful* discourse by the fact that it does not want to show univocally what is actual, but rather what is possible. The pseudonyms disguise the true Kierkegaard and—dialectically—also picture him from a distance, working as a re-creation of the existential possibilities that concern every human being. This is not a postmodern claim but rather, as Paul Ricoeur has shown in several of his works,[7] a condition of fictional statements, an open possibility of participation already present in those remote Aristotelian implications of *mimesis* and, of course, in the almost contemporary notion of *Bildungsroman* so fundamental to the poetics of the nineteenth century. In this sense, the reader of Kierkegaard's pseudonymous works is supposed to complete the message, to decide for himself, and thereby discern the seriousness behind the fictitious and yet real game, just as in Socrates' ironical discourse. In his dissertation, Kierkegaard noted Talleyrand's witty comment on the equivocalness of language, namely, that "man did not acquire speech in order to reveal his thoughts but in order to conceal them."[8] Thus, the attribution of the pseudonymous authors' thoughts to Kierkegaard himself may certainly be problematic if done univocally, but then again this problem reveals a fruitful way of understanding his literary purpose: "I find it ironically in order that the honorarium,

---

4   *SKS* 13, 13–14 / *PV*, 7.
5   *SKS* 17, 250, DD:89 / *KJN* 1, 240.
6   *SKS* 13, 18 / *PV*, 12.
7   Paul Ricoeur, *La métaphore vive*, Paris: Seuil 1975; cf. Paul Ricoeur, *Temps et récit. Tome III: Le temps raconté*, Paris: Seuil 1985; Paul Ricoeur, *Soi-même comme un autre*, Paris: Seuil 1990.
8   *SKS* 1, 292 / *CI*, 253.

at least, in virtue of the production and of my equivocal [*tvetydige*] authorship, has been rather Socratic."[9]

II. Alternatives to Philosophy (Irony)

Kierkegaard was well acquainted with Hegel's philosophy, which was dominant in the period. According to Hans Lassen Martensen, one of Kierkegaard's teachers, Hegel's "philosophy is the present, because the whole philosophical attitude is permeated with this philosophy, so that nothing can be written without being traceable to it." His approach "is used even by his opponents."[10] One of the first critical voices to reflect on Kierkegaard's thought, Theodor W. Adorno, supported the idea of this interdependence, suggesting that Hegel had found his posthumous mortal enemy after having somehow invented him prophetically. Adorno was thinking of Kierkegaard's subjectivity in terms of the Hegelian *unhappy consciousness* (a redoubled consciousness that desperately looks for itself in such a way that it can only be confirmed as split, incomplete and therefore unrealized). According to him, the anti-Hegelianism of Kierkegaard is trapped in the mud and pretends to get out of it by employing its own dialectical procedures but in an unconscious manner: "truth becomes ambiguous as the quintessence of dialectical movement without being its measure."[11]

It is known that many of Hegel's followers and detractors only had a second-hand knowledge of his philosophy. This applies somewhat to Kierkegaard, who, despite his own reading of Hegel, mainly knew about *the system* through Martensen's lectures. The notes that Kierkegaard took then do not quite reflect the depth of Hegel's thought (he "did not grasp entirely the fine nuances and he occasionally missed the context").[12] While Kierkegaard detects something positive in Hegel's interpretation,[13] he stresses the absolute negativity of irony. Socrates' irony pushes coherence to its limit, projecting him towards an inescapable death and into misunderstanding by later generations. In the introduction to his dissertation, Kierkegaard affirms that Socrates "left nothing by which a later age can judge him; indeed, even if I were to imagine myself his contemporary, he would still always be difficult to comprehend…what Socrates said meant something different."[14] Hegel's *Philosophy of Right*, a work that Kierkegaard has in mind in several passages of his dissertation, is treated in an ambiguous way: Kierkegaard employs Hegel's category of *universalized subjectivity* applied to Socrates and discusses the relation between morality and ethics,[15] but at the same time defies the rationality that is supposed to sustain reality, as explained by Hegel in the prologue of that work.

---

[9]   *SKS 7*, 572 / *CUP1*, 628.
[10]   Quoted from Niels Thulstrup, *Kierkegaard's Relation to Hegel*, trans. by George L. Stengren, Princeton: Princeton University Press 1980, p. 136.
[11]   Theodor W. Adorno, *Kierkegaard: Construction of the Aesthetic*, trans. and ed. by Robert Hullot-Kentor, Minneapolis: University of Minnesota Press 1989, p. 73.
[12]   Thulstrup, *Kierkegaard's Relation to Hegel*, p. 133.
[13]   Ibid., p. 242.
[14]   *SKS* 1, 74 / *CI*, 12.
[15]   Thulstrup, *Kierkegaard's Relation to Hegel*, p. 217.

Hegel's *Lectures on the Philosophy of History* also appears to be closely followed by Kierkegaard in his attempt to understand the Greek paradigm but only to a certain point, namely, when the Socratic concept of irony is introduced:

> The objective power of the state, its claims upon the activity of the individual, the laws, the courts—everything loses its absolute validity for him [sc. Socrates]….and he himself hovers over it in ironic contentment, borne up by the absolute self-consistency of infinite negativity.[16]

What is affirmed in Socrates' life and death is a void, a suspension of criteria and a radical alternative to the *status quo* of positive truth. In this way, Kierkegaard tends to employ *Hegel against Hegel*, perhaps without being fully conscious at this early point. What is certain in any case is that Socrates' death, narrated in Plato's *Phaedo*, leaves room for uncertainty. In *The Concept of Irony* Kierkegaard refers to the "ambiguity" (*Tvetydighed*)[17] of Socrates' words, taken from the *Apology*: "now it is time that we are going, I to die and you to live, but which of us has the happier prospect is unknown to anyone but the god."[18] As for the *Phaedo*, the dying Socrates' reminder of the need to sacrifice a cock for Asclepius (the god of health and medicine) is equally ambivalent or ironic—an acknowledgment of death as a "cure" for life.

Not having a "positive system," Socrates made possible all positivity by the pressure of the "infinite negativity"[19] of his procedure, a way of suspending judgment about what is supposedly known, and simultaneously opening the possibility for an inner, absolute knowledge. Still, according to Kierkegaard, Socrates' dialectical praxis "has the very ambiguity [*Tvetydighed*] that it can both polemically turn against the finite and be stimulative for the infinite."[20] In his loose papers he observes: "This self-overcoming of irony is the crisis of the higher spiritual life."[21] Irony suspends "all the qualifications of substantial life";[22] the "established order of things" is negated, consequently offering a new possibility—a positive, existential movement which is not only qualified as free but also as "infinitely ambiguous [*tvetydig*]."[23]

III. Sin's Anxiety

Socrates would remain a major reference point for Kierkegaard, even being mentioned at the end of his lifetime in some of his explicitly religious works as the "true martyr of intellectuality."[24] Irony is diagnosed by Kierkegaard as something rare, too sly to be really understood, and yet powerful: "Occasionally we still meet

---

16   *SKS* 1, 243 / *CI*, 196.
17   *SKS* 1, 142 / *CI*, 85.
18   Ibid.
19   *SKS* 1, 261 / *CI*, 216.
20   *SKS* 1, 261 / *CI*, 217.
21   *SKS* 27, 157, Papir 209 / *JP* 2, 1688.
22   *SKS* 1, 262 / *CI*, 217.
23   *SKS* 1, 262 / *CI*, 218.
24   *SKS* 13, 405 / *M*, 341.

a representative of that vanished age who has preserved that subtle, sententious, equivocally [*tvetydigt*] divulging smile,"[25] a mysterious smile that Kierkegaard compared to that of the fisherman upon sensing the nibble of a fish.[26] There is an understanding through irony, but of a very peculiar kind, expressed as a silent assumption about the negation of actuality. Nothingness emerges and becomes a real-though-imaginary possibility: "the ironic nothing is the dead silence in which irony walks again and haunts (the latter word taken altogether ambiguously)."[27]

Only three years later Kierkegaard would reflect in *The Concept of Anxiety* about that absolute openness of negativity, the condition for the self's positive freedom, understanding it also as a cause of spiritual, psychosomatic distress in its actualization of nothingness. In this case, there is—as the subtitle indicates—a theological issue involved, specifically concerning the *Dogmatic Issue of Hereditary Sin*, which is "psychologically" focused even if sin itself is not a matter of psychology: "Sin has its specific place, or more correctly it has no place, and this is its specific nature."[28] Kierkegaard considers it necessity to present an explanation of the undeterminable and yet absolute reality of sin that is neither systematic nor philosophical, but rather constructed according to the intimate way it affects every individual's actuality: "The psychological explanation must not talk around the point but remain in its elastic ambiguity [*elastiske Tvetydighed*], from which guilt breaks forth in the qualitative leap."[29] Anxiety, being an affect of the soul, must be described from a psychological perspective due to the impossibility of referring to it as a mere object. It cannot be understood straightforwardly, since it is a response to the ineffable reality of guilt: "because Adam has not understood what was spoken, there is nothing but the ambiguity of anxiety."[30] Kierkegaard employed a celebrated and yet ambivalent expression to define it: "anxiety is *a sympathetic antipathy* and *an antipathetic sympathy*,"[31] a state of attraction and repulsion that reveals suffering and grace, a superior force that tempts and posits the spiritual transcendence as well as freedom.[32]

These theological reflections—attributed to Vigilius Haufniensis—must have held a personal interest for Kierkegaard, preoccupied as he was for so long about the reality of guilt. From a biographical perspective it has been suggested that he inherited this preoccupation from his father, who was apparently responsible for some unconfessed mortal sin that he thought would cause his children to die before he did: "Then I surmised that my father's old-age was not a divine blessing, but rather a curse….A guilt must rest upon the entire family."[33] The anxiety of the young Kierkegaard, who experienced the loss of his brothers and sisters, remained even after he realized that the prophecy could not be fulfilled. Three days after his father's death Kierkegaard constructed a Christian explanation with a dialectical logic based

---

[25]   *SKS* 1, 285 / *CI*, 247.
[26]   *SKS* 20, 307, NB4:39 / *KJN* 4, 307.
[27]   *SKS* 1, 296 / *CI*, 258.
[28]   *SKS* 4, 321 / *CA*, 14.
[29]   *SKS* 4, 347 / *CA*, 41.
[30]   *SKS* 4, 350 / *CA*, 45.
[31]   *SKS* 4, 348 / *CA*, 42.
[32]   *SKS* 4, 350 / *CA*, 45.
[33]   *SKS* 27, 291–2, Papir 305:3 / *JP* 5, 5430.

on guilt and grace: "I regard his death as the last sacrifice of his love for me, because in dying he did not depart from me but he *died for me*, in order that something, if possible, might still come for me."[34] Such wishful thinking would nevertheless soon turn dark—actually, for the rest of his life, in several episodes of melancholy related to a sense of sinfulness. Kierkegaard would often complain in the journals of his fragile physical nature and mention the ambiguous, biblical expression of the *thorn in the flesh* (*Pælen i Kjødet*), an ambiguous suffering that nobody could know about, since—according to his words—it explained his most intimate reality.[35]

Paul's epistles (especially the second addressed to the Corinthians) relate how that specific suffering was sent to him so he would remain close to his duty, in order to be uplifted from an anguished and feeble condition. Luther's reading of this same passage reappears in Kierkegaard's ambiguous explanation of the cause for his sufferings. In 1844 he wrote an edifying discourse on this topic, stressing the correspondence between spiritual beatitude and the absolute, personal reality of the *thorn in the flesh*. While Luther employs the metaphor of the palm tree,[36] Kierkegaard considers—in similar vein—that believing is precisely becoming light thanks to the weight that one carries,[37] believing that God is powerfully present in the individual who does not avoid the sufferings described by Paul. In spite of the uncertainty of the approach, a conscience in anxiety is the condition *sine qua non* (a necessary though not sufficient condition) for the faith that Kierkegaard sustains.

IV. Unambiguous as a Bird? (A Possible Conclusion)

Ambiguity might be (1) the medium, the literary device to communicate indirectly a real, subjective presence; or ambiguity might be (2) the philosophical, universal approach to truth, ironically focused; or, due to its ineffability, ambiguity might be (3) the experience of anxiety, a spiritual suffering felt as a responsibility or as actualization of sin in oneself. But in spite of these three forms of ambiguity, Kierkegaard believes in the need to remain beyond all equivocation in relation to spiritual truth.

There are some poetical images that Kierkegaard employs in order to communicate what—according to him—is a natural, unmistakable reality, that is, the absolute dependence of human beings on God, the need to accept and follow God's plan just like *the lily in the field and the bird in the air*. One word captures the proper attitude before God: "obedience" (*Lydighed*). With this word Kierkegaard seems to annihilate all his dialectical procedures. "Out there with the lily and the bird, we said, there is silence. But this silence…is the first condition to be able to obey."[38] Silence is not the pattern for an equivocal praxis but the condition for a higher participation in transcendence, a submission comparable to Abraham's faith that *should not*—and

---

[34]   *SKS* 17, 258, DD:126 / *KJN* 1, 249.
[35]   *SKS* 22, 196, NB12:100 / *JP* 6, 6468.
[36]   Martin Luther, *The Sermons of Martin Luther*, trans. and ed. by John Nicholas Lenker, Grand Rapids, Michigan: Baker Book House 1983, pp. 117–18.
[37]   *SKS* 20, 56, NB:65 / *KJN* 4, 55.
[38]   *SKS* 11, 29 / *WA*, 24.

cannot—be a matter for rational, objective, scientific inquiry. Also in his discourse "No One Can Serve Two Masters," published in 1849, Kierkegaard explicitly tries to erase all possible forms of "ambivalence" (*Tvetydighed*) and establishes "simplicity" (*Eenfoldighed*) as the key to avoid Satan's "craftiness."[39]

The dialectic of suffering seems to stand in an uneasy relation to this preaching of unequivocal obedience: "Wherever there is ambivalence [*Tvetydighed*], there is temptation…there is in one way or another also disobedience underneath at the base."[40] *One way or another* is a rather ambiguous expression, but it is absolutely adequate, nevertheless, if one takes into account the impossibility of detecting the real work of love.[41] It belongs to the very essence of Kierkegaard's idea of subjectivity, imbued with religious pathos, that even the *simplicity* of faith has to endure some severe crisis (Christ's suffering on the cross, an absurd separation from the Father, is the most radical and explicit example of this). Therefore, even inner reality may also seem for a moment *unbelievable* for the person involved. Kierkegaard's struggle for simple faith and obedience cannot eliminate the ambiguity in the dialectic implicit in his subjective and spiritual conception of existence.

See also Absurd; Actuality/Ideality; Anxiety; Contradiction; Freedom; Irony; Love; Paradox; Pathos/Passion; Sin.

---

[39] *SKS* 11, 37 / *WA*, 32.
[40] *SKS* 11, 37 / *WA*, 33.
[41] *SKS* 9, 21 / *WL*, 13.

Anonymity

Joseph Westfall

Anonymity (*Anonymitet*—noun; *Navnløshed*—noun; *Anonym*—noun; *anonym*—adjective)

The lexical meaning of the Danish word (from the Latin *anonymus*, following the Greek ἀνώνυμος) is the quality of lacking or refraining from using a name with regard to one's public activities, perhaps especially as they may relate to the creation of literary or otherwise artistic works.[1] An anonym (literally, "without a name") is a designation or mark, sometimes alphabetic or alphanumeric, used to conceal the name of the author of a written work without substituting a pseudonym for the author's real name. In addition to being marked with an anonym, an anonymous work can (and often does) simply lack any ascription of authorship, or the author can be straightforwardly designated as "Anonymous." As in the case of pseudonymity, anonymous authorship may originate in an intention to conceal, but with regard to historical texts it is often instead the consequence of a loss of knowledge of the author's name with the passage of time.

Although Kierkegaard employs anonymity on occasion, in the Kierkegaardian *corpus* anonymity is most frequently discussed in the context of other anonymous authors. Most of the relevant references appear in *A Literary Review of Two Ages*; some others appear in newspaper articles from 1836 and in *The Point of View for My Work as an Author*. In Kierkegaard's understanding of the concept, anonymity consists of three essentially related notions: (1) the socio-political phenomenon of individual anonymity in public or popular movements; (2) the literary phenomenon of authoring newspaper articles and books without appending one's name—or any name—as author; and (3) the ethical-existential phenomenon of actions lacking any genuine connection to the lives of the persons who perform them. In Kierkegaard's writings, these three senses of anonymity regularly coincide.

I. Socio-Political Anonymity

Kierkegaard's earliest comments on anonymity appear in a mostly anonymous journalistic altercation between Kierkegaard (writing as the anonym, "B") and the Danish activist and popular reformer Orla Lehmann (writing anonymously without a specific anonym). The ostensible matter of debate is the freedom of the press,

---

[1] *Ordbog over det danske Sprog*, vols. 1–28, published by the Society for Danish Language and Literature, Copenhagen: Gyldendal 1918–56, vol. 1, columns 668–9.

and Lehmann's anonymous articles were written to incite public opposition to more stringent censorship laws. B's articles take issue primarily with the anonymous manner in which the reform movement was taking place in Denmark. In B's last anonymous contribution to the controversy, he writes: "Where, then, is that energetic, that serious, reforming spirit? Is it identical with those anonymous reformers (I can hardly say these words in one breath) who have their prototype in that anonymous or rather pseudonymous reformer, the snake of Eden?"[2]

Here, B unifies three anonymities into a criticism of Lehmann's movement: the anonymity of individual members of public or mass movements, wherein the particularities of the individuals involved tend to be blurred together into something we might call "the crowd," "the public," or "the movement"; the anonymity of Lehmann and other like-minded authors (such as Johannes Hage, also participating—to a much more limited extent than Lehmann or Kierkegaard—in the newspaper dispute), who write articles meant to encourage political action without signing their names to their provocations; and an anonymity of irresponsible manipulation, compared here to the snake in the book of Genesis, who is understood in popular readings of the Bible to be the devil appearing in the form of a serpent. While one might consider such a comparison unduly harsh, it does nevertheless make B's point: that one might by way of anonymity attempt to encourage others to engage in destructive if not evil actions while leaving one's own role and responsibility ambiguous.

The charge against an anonymous reform movement, then, has everything to do with the manipulative potential of public writings—in this case, newspaper articles— and the freedom anonymous authors have from responsibility for the socio-political consequences of their words. Following from the passage quoted above, B continues, noting that the anonymous reformers writing in *Kjøbenhavnsposten* have evaded responsibility for their actions, leaving it to others (in this case, the newspaper's editor, Andreas Peter Liunge) to suffer whatever consequences might come.[3] The anonymous reformers are actually saying something in their articles, something for which someone needs to be able to be held accountable, B argues; contrariwise, the named editor might as well have no name, since his role is simply to take the blame for whatever the anonymous authors say in their articles.

According to this early view, anonymity is anything but good. Despite the fact that Kierkegaard is waging his public war on anonymity anonymously, his perspective on anonymity is very clear: if one wishes to write publicly about matters of political or social concern, and if one wishes to do so in a way that advocates reform, then one must do so under one's own name. The exemplars of such reform are lofty indeed— Moses, Martin Luther, Daniel O'Connell[4]—but this only serves to re-emphasize the basic point: it matters what one says in public, all the more so if what one says is politically controversial and might result in reformist or revolutionary action. In the closing salvos of their battle, Kierkegaard makes clear that he understands this

---

[2]   *SKS* 14, 15 / *EPW*, 10. Except where otherwise indicated, Kierkegaard uses the term *anonym* and its variants, rather than other synonymous terms for anonymity available in the Danish language.

[3]   *SKS* 14, 16 / *EPW*, 10.

[4]   Ibid.

point, taking responsibility in his own name for all of the articles previously ascribed to the anonym, B; Orla Lehmann does not, as Kierkegaard notes in his concluding criticism of the man's role in the whole affair.[5]

II. Literary Anonymity

While there are non-literal senses of the terms "anonymity" and "anonymous" in Kierkegaard, even most of these have some direct and literal connection to the most common, literary concept of anonymity: authorship without ascription. While B and Kierkegaard were apparently entirely opposed to the socio-political practice of anonymity, even when that practice took the form of literary or journalistic productivity, Kierkegaard's stance on literary anonymity as such is decidedly more mixed. We might divide the anonymous authors treated in Kierkegaard's writings into three loose groups: (a) anonymous newspaper authors, such as Orla Lehmann, (b) "the author of *A Story of Everyday Life*," a descriptor used as an anonym by the Danish novelist, Thomasine Gyllembourg, and (c) Kierkegaard's own anonyms. Kierkegaard writes most critically of (a) in his various newspaper articles, at greatest length and most approvingly of (b) in *A Literary Review of Two Ages*, and makes only one passing but telling reference to (c) in *On My Work as an Author*.

In addition to the freedom of the press affair, wherein Kierkegaard set forth (first anonymously, then in his own name) his initial position on journalistic and political anonymity, there is another crucially important instance in Kierkegaard's authorship where authorial anonymity in the newspapers takes centerstage. "An Explanation and a Little More" (*Fædrelandet*, 1845) is Kierkegaard's published response to "an anonymous article in the *Berlingske Tidende*, no. 108,"[6] wherein the author suggests that Kierkegaard is the author of the pseudonymous books. There, after discussing the article's assertions, Kierkegaard notes that "since, as a matter of fact, that reviewer…is anonymous [*Anonym*]," it follows that the author is "thus divested of the trustworthiness of authority."[7] In what amounts to a significant critique of anonymity, Kierkegaard says in this passage that, without a name, an author lacks authority and authority's trustworthiness. In this article, Kierkegaard is referring specifically to literary authority, the standing in the world of literature either to confer or deny membership in the country's literary elite upon another author. Nevertheless, the principle underlying Kierkegaard's claim is more wide ranging than its context makes it seem. Ultimately, anonymous authors lack authority because they lack substantial, real identities for their readers. From the reader's perspective, an anonymous author could be anyone—and thus actually is no one, or at the very least, no one in particular.

This criticism of anonymity is matched, however, by a sort of praise for anonymous authorship in another work—*A Literary Review*—also signed by Kierkegaard, and also appearing in print in 1845. In this book, Kierkegaard offers a review of a new novel by an anonymous Danish author, "the author of *A Story of*

---

[5]   *SKS* 14, 35 / *EPW*, 34.
[6]   *SKS* 14, 65 / *COR*, 24.
[7]   *SKS* 14, 66 / *COR*, 26.

Everyday Life," believed by some at the time to have been the Danish litterateur Johan Ludvig Heiberg, but in fact having been Heiberg's mother, Thomasine Gyllembourg. Gyllembourg published the novels for which she became famous in Copenhagen literary circles anonymously. (Heiberg was, however, named on the title page of Gyllembourg's novel as its editor.) In this context, with reference to Gyllembourg's anonymity and Heiberg's fame, Kierkegaard writes:

> The editor has not become famous because of [these stories], he was already famous; but the stories, which themselves have won a name for themselves next to the editor's, one of the most important of names, nevertheless with the deference of anonymity [*Navnløshedens Hengivelse*] continue to seek a place among the renowned.[8]

The accuracy of Kierkegaard's literary criticism aside, the concept of anonymity at work in this passage mitigates against the heretofore uniformly negative stance on anonymous authorship taken in the Kierkegaardian authorship. Whereas in prior cases anonymity is seen as manipulative and deceptive, here it is the mark of deference. Importantly, it is not simply that Gyllembourg's novels overcome the deficiency of anonymity to become something better, but instead that the anonymity Gyllembourg employs is itself the deference Kierkegaard admires.

One final use of the concept in Kierkegaard helps us to make the relevant distinction in his thought between praiseworthy and blameworthy anonymities. In *On My Work as an Author*, Kierkegaard makes reference in a footnote to an instance of his own use of anonymity:

> And a little earlier in that same year, there appeared a little book: *Two Ethical-Religious Essays* by H.H. The significance of this little book (which does not stand *in* the authorship as much as it relates totally *to* the authorship and for that reason also was anonymous, in order to be kept outside entirely) is not very easy to explain without going into the whole matter.[9]

Without going into the whole matter, we can see that anonymity here serves in Kierkegaard's understanding at least two functions: to distance the anonymous work from Kierkegaard himself, and to confine the work to a special but highly circumscribed place in Kierkegaard's authorship. In lacking an author's name to whom to ascribe responsibility for the work, *Two Ethical-Religious Essays* cannot be legitimately understood as anyone's literary responsibility; it remains outside such considerations, and thus must and can only be taken for what it says, not for what it is (or to whom it belongs). In short, in lacking a name, H.H. lacks an identity—and thus lacks any authority of any sort whatsoever.

In publishing the work under an anonym, however, Kierkegaard claims to be able to use *Two Ethical-Religious Essays* to achieve an end that no named author—whether Kierkegaard or a pseudonym—could achieve, namely, to set a "boundary"[10] for the whole Kierkegaardian authorship. No work authored by Kierkegaard could

---

[8]   *SKS* 8, 19–20 / *TA*, 16.
[9]   *SKS* 13, 12n. / *PV*, 6n.
[10]   Ibid.

do this since any such work would operate entirely within the authorship and thus would lack the vantage from which clearly to mark the authorship's boundary. And no pseudonymous work could achieve this purpose, either, since every pseudonymously authored work would have to be either ascribed ultimately to Kierkegaard, and thus would be a work within the authorship, or remain unremittingly pseudonymous, and thus constitute (or begin to constitute) a separate authorship by a separate author who would thus lack the authority to say anything final about Kierkegaard's authorship.

In any case, anonymity in both Gyllembourg's and Kierkegaard's cases seems, for Kierkegaard, to be acceptable in a way that it was not for the anonymous reviewer in the *Berlingske Tidende* and Orla Lehmann. This seems to have everything to do with the notions of authority and responsibility in Kierkegaard. In cases where what is said in a work depends upon the person who has said it to be one particular person (or sort of person) or another, and in related cases, where it matters who has said what is said in the work, anonymity is entirely inappropriate—bordering upon, and in at least some cases becoming, ethically irresponsible. This is no less true in the aesthetic case of the *Berlingske Tidende* article than it is in Lehmann's anonymous reform movement. In cases where it does not matter who the author is, however, or cases such as Kierkegaard's own, where what matters is that no one in particular be ascribed authorial responsibility for the work, then anonymity is not only not problematic, but it may even be beneficial to reader and work. Gyllembourg's anonymity, for example, is for Kierkegaard a gratifying mark of humility in the author, and thus a sign of good moral character—exactly the opposite of the conclusion Kierkegaard draws from Lehmann's anonymity.

III. Ethical-Existential Anonymity

The relative praiseworthiness or blameworthiness of any instance of anonymity, then, seems to depend essentially upon the relationship between the author's character and the nature of the anonymous work. This relationship—more generally understood as the relationship between actor and action—forms the context within which the final sense of anonymity in Kierkegaard's use of the concept appears in the authorship. Most of the instances of this sense of the concept in Kierkegaard appear in *A Literary Review*, and although they constitute a relatively small portion of the book, they nevertheless form a significant element of the argument therein.

In what is by far Kierkegaard's most extended direct treatment of the concept of anonymity anywhere in his authorship, he notes that in his age "not only do people write anonymously, but they write anonymously over their signature, yes, even speak anonymously."[11] That is to say, ultimately, that "it is possible actually to speak with people, and what they say is admittedly very sensible, and yet the conversation leaves the impression that one has been speaking with an anonymity. The same man can say the most contradictory things, can coolly express something that, coming from him, is the bitterest satire on his own life."[12] Less than a page later, Kierkegaard

---

[11]   *SKS* 8, 98 / *TA*, 103.
[12]   Ibid.

clarifies: "The comments become so objective, their range so all-encompassing, that eventually it makes no difference at all who says them."[13] He concludes with a somewhat comic turn of the same theme: "In Germany there are even handbooks for lovers; so it probably will end with lovers being able to sit and speak anonymously to each other."[14]

Clearly, in Kierkegaard's analysis and diagnosis of anonymity in *A Literary Review*, he has moved beyond a strictly literal concept of anonymity, whether socio-political or literary in nature. The kind of anonymity he criticizes here is not merely the absence of an author's (or actor's) name, the disappearance or evasion of accountability for one's words and actions. Rather, as he notes quite explicitly in the passages quoted above, one can be anonymous in this new sense while retaining one's name. Anonymity, then, ceases to mean exclusively namelessness; it now becomes the absence of particularity, of idiosyncrasy, of individuality altogether. In the modern age, there is a very real sense that individuals ought to be striving for uniformity with other individuals: that one ought to choose for oneself what anyone in a similar situation ought to choose. On this view of anonymity, one does not merely refuse to take authorial responsibility for one's writings, nor does one merely use an anonym; more fundamentally, one becomes an anonym.

The most cutting and direct expression of this criticism comes not in *A Literary Review*, however, but in Kierkegaard's unpublished *The Point of View for My Work as an Author*. There, Kierkegaard neatly unifies the three senses of anonymity discussed so far into a single, modern, demoralizing phenomenon. As he notes, "anonymity, the highest expression for abstraction, impersonality, impenitence, and irresponsibility, is a basic source of modern demoralization."[15] We could counteract the modern power of anonymity, however, "if we turned back once again to antiquity and learned what it means to be an individual human being, no more and no less."[16] The failure Kierkegaard dubs "anonymity" is a failure of subjectivity, a failure associated with the notion, popular in Kierkegaard's day, that one ought as far as possible to strive to become as objective (and thus impersonal) as possible. Ultimately, Kierkegaard comes to view even purely literary or journalistic instances of anonymous authorship as indicative of the decline of the classical understanding of individuality, and thus treats almost all anonymous authors as problematically irresponsible.

The two most prominent exceptions to Kierkegaard's criticism of anonymity are, once again, Thomasine Gyllembourg and Kierkegaard himself. Both of these authors try—according to Kierkegaard—to do whatever they can to imbue the anonyms and their anonymous works nevertheless with personality rather than impersonality, the subjective rather than the objective. It is this commitment to subjectivity that seems, ultimately, to ground Kierkegaard's tacit argument that neither Gyllembourg nor he himself, when writing anonymously, is truly anonymous. Gyllembourg's writings,

---

13   *SKS* 8, 98 / *TA*, 104.
14   *SKS* 8, 99 / *TA*, 104.
15   *SKS* 16, 38 / *PV*, 57.
16   Ibid.

through their consistency and dedication, have "won a name for themselves"[17] despite their anonymity. And Kierkegaard's anonymity, at least in the cases of B and H.H., is depicted as purely strategic—and, in both cases, easily revoked. Although their works are anonymous, neither is essentially an anonym—and it is the modern predilection for allowing impersonality and anonymity into the heart of one's work and oneself that seems to be Kierkegaard's greatest concern.

See also Aesthetic/Aesthetics; Authority; Authorship; Crowd/Public; Individual; Objectivity/Subjectivity; Personality; Politics; Press/Journalism; Pseudonymity; Writing.

---

[17]   *SKS* 8, 20 / *TA*, 16.

Anthropology

Sean Anthony Turchin

Anthropology (*Anthropologie*—noun)

From the Greek ἄνθρωπος (human being) and the suffix -λογία (study of), the lexical meaning of *Anthropologie* in Danish is the science or study of humankind. The study of anthropology is one that encompasses the physical, spiritual and social aspects, as well as the origin of the human being.[1]

The word *Anthropologie* appears only five times in Kierkegaard's works, all found in his journals and notebooks. Indeed, the term is entirely confined to Kierkegaard's notes on lectures given by Henrik Nicolai Clausen,[2] Philipp Konrad Marheineke,[3] and notes on two works on anthropology: one by Henrich Steffens[4] and the other by Carl Daub.[5] Although these notes tell us little about Kierkegaard's own anthropology, the concept itself is one that he explored throughout his *corpus*. The concept of anthropology occurs more or less equally in Kierkegaard's *The Sickness unto Death*, *Either/Or*, the edifying discourses of 1843 and 1844, *Philosophical Fragments*, and the *Concluding Unscientific Postscript to Philosophical Fragments*.

At the heart of Kierkegaard's anthropology stands the concept of the *single individual*, which encapsulates what it means to be a human being. In sum, to be a single individual means to exist in relation to the eternal; this criterion is for Kierkegaard nothing more than what is demanded by the New Testament.[6]

But this criterion presupposes a point of access between the human being and God. In short, the criterion presupposes a specific constitution of the self as a self who can relate to God by virtue of this constitution, namely, that a "human being is a synthesis of the infinite and the finite, of the temporal and the eternal."[7] Thus, a "human being is spirit…and…Spirit is the self."[8]

However, there are factors that inhibit the process of the individual becoming what he or she is meant to be as a result of the human and divine relation. First, Kierkegaard's examinations of the self in *Philosophical Fragments* and *The Sickness*

---

[1]   *Ordbog over det danske Sprog*, vols. 1–28, published by the Society for Danish Language and Literature, Copenhagen: Gyldendal 1918–56, vol. 1, columns 638–9.
[2]   *SKS* 19, 81, Not1:9 / *KJN* 3, 78–80.
[3]   *SKS* 19, 255, Not9:1 / *KJN* 3, 249–50.
[4]   *SKS* 20, 424, NB5:136.a / *KJN* 4, 426.
[5]   *SKS* 17, 216, DD:5 / *KJN* 1, 208.
[6]   *SKS* 25, 342, NB29:81 / *JP* 2, 1802; *SKS* 21, 105–6, NB7:59 / *KJN* 5, 109–10.
[7]   *SKS* 11, 129 / *SUD*, 13; *SKS* 7, 274 / *CUP1*, 301.
[8]   *SKS* 11, 129 / *SUD*, 13.

unto Death share the same diagnosis of the human condition: that without God there is no true selfhood. Furthermore, these two works share the view that the self is unable by its own powers to reconcile itself either to itself or to God. Insofar as every human being exists before God as a sinner, the self is *infinitely qualitatively distinct* from God.[9] The infinite distance that separates us from God therefore disrupts our autonomous attainment of selfhood since, according to Kierkegaard, only in relationship to God can the self attain true selfhood.[10] He writes, "Paganism required: Know yourself. Christianity declares: No, that is provisional—know yourself—and look at yourself in the mirror of the Word in order to know yourself properly. No true self-knowledge without God-knowledge or [without standing] before God. To stand before the mirror means to stand before God."[11]

"Such an individual who relates himself to God in this way becomes an authentic individual."[12] However, as stated earlier, our ability to relate to the eternal is inhibited by sin. Only by God's revelation can the self become aware of its situation.[13] It is here, with the necessity of revelation in order to make known the infinite qualitative difference and its consequences for the self, where Kierkegaard takes up the notion of human despair.

For Kierkegaard, a human being is conditioned by sin and therefore exists before God in a state of despair. This is seemingly inescapable, since either in despair one does not will to be oneself, or before God in despair one does will to be oneself.[14] Despair is subject to a dialectical development, as is sin. On one hand, one does not will to be one's true self (born anew in faith) over and against the old self conditioned by sin; on the other hand, one does will to be oneself, but despairs of being able to do so because of one's sinfulness. Concerning the first notion of despair, Kierkegaard posits the self as one who is unaware of the chasm that separates it from God. Unaware of its separation, the self continues in the delusion that it is established by itself.[15] In other words, the self, unaware that it can only become a self in relation to God, thinks that it is a self by virtue "of a synthesis that relates itself to itself," and this misrelation is one aspect of our despair.[16]

It is this notion of the utter powerlessness of the self to discover the truth about itself in relation to God that Kierkegaard discusses in *Philosophical Fragments*. There, Johannes Climacus argues that the human condition is one of sinfulness and thus the human being exists in untruth, unable to reconcile itself by its own powers to the eternal. In positing the individual as being in untruth, Climacus argues against the Socratic conception of the truth as the recollection of something already within the human as a result of its former coexistence with the eternal.[17]

---

9   *SKS* 11, 232 / *SUD*, 121.
10 *SKS* 11, 145 / *SUD*, 29–30.
11 *SKS* 24, 425, NB24:159 / *JP* 4, 3902.
12 *SKS* 24, 41, NB21:55 / *JP* 3, 3019.
13 *SKS* 11, 208 / *SUD*, 96.
14 *SKS* 11, 194 / *SUD*, 81.
15 *SKS* 11, 129 / *SUD*, 13.
16 *SKS* 11, 131 / *SUD*, 15.
17 *SKS* 4, 221 / *PF*, 11.

However, Kierkegaard poses the question of whether the human being has the truth at all.[18] If it is the case that the human being is not in possession of the truth, the question is how can the human being obtain the truth. "Christianity," he states, "begins in another way: man has to learn what sin is by revelation from God; sin is not a matter of a person's not having understood what is right but of his being unwilling to understand it, of his not willing what is right."[19] His solution to the problem is explicated in his notion of the "teacher."

But one might question what role the teacher would have in the Socratic method, for one who needs only to be reminded rather than taught. Kierkegaard writes that the "teacher merely helps the pupil to realize what he had known all along. In such a case, the individual is in the truth rather than in error."[20] With the Socratic approach the teacher, ultimately, is insignificant. The teacher does not teach or present new truth but serves only as an occasion for the individual to recall what he has forgotten. However, if the human being is in untruth, then what would this approach achieve?

Kierkegaard's response is that what would be achieved is untruth.[21] Our existence outside the truth is grounded in our unawareness of our ignorance. In order to be made aware of the truth, it has to be presented to us, along with the necessary conditions for our learning the truth:

> Now if the learner is to obtain the truth, the teacher must bring it to him, but not only that. Along with it, he must provide him with the condition for understanding it, for if the learner were himself the condition for understanding the truth, then he merely needs to recollect because the condition for understanding the truth is like being able to ask about it—the condition and the question contain the condition and the answer.[22]

Kierkegaard's point here is that human beings alone cannot serve each other in discovering the truth of their existence, nor diagnose the absence of truth or find its remedy. Such endeavors, Kierkegaard thinks, reflect the despair of not knowing that we are in despair.

At this point, Kierkegaard proposes that if the teacher is to be any help at all then he must be more than a mere human being conditioned in sin: "The teacher, then, is the god, who gives the condition and gives the truth. Now, what should we call such a teacher, for we surely do agree that we have gone far beyond the definition of a teacher...let us call him a *savior*, for he does indeed save the learner from unfreedom, saves him from himself."[23]

The role of the savior in Kierkegaard's discussion of the human condition cannot be overemphasized. Even with the condition for the truth, without the truth itself, the self is left to its own despair insofar as the condition only initiates the process of the self's achieving true selfhood. Thus, if one is unaware of being sick then one will fail to seek a remedy, and this is to despair. But understanding what it is to be human

---

18   *SKS* 4, 223 / *PF*, 13.
19   *SKS* 11, 207 / *SUD*, 95.
20   *SKS* 4, 224 / *PF*, 14.
21   Ibid.
22   Ibid.
23   *SKS* 4, 224–6 / *PF,* 15–17.

extends beyond a mere awareness of an ideal notion of true selfhood as a result of the human relation to the divine. Our ability to understand ourselves correctly is also maintained in the manner in which we relate to each other and ourselves.

According to Kierkegaard, most people believe that, with respect to some accidental quality, they cannot be otherwise. Providence usually confirms them in this belief.[24] Yet to become a self as spirit, a human being must recognize his or her infinitude as well as finitude, his or her possibility as well as necessity. This does not necessarily mean being able to be otherwise, but to realize the possibility of purposefully grasping one's necessity, of infinitizing one's finitude.[25] A self must have an infinite interest in his or her own existence.[26] But this is not merely to think about existing in some abstract manner. Rather, "for the existing person, existing is for him his highest interest, and his interestedness in existing is his actuality."[27] "Actuality is interestedness by existing in it."[28] Seeking to understand what it means to be "human" must extend beyond a mere understanding of existence to that of an actual participation in existence.

Truly to exist one must move beyond the stance of a spectator of existence; existence is not something that should be left merely to thinking.[29] If existence is defined as the individual's infinite interest, to exist as a participant who understands the ethical dimension of existence, then existing requires a subjective interest, an interest that demands the depths of human subjectivity and thus has no room for objective observance alone.[30] If the truth is something that human beings acquire in participation, in doing rather than knowing, then "subjectivity is truth; subjectivity is actuality."[31] Insofar as a human being expresses this participation, to exist in actuality is to exist ethically and this requires participation.[32]

As ethical beings, Johannes Climacus maintains that only in action can the ethical be actualized.[33] Indeed, the task of existing is difficult. The difficulty of existence is for the existing individual "to permeate one's existence with consciousness, simultaneously to be eternal, far beyond it, as it were, and nevertheless present in it and nevertheless in a process of becoming."[34] To accomplish this is truly to exist.[35] However, since there is much that inhibits the individual's ability to actualize his or her existence, one must take on this task with the utmost passion.[36]

Being human is, for Kierkegaard, something that is intrinsically linked to the concept of passion; one must exist in passionate activity. We struggle to rise above

---

24   *SKS* 21, 180, NB8:84 / *KJN* 5, 188.
25   Ibid.
26   *SKS* 7, 275 / *CUP1*, 302; *SKS* 7, 283 / *CUP1*, 311; *SKS* 7, 285 / *CUP1*, 313.
27   *SKS* 7, 286 / *CUP1*, 314.
28   *SKS* 7, 311 / *CUP1*, 340.
29   *SKS* 7, 275 / *CUP1*, 302.
30   *SKS* 7, 314 / *CUP1*, 343.
31   Ibid.
32   *SKS* 7, 288 / *CUP1*, 316.
33   *SKS* 7, 291 / *CUP1*, 319–20.
34   *SKS* 7, 280 / *CUP1*, 308.
35   Ibid.
36   *SKS* 7, 283 / *CUP1*, 311.

the weight of the world and our circumstances that restrict a meaningful existence. A meaningful existence is lived in absolute relation to the ideal, that is, as the single individual before God. Thus, "God is the *I*, the subject who in relation to men must emphasize his *I* in such a way that it is only the object of faith."[37]

Faith is the greatest expression of human existence insofar as it focuses human imagination and will on God, against reason, for "imagination is what providence uses to take men captive in actuality."[38] Imagination engages human beings by taking them "far enough out, or within, or down into actuality."[39] Faith is therefore the use of imagination and will to engage with the actuality of God.

Such engagement in actuality makes human existence more concrete, so that the individual learns "what it means to be a human being."[40] "Only when a person has become so unhappy or has penetrated the wretchedness of this existence so deeply that he must truly say: For me life has no value—only then can he make a bid for Christianity. And then life can get its highest value."[41] However, for Kierkegaard, faith does not supplant the need for the individual to come into authentic existence. Instead, faith guarantees the inability of the individual to "interpret the qualitative Christian existing as something meritorious."[42]

But most of us do not have the "courage to believe existentially in the ideal."[43] Rather, the self retreats from "life's terrors," thus betraying a lack of character, which allows it to be "ground down into conformity."[44] Nevertheless, despite the struggle of existence, the individual's task is to "measure himself before God by the requirement of ideality."[45] Of course, the individual must recognize his or her weakness in order to rely on grace.[46] "Every step forward toward the ideal is a backward step, for the progress consists precisely in my discovering increasingly the perfection of the ideal—and consequently my greater distance from it."[47] This is a movement of faith, and "faith certainly requires an expression of the will."[48]

Furthermore, the movement of faith is one from immediacy to reflection and then to a higher immediacy: for "Christianity is opposed to spontaneous, immediate human nature (the immediate natural)."[49] However, most human beings will only ever exist in immediacy or spontaneity; they will never reach the higher immediacy of faith. Instead, their lives will give evidence of an enduring preoccupation with immediacy,

---

[37]   Ibid.
[38]   *SKS* 25, 470, NB30:103 / *JP* 2, 1832.
[39]   Ibid.
[40]   *SKS* 20, 362, NB4:159 / *KJN* 4, 362.
[41]   *SKS* 26, 281, NB33:38 / *JP* 2, 1152.
[42]   *SKS* 24, 264, NB23:119 / *JP* 2, 1143.
[43]   *SKS* 22, 199, NB12:103 / *JP* 2, 1781.
[44]   *SKS* 21, 181, NB8:84 / *KJN* 5, 188.
[45]   *SKS* 23, 399, NB20:15 / *JP* 2, 1785.
[46]   Ibid.
[47]   *SKS* 24, 47, NB21:68 / *JP* 2, 1789.
[48]   Ibid.
[49]   *SKS* 24, 467, NB25:46 / *JP* 2, 1943.

followed by little reflection, and then death. But, according to Kierkegaard, what should follow reflection is the higher immediacy of faith.[50]

Reflection brings the individual to a point of decision as to whether faith will follow reflection. Whether or not faith will follow the individual's reflection is a matter of one's willing to believe. "Faith is essentially this—to hold fast to possibility."[51] Insofar as the demand of faith is to hold fast to possibility (the possibility that appears contrary to what is actual), Kierkegaard views the individual's relation to faith as a "character task." The challenge of this task reveals whether or not a human being will be "unconditionally obedient to God" in realizing that what is to be believed is not an object to be comprehended.[52]

The essential task of human existence is to exist in relation to God, which demands an expression of the will to believe what is incomprehensible.[53] This requires that the individual face faith and despair as existential options.[54] Kierkegaard is keen to correct the misguided notion that "first one must have faith and then existing follows."[55]

In short, the development of human existence is one that commences with immediacy, is followed by reflection, and then by the choice between faith and despair.[56] If faith is the victor then the human being becomes a self by existing before God. "The greatest emphasis a man can put upon himself, upon his *I*, upon the fact that *I* am the one with whom you are dealing—is to require faith."[57]

Kierkegaard's anthropology explains what it is to be human in terms of existing in relation to God. Insofar as existence denotes actuality, this relation requires active and passionate participation in the struggle of existence.

See also Contingency/Possibility; Existence/Existential; Faith; God; Immanence/Transcendence; Individual; Passion/Pathos; Reason; Revelation; Sin.

---

[50]   *SKS* 20, 362, NB4:159 / *KJN* 4, 362.
[51]   *SKS* 21, 101, NB7:54 / *KJN* 5, 106.
[52]   *SKS* 22, 42, NB11:68 / *JP* 2, 1129.
[53]   *SKS* 22, 43, NB11:70 / *JP* 2, 1130.
[54]   *SKS* 24, 260, NB23:111 / *JP* 2, 1142.
[55]   Ibid.
[56]   Ibid.
[57]   *SKS* 24, 431, NB24:169 / *JP* 2, 1144.

Anxiety

William McDonald

Anxiety (*Angest*—noun; *angest*—adjective)

Angest is a loan word from the Middle Low German *angest*. The Old High German *angust* is closely related to the Latin *angustiae* (narrowness, tightness, difficulty). The Danish word may refer to a dangerous or difficult situation, as it frequently does in biblical usage. More generally, though, it describes a feeling of unease brought on by the thought of a real or imagined danger. The *Ordbog over det danske Sprog* adds that the term denotes a feeling of oppression of spirit distinct from, and stronger than, fear, citing the following passage from Kierkegaard's authorship: "The concept of anxiety…is altogether different from fear and similar concepts that refer to something definite…."[1] *Angest*, in Kierkegaard's work, is also sometimes translated as *anguish* or *dread*.

Kierkegaard concerned himself with the concept of anxiety throughout his *oeuvre*, partly because of the intensity of his own feelings of anxiety and partly because of the potential he saw in the concept for articulating a relation between time, freedom, sin, and individual responsibility for becoming a self. While the concept of anxiety had received a considerable amount of philosophical attention— from Hamann, Hegel, and Schelling among others—it had not been connected to these other concepts previously. Kierkegaard had a penchant for "ordinary language philosophy,"[2] in wanting to plumb the resources of everyday discourse for its conceptual potential, in contrast to the specialized jargon of speculative philosophy. The word *Angest* was prime material for clarification and rigorous renewal.

Although the concept of anxiety is widely distributed in Kierkegaard's writings, it is most fully developed in *The Concept of Anxiety*. It is largely supplanted by the related notion of *despair* in *The Sickness unto Death* and subsequently, though it recurs even in *The Moment*.[3] The concept as presented in *The Concept of Anxiety* must be understood in the light of that book's subtitle: "A Simple Psychologically Orienting Deliberation on The Dogmatic Issue of Hereditary Sin." The work is a "deliberation" (*Overveielse*), which Kierkegaard later says,

---

[1]   *Ordbog over det danske Sprog*, vols. 1–28, published by the Society for Danish Language and Literature, Copenhagen: Gyldendal 1918–56, vol. 1, columns 607–8. The citation from Kierkegaard refers to *SKS* 4, 348 / *CA*, 42.

[2]   Cf. *Pap.* V B 50 / *CA*, Supplement, 183–4.

[3]   E.g. *SKS* 13, 361 / *M*, 302.

does not presuppose the definitions as given and understood; therefore, it must not so much move, mollify, reassure, persuade, as awaken and provoke people and sharpen thought. The time for deliberation is indeed before action, and its purpose therefore is rightly to set all the elements in motion…irony is necessary here and the even more significant ingredient of the comic.[4]

The concepts under consideration are set in motion from a psychological point of view, but run up against the boundary of dogmatics, which is the proper discipline for treatment of the notion of hereditary sin. Psychology is characterized as the science of subjective spirit, ethics as the science of objective spirit, and dogmatics as the science of absolute spirit.[5] Dogmatics "does not prove hereditary sin, but explains it by presupposing it."[6] Accordingly, *The Concept of Anxiety* does not presuppose the category of sin as actual, but only aims to awaken the reader's subjective spirit and orient it towards dogmatics by setting the relevant concepts in motion.

As early as *Either/Or*, Part One, Kierkegaard had characterized anxiety as a category of reflection—which means it must have an intentional object. It also contains a reflection on time. One must be anxious about something, and that something is either the past or the future, never something present and concrete.[7] Yet anxiety is later differentiated from fear precisely by not having a determinate object, or by having as its object "nothing."[8] These two assertions are reconcilable if we take anxiety to have an indeterminate intentional object, which is nothing actual. This allows possible future and past states to be proper intentional objects of anxiety.

By having past and future as intentional objects, anxiety relates itself to its own temporality. Time is the element in which the self acquires, or loses, integrity and it is the individual's responsibility to acquire and maintain a sense of continuity between his or her own past and future. The acts of repetition thereby entailed require seriousness, and this dread weight of responsibility for oneself is the source of anxiety. No individual is born anxious. Each is born in immediacy, and responds spontaneously to the world through the senses and the psyche. But to become a self the individual needs to become aware of his or her spirit, for the self is conceived as a synthesis of body and mind sustained by spirit.[9] Anxiety, as instrumental in the task of becoming a self, is a qualification of spirit—but, at least initially, this is only "dreaming spirit," not fully self-conscious spirit.[10] Truly to become a self requires alienation from one's immediate sensate and psychic existence by means of reflection, then ultimately a reintegration of oneself in a "higher immediacy" by means of self-conscious spirit (via a relationship to God). It is by means of anxiety that the possibility of self-alienation is sensed, indefinitely, as the frightening first

---

4   *SKS* 20, 211, NB2:176 / *KJN* 4, 210.
5   *SKS* 4, 331 / *CA*, 23. See also *Pap*. V B 49:17 / *CA*, Supplement, 183.
6   *Pap*. V B 49:11 / *CA*, Supplement, 182.
7   *SKS* 2, 154 / *EO1*, 155.
8   *SKS* 4, 348–9 / *CA*, 42–3.
9   *SKS* 4, 423 / *CA*, 122.
10   *SKS* 4, 347 / *CA*, 41.

step on the path to freedom. For anxiety is "freedom's actuality as the possibility of possibility."[11]

To learn to be anxious, then, is a task for every individual in quest of selfhood, but if one fails to learn in the right way one risks being lost, either by virtue of never having been in anxiety or by virtue of sinking irretrievably into anxiety.[12] The usual awakening of a sense of anxiety occurs in puberty, when through the dawning of sexual desire, the individual becomes self-conscious. The first intimations of this are in feelings of bashfulness, shame, and modesty, when "spirit is not merely qualified as body but as body with a generic difference."[13] In shame and modesty the individual becomes aware of a tension, or contradiction, between his or her own somatic and psychic elements. But this shame has no determinate object, only an indeterminate presentiment of possibilities, and therefore generates anxiety. Since the self is conceived as a task of synthesis sustained by spirit, when the elements of that synthesis are centrifugally flung to their extremities, the spirit has most work to do. In particular, anxiety is greatest when the sensuous is most accentuated—hence woman, being more sensuous than man, is more anxious.[14]

The anxiety of shame and modesty is the beginning of experiencing oneself as another. With the onset of the full sexual drive one's difference in relation to the other sex is posited.[15] This arouses the possibility of erotic love. But anxiety can work positively or negatively in erotic love: anxiety might make the individual aware of himself or herself in relation to the other person, or the individual might flee inwards, thereby shutting the other out (and shutting otherness out of himself or herself). This "inclosing reserve" (*Indesluttethed*) as a defensive response against otherness is one of the definitions of the demonic.

Spirit is present in erotic love, "but it cannot express itself in the erotic."[16] Erotic love is an attraction based on beauty, which is understood as "the unity of the psychic and the somatic."[17] This unity, however, is not sustained by spirit, which "feels itself a stranger…this precisely is anxiety, and modesty as well."[18] In other words, while erotic attraction arouses the recognition of otherness, its alienation of spirit causes an anxiety with respect to the quest for selfhood. Erotic love typically seeks to assimilate the other to oneself, rather than respecting the otherness of the beloved—and is ultimately a form of self-love. Attainment of selfhood demands a fully spiritual understanding of love. This is expressed in *Works of Love* as "love of the neighbor [which] is love between two beings eternally and independently determined as spirit."[19] Once one has recognized another person as truly other, one can recognize oneself as another—which is a necessary stage in the dialectical

11   *SKS* 4, 348 / *CA*, 42.
12   *SKS* 4, 454–6 / *CA*, 155–7.
13   *SKS* 4, 372 / *CA*, 68.
14   *SKS* 4, 370 / *CA*, 66.
15   *SKS* 4, 373 / *CA*, 69.
16   *SKS* 4, 375 / *CA*, 71.
17   *SKS* 4, 373 / *CA*, 69.
18   *SKS* 4, 375 / *CA*, 71.
19   *SKS* 9, 63 / *WL*, 56.

progress from immediacy, through self-alienation, to higher immediacy (or from innocence, through the fall, to atonement).

Considered dialectically, anxiety is psychologically ambiguous, inducing both "a sympathetic antipathy and an antipathetic sympathy."[20] In the course of the dialectical evolution of the self, anxiety oscillates between these alternatives and finally loses the ambiguity only "when sin is posited in the particular individual by the qualitative leap."[21] This is true of the anxiety that characterizes cultural epochs as well as individuals. Paganism corresponds to the "dreaming spirit" of innocent pubescence. Its essence lies in its sensuousness, since it has not yet posited spirit as spirit. But the possibility of spirit is present as anxiety. The object of pagan anxiety, like that of other dreaming spirits, is "nothing." "But what then does the nothing of anxiety signify more particularly in paganism? This is fate."[22] Fate is conceived as "the unity of necessity and the accidental" and as having an external relation to spirit.[23] Fate is not compatible with the idea of guilt or sin, in which the individual assumes responsibility for his or her actions. Guilt and sin are indices of freedom, which is the essence of spirit. Fate and anxiety are canceled as soon as spirit is posited, "for thereby providence is also posited."[24]

The next phase of the dialectic of anxiety in terms of cultural epochs is Judaism, which is characterized as "the standpoint of the law."[25] The object of anxiety in Judaism is guilt, which the Jew seeks to assuage by means of sacrifice. But since the category of sin has not yet emerged, the sacrifice is an ambiguous possibility only, not an actual relation to the divine. The ambiguity of the sacrifice is implicitly acknowledged with its constant repetition, which reveals an underlying skepticism about its efficacy.[26]

An intermediate step towards Christian sin-consciousness is to recognize that the opposite of freedom is not necessity but guilt. When freedom fears guilt, it fears its own capacity to become guilty through a free act. The appropriate Christian response to this is not sacrifice, but repentance. Once the individual becomes aware of sin, the object of anxiety ceases to be indeterminate. Instead it becomes "the distinction between good and evil...posited *in concreto*—and anxiety therefore loses it dialectical ambiguity."[27] Nevertheless, anxiety is still present. When the individual is anxious about doing evil, he or she is conscious of sin as a possibility of freedom from the standpoint of being in the good. But when the individual is anxious about the good, he or she is demonic.[28] The demonic individual regards the good as something outside, which "signifies the restoration of freedom, redemption, salvation, or whatever one would call it."[29]

[20]   *SKS* 4, 348 / *CA*, 42.
[21]   *SKS* 4, 414 / *CA*, 112.
[22]   *SKS* 4, 399 / *CA*, 96.
[23]   *SKS* 4, 400 / *CA*, 96.
[24]   *SKS* 4, 400 / *CA*, 97.
[25]   *SKS* 4, 405 / *CA*, 103.
[26]   *SKS* 4, 406 / *CA*, 104.
[27]   *SKS* 4, 413–4 / *CA*, 111–12.
[28]   *SKS* 4, 421 / *CA*, 119.
[29]   Ibid.

It is necessary for every human being to pass through these dialectical stages in order to become a self before God. To learn to be anxious in the right way is to learn to be anxious about sin, rather than about sex or fate or guilt or the good. This is only possible because human beings are a synthesis. "If a human being were a beast or an angel, he could not be in anxiety."[30] Becoming a self is a matter of coming to know each of one's components (finitude/infinity, temporality/eternity, possibility/ necessity, body/mind) and sustaining them in proper equilibrium by means of the spirit before God. Anxiety educates the individual about possibility, which is the category of the infinite.[31] Sin-consciousness makes one aware of the absolute difference between humans and God. This difference is underscored twofold: (1) by consciousness of the sinfulness inherent in the human species, as a capacity for sinning; and (2) by consciousness of one's own capacity as an individual to sin. It is only by faith, which is the antidote for both anxiety and despair, that the individual can be brought to rest in providence.[32]

There is a close relation between anxiety and despair. Both take as their point of departure the notion that the self is a synthesis, whose achievement is a task for spirit. But whereas anxiety starts with nothing determinate as its object, despair always has only one object: the self. The main discussion of despair occurs in *The Sickness unto Death*, in which it is claimed that the "dizziness" that characterizes anxiety is a psychic phenomenon rather than a spiritual one.[33] This seems to contradict the claim in *The Concept of Anxiety* that anxiety is a qualification of spirit, but is perhaps reconcilable with the idea that anxiety contains only a presentiment of spirit. It may also be explained in terms of the different narrative points of view contained in the respective pseudonymous works, with *The Concept of Anxiety* being a psychological work (even when it analyzes the concept of spirit) and *The Sickness unto Death* representing an idealized Christian point of view. The analysis of anxiety in *The Concept of Anxiety* seems to take us to the threshold of an understanding of despair, and the discussion of despair in *The Sickness unto Death* takes off from the analysis of anxiety. Anxiety and despair undertake parallel movements, which both end in demonic inclosing reserve, from which the individual is saved only by faith in the God of love.

Although Kierkegaard worked on the concept of anxiety from as early as 1842 until as late as 1855, it is not clear that the concept was always used consistently. In particular, some uses of the term in *Fear and Trembling* seem anomalous. Johannes de silentio avers that what is left out of Abraham's story is the anxiety.[34] Vigilius Haufnienesis has allowed the possibility of anxiety within Judaism, and precisely under the aspect of sacrifice. So we could consistently understand Abraham's anxiety to be expressed over his imminent sacrifice of Isaac. Yet de silentio also presents Abraham as the "father of faith," while Haufniensis regards faith as that which dispels anxiety. Perhaps the difference lies in the object of faith in each

---

30   *SKS* 4, 454 / *CA*, 155.
31   *SKS* 4, 455 / *CA*, 156.
32   *SKS* 4, 459 / *CA*, 161.
33   *SKS* 11, 132 / *SUD*, 16.
34   *SKS* 4, 124 / *FT*, 28.

case: whereas Abraham has faith in the God of power and vengeance who demands sacrifices, the Christian has faith in the self-sacrificing God of love. Love might well be an antidote to anxiety, while power and vengeance are not.

See also Ambiguity; Despair; Demonic; Dialectic; Duty; Ethics; Evil; Faith; Finitude/Infinity; Freedom; Good; Governance/Providence; Guilt; Immediacy/Reflection; Judaism; Love; Paganism; Personality; Self; Sin; Spirit; Stages; Time/Temporality/Eternity.

Aphorisms

Henrike Fürstenberg

Aphorism (*Aphorisme*—noun; *aphoristisk*—adjective)

The word *Aphorisme* comes from the Greek ἀφορισμός, where it means "definition, distinction," from ἀφορίζειν, "to mark-off, to limit." An aphorism is a peculiar thought expressed in concise form, or a splinter of thought.[1] Aphorisms were extensively used by philosophers and writers who were contemporaries of Kierkegaard, for example, Schopenhauer, Feuerbach, and Stendhal. A basic distinction is to be made between Kierkegaard's use of aphorisms as a genre of literary-philosophical text, and his use of the terms "aphorism" and "aphoristic." Regarding the latter, one has to distinguish between a designation of a particular text genre and a designation of a particular mode of existence. Thus, in Kierkegaard, the term has two different points of reference: one literary and one existential.

In Kierkegaard's published work, one finds both original aphorisms and aphorisms quoted from other authors. Sometimes aphorisms can be found as direct quotations, for example, as mottos.[2] Frequently Kierkegaard also quotes aphorisms indirectly, such as in the following sentence from *Prefaces* that refers to a popularized aphorism by Hippocrates: "Life is short; would therefore that the art not be made too long for me, above all not longer than life."[3] The most prominent and extensive use of the genre occurs in the "Diapsalmata," which opens the first volume of *Either/Or*. Additional original aphorisms are to be found in short texts entitled "Brief and to the Point" in *The Moment* (no. 6),[4] and in texts entitled "Minor Remarks" in *The Moment* (nos. 6 and 10).[5] Just as most of the "Diapsalmata" can be traced back to drafts noted in the journals,[6] abundant text fragments are spread throughout the journals and notebooks that qualify as aphorisms according to the foregoing definition. In part, they appear under titles

---

[1]   *Ordbog over det danske Sprog*, vols. 1–28, published by the Society for Danish Language and Literature, Copenhagen: Gyldendal 1918–56, vol. 1, column 231.
[2]   Cf. *SKS* 6, 16 / *SLW*, 8.
[3]   *SKS* 4, 516 / *P*, 56.
[4]   *SKS* 13, 257 / *M*, 203.
[5]   *SKS* 13, 274 / *M*, 221; *SKS* 13, 412 / *M*, 348.
[6]   *Pap.* III B 179.

like "Aphorisms"[7] or "Epigram."[8] Sometimes, Kierkegaard himself labeled shorter notes as aphorisms.[9]

Particularly in the *Journal FF* one finds a wealth of aphoristic reflections and fragmentary observations from the years 1836–38 that shed (an often ironic) light on human ambition, presented in a highly condensed language. The records beginning in about 1846 contain a large number of scattered aphorisms with predominantly religious content and an often polemical tone, which frequently juxtapose Christianity with subtle attacks on his contemporaries. Volume 27 of *Søren Kierkegaards Skrifter* contains an enormous amount of aphoristic writings from different periods, published posthumously.[10] In general, Kierkegaard uses the genre of aphorism to make pointed observations about contemporary society. These are often formulated provocatively, and their focus becomes increasingly religious. Over the course of this development one can observe a movement from irony to polemic. While the tone of the earlier records often delivers surprising punch-lines in elegant turns, the aphorisms of later journal records are sharp attacks displaying a fine eye for the internal contradictions of prevailing conditions, particularly in the contemporary church and Christianity; this kind of aphorism was perfected in *The Moment*.

The most important collection of aphorisms among Kierkegaard's writings, the "Diapsalmata," is described in Victor Eremita's preface to *Either/Or* as "aphorisms, lyrical utterances and reflections."[11] The texts are marked by contradictions. They appear isolated, fragmentary, and unconnected. Though some correlations among them exist, they constitute self-sufficient microcosms and sometimes even revoke one another. They oscillate between ironic distance and intimate subjectivity, fragments of a splintered world without orientation. Thus, by their very form, they shape and style A's aesthetic personality and reveal flashes of a consciousness that cannot grasp itself: the unrestrained absorption with singular moods makes it impossible for any identity—in the sense of a congruity between two different points in time—to establish itself, or to achieve genuine self-consciousness. A, the aesthete, creates the opposite of a coherent narrative. Correspondingly, his existence comes across as incoherent and fragmented, without access to any unifying context of meaning. In this way, the aphoristic style of writing highlights the limits of the possibility of poeticizing one's own life. Moreover, the "Diapsalmata" often display ironically tinged contradictions between general maxims and purportedly

---

[7]   *SKS* 22, 215, NB12:121 / *JP* 3, 3558.

[8]   *SKS* 25, 228, NB28:18 / *JP* 1, 402.

[9]   Cf. *SKS* 22, 25, NB11:30 / *JP* 6, 6398. The heterogeneous form and content of the shorter texts in Kierkegaard's records though defy simple classification; it is not always possible to distinguish aphorisms from other short text genres such as anecdotes, parables or fragments.

[10]   Cf. *JP* 5, 5181 footnote 245, for a list of entries in the *Papirer* in which Kierkegaard drafts diapsalmata-like aphorisms.

[11]   *SKS* 2, 15 / *EO1*, 7. A sharp distinction between the three different types of text seems inappropriate; the concepts rather overlap one another. Not all of the texts can, strictly speaking, be called aphorisms. But some of them conform almost classically to the conventions of the genre: "Old age fulfills the dreams of youth. One sees this in Swift: in his youth he built an insane asylum; in his old age he himself entered it" (*SKS* 2, 29 / *EO1*, 21).

explanatory examples, which, in effect, revoke the validity of the particular maxim.[12] The abridged, laconic form of the aphorism, as well as the often surprising turn from maxim to example, provide the author with a means of depicting the dissolution of any sense of meaning and refuting generally accepted human notions of purpose. "Aphoristic" therefore primarily means: incongruous and external to any context.

When Kierkegaard uses the word "aphorism" *as a genre name*, it is in most cases purely a genre label consistent with the definition given above.[13] An aphorism for Kierkegaard is primarily something isolated, singular, and conceived in opposition to systematic, consistent discussion. The special potential that Kierkegaard saw in the genre, and that explains his appreciation for it, is evident from an idea of his, stemming from the year 1847, for a book that would put to use the theological reflections contained in the journals: "A book could be written: *Clues to Illuminate the Modern Religious Confusion in Aphorisms*. Perhaps this form (glimpses) would be most illuminating; a rigorous development of certain concepts that the age has completely forgotten might be nourishing for the sickness: didacticism."[14] The peculiar quality of aphoristic writing, that is, not to develop ideas in a logically coherent way, but to indicate them instead through pithy splinters of thoughts, is closely related to the basic intention of indirect communication strategies: the active, existential adoption by the reader of whatever is depicted. Whereas a pontificating style is unsuitable for conveying any message regarding existence, aphoristic texts, which give only the glimmer of an idea, stimulate by their very terseness the reflexive productivity of the reader. Similarly, Kierkegaard understands aphorisms as a genre primarily antithetical to—and defined negatively in contradistinction to—a logical-argumentative, coherent development of ideas.[15] As a definition of sorts, he compares aphorisms to fossilized remains of once fertile or productive roots of words and genres.[16] An aphorism is thus indeed undergirded by a coherent development (of thoughts or stirrings of the consciousness) to which it testifies, but from which, as an organic process, it also liberates itself. Elsewhere, Kierkegaard also uses the word "aphoristic" to describe an idea that is dissociated from any living context of existence.[17] At the same time, the quality of aphorisms for Kierkegaard lies in their potential to open up a space—precisely through their fragmentariness—in which one's thought can range widely. For example, he describes how his fascination with the title of a book stimulates his mental activity to the extent "that I pause at the title and almost do not get the book read."[18] This enthusiasm for the fragmentary is particularly apparent in A's aesthetic writings in *Either/Or*, where it is connected to the arbitrary. The same idea reappears in a passage from "The Unhappiest One":

---

[12] Cf. *SKS* 2, 29 / *EO1*, 21.
[13] Cf. *SKS* 7, 118 / *CUP1*, 122; *SKS* 20, 80, NB:103 / *KJN* 4, 79; *SKS* 22, 375, NB14:51 / *JP* 2, 1559.
[14] *SKS* 20, 267–8, NB3:42 / *KJN* 4, 268.
[15] *SKS* 1, 342 / *CI*, 309; *SKS* 12, 61 / *PC*, 48; *SKS* 17, 228, DD:26 / *KJN* 1, 219.
[16] *SKS* 18, 111, FF:188 / *KJN* 2, 102.
[17] *SKS* 17, 25, AA:12 / *KJN* 1, 20.
[18] *SKS* 18, 11, EE:14 / *KJN* 2, 7.

"a title in itself can be so thought-laden, so personally appealing, that one will never read the book."[19]

In addition to this genre-related use of the term, which mainly refers to the isolation of the aphorism as opposed to broader contexts, Kierkegaard exhibits a second level of meaning: one in which the genre name undergoes a transfer to existential categories. Aphorism here appears as *a term for a way of life or mode of existence*. When transposed into human-existential categories, that which exists outside of a context turns out to be that which exists outside the community. This criterion of the exceptional, the "aphoristic" way of life, is, on the one hand, fulfilled by the chosen one on the religious level, but, on the other hand, by the aesthete, who positions himself outside meaningful human contexts.

This transition appears for the first time in a note from April 23, 1839: "The Christian life has aphorisms with their own characteristic quality which falls outside the range of all aesthetic qualifications—for example, Paul in Romans 1:1: ἀφωρισμένος εἰς εὐαγγέλιον."[20] The Greek quotation can be translated as "selected/chosen to [promulgate] God's Gospel."[21] Even though the Christian "aphorisms" drop out of all aesthetic determinations, the characteristics of the genre name still resonate in the metaphor, so the Christian life itself appears detached from a given (social) context. The exceptional Christian is selected for a certain task, and extracted from the masses.

The word ἀφωρισμένος in this sense appears in three other locations in Kierkegaard's writings, once in "In Vino Veritas"[22] and twice in private records from the years 1847[23] and 1850.[24] It designates the state of existence of the religious exception as external to the common and the general. In this sense, Kierkegaard also sees himself as an embodiment of ἀφωρισμένος: "Paul speaks of being ἀφωρισμένος—this I have been since my earliest childhood."[25] The essence of this separation is very clearly and compactly expressed in a third record from the year 1854: "O, when I consider how from earliest childhood I have been isolated in special torments appointed for the extraordinary."[26] Kierkegaard conceives himself as inevitably being set apart from the ordinary by God's determination. The ambivalence of the condition is reflected in the twin aspects of existing separately from the multitude of people: on the one hand, it is an accolade that obliges the chosen one to fulfill a particular task—in Kierkegaard's case, to focus on the religious existence, on eternal and not ephemeral goals. On the other hand, it is an extremely painful condition whereby the suffering results not so much from the exclusion from a community as from the wistful nature of the soul of the exceptional one.

---

[19] *SKS* 2, 213 / *EO1*, 219.
[20] *SKS* 18, 22, EE:47 / *KJN* 2, 18.
[21] Cf. *SKS* K18, 38.
[22] *SKS* 6, 319 / *SLW*, 342.
[23] *SKS* 20, 171–2, NB2:73 / *KJN* 4, 170.
[24] *SKS* 23, 173, NB17:14.
[25] *SKS* 20, 172, NB2:73 / *KJN* 4, 170.
[26] *SKS* 26, 285, NB33:43 / *JP* 3, 2573.

Among the published writings, the most important uses of the concept in terms of existence are found in the writings of A, the aesthete, in *Either/Or*. In the course of his call for pilgrimage to the empty grave of the unhappiest one, A proclaims the aphoristic to be the guiding principle of the society of Συμπαρανεκρωμένοι, the "ones who also died":

> Or may it be that such deliberation is not a worthy subject for consideration by us, whose activity, in compliance with our society's sacred custom, is a venture in aphoristic, occasional devotion—we who do not think and talk aphoristically but live aphoristically; we who live ἀφωρισμένοι and *segregati*, as aphorisms in life, without association with men, having no share in their griefs and their joys....[27]

"Aphoristic" no longer refers to a mode of expression, a mode of verbally realizing the contents of consciousness (as indicated by "think and talk"), but refers to a category of existence, indeed to the only such category. The society of Συμπαρανεκρωμένοι, that illustrious circle of pain-proven and pain-seeking aesthetes, refuses any continuity or commitment on the grounds that it lacks meaning. A declares that they are not integrated into the context of society or even of humanity. Thus, here too the aphoristic is that which is isolated and external, the exception. As such, however, it is not distinguished by any distinctive determination but is, by virtue of its connection to the random and the accidental, the epitome of indetermination and arbitrariness. First, the aphoristic behaves in opposition to the universally human; second, it is characterized by its breach with any kind of order and thus embodies the aesthetic consciousness and way of life.

This is also apparent in a passage from "The Tragic in Ancient Drama Reflected in the Tragic in Modern Drama."[28] Although the word "aphoristic" only appears once here, it can be understood as a generic term for the forms of dissociation that A favors in opposition to perfected, cohesive, result-oriented reasoning: the ephemeral, fragmentary, incomplete, random and unsystematic; that which only allows the idea to flash, but not to mature. The aphoristic is approached as a principle of speech and writing, yet it is based in the fragmentary nature of human ambition, which must remain aimless and without direction. "Aphoristic" is consolidated as something contrary, a recalcitrant counterpart to the prevailing idea of some meaningful context which would permit or produce a sense of orientation. What is aphoristic cannot be integrated. Thus, the connection between the formal and the existential application of the concept of the aphoristic appears clearly in light of the congruence between the demand for fragmentary writings and the rejection of coherent writings, on the one hand, and the principles of a society that rejects any form of commitment, on the other. Since the parentheses in A's speech are qualified as "willfully" aphoristic,[29] a further specification of the concept emerges: aphoristic representations of thoughts do not serve any extrinsic goal and do not promote any major ideas. Instead, they amount to nothing beyond themselves in their fragmentariness. So whereas the term

---

[27]   *SKS* 2, 214 / *EO1*, 220.
[28]   Cf. *SKS* 2, 150–2 / *EO1*, 151–3.
[29]   *SKS* 2, 151 / *EO1*, 152.

"ἀφωρισμένος" in the journals and in "In Vino Veritas" accounts precisely for a particular determination of a life's purpose, in A's aesthetic writings it lacks such a definite import and even bears as its essential feature the absence of any such determination or definition.

To summarize, Kierkegaard conceives aphorisms primarily negatively in contradistinction to coherent argumentation. His use of aphorisms thus plays a crucial role in the link between Kierkegaard's thinking and writing: as a strictly non-systematic genre, they can be seen as a protest against systematic philosophy; as an existential concept, the aphoristic emerges as the antithesis of the general. The features of the aphorism accentuated by Kierkegaard provide the coordinates for the concept as transposed into terms of existence.

Since both the genre and the existential concept are featured extensively in A's aesthetic writings in *Either/Or*, a close connection between the concept and the aesthetic attitude to life can be affirmed. First, the term "aphoristic" applies to the special existential conditions of an aesthetic consciousness; second, the fragmentary, contradictory form, which stands absolutely and for itself, reflects this consciousness. At the same time, the term "ἀφωρισμένος" expresses, especially in the last decade of Kierkegaard's life, the religious exception of a chosen one, as Kierkegaard understood himself. In the concept of the exception, the outlier, the aesthetic and religious life-models meet. But whereas the religious exception is substantially defined, a chosen one with a certain existential mission, the aesthetic condition of being ἀφωρισμένος is to be understood as dissociation from any meaningful orientation and amounts to nothing more than a counterpoint to an (apparent) sense of purpose in the context of a philistine society, contradictory in itself.

The wealth of aphoristic texts in Kierkegaard's writings reveals a penchant for aphoristic writing that may have two causes. First, it may be related to Kierkegaard's strategies of indirect communication. Second, the form allows a verbal genius such as Kierkegaard to deliver pointed attacks on philistinism and the Danish State Church, and to do so with exceptionally explosive power.

See also Aesthetic/Aesthetics; Asceticism; Communication/Indirect Communication; Epic; Epigram; Exception/Universal; Existence; Story-Telling; Writing.

Apologetics

Curtis L. Thompson

Apologetics (*Apologetik*—noun; *Apologie*—noun)

The Danish word *Apologie* derives from the Greek ἀπολογία, meaning "a speech in defense," which in the Greek legal system often functioned as an explanation in reply to charges. In its most general sense, the term "apology" refers to a defense made in speech or writing,[1] while "apologetics" refers specifically to that branch of theology which deals with the intellectual defense of Christianity. Acts 26:2 presents St. Paul as using the word ἀπολογία in making his "defense," and it is also used in 1 Peter 3:15, where Christians are exhorted always to be ready to make a "defense" to anyone who demands it for the hope that is within them.

Kierkegaard's writings reveal an ambivalence regarding the concept of apologetics. On the one hand, he has great contempt for apologetics as it is practiced in his day. One finds the Socratic Dane bemoaning how apologetics of the old variety reduces the Christian faith to an intellectual affair and relegates existential passion to unimportant status. Apologetics is part of the whole complex edifice of Christendom or cultural Christianity that has betrayed the genuine Christianity of the New Testament. On the other hand, Kierkegaard appreciates the apologies of the ancient writers and expends much energy on developing a brand new type of apologetics that he thinks is demanded by his time. This different genre of apologetics calls for transforming the very mode by which one communicates. Indeed, Kierkegaard's whole authorship can be viewed as the creation of a new sort of apologetics. Thus one finds a significant Christian theologian of the twentieth century describing Kierkegaard as "incomparably the greatest apologist" of the Protestant Christian faith, because of the way he contrasted Christian faith to "all the 'immanental' possibilities of thought with such clarity and intensity."[2]

Kierkegaard does not use the term "apologetics" very frequently in his writings. We find very few uses of it in his books and a little more in his journals and notebooks. From earlier drafts of *Philosophical Fragments* we know that Kierkegaard had contemplated as a subtitle for that work, "The Apologetical Presuppositions of

---

[1]   *Ordbog over det danske Sprog*, vols. 1–28, published by the Society for Danish Language and Literature, Copenhagen: Gyldendal 1918–56, vol. 1, column 774.

[2]   Emil Brunner, *Die christliche Lehre von Gott*, Zurich: Zwingli-Verlag 1946 (vol. 1 in Emil Brunner, *Dogmatik*, vols. 1–3, Zurich: Zwingli-Verlag 1946–60), p. 108. (English translation: *The Christian Doctrine of God*, trans. by Olive Wyon, Philadelphia: Westminster Press 1950, p. 100.)

Dogmatics or Thought-Approximations to Faith," although he did not follow through with the idea.[3] Thoughts on apologetics as an introductory discipline to be used in the treatment of faith's presuppositions are also mentioned in passing by Johannes Climacus in the *Concluding Unscientific Postscript* in discussing the issue of the *Fragments*:

> In treatise form, the issue could be formulated less problematically this way: the apologetical presuppositions of faith, approximational transitions and overtures in faith, the quantifying introduction to the decision of faith. What would then be treated would be numerous considerations that are discussed or have been discussed by theologians in introductory disciplines, in the introduction to dogmatics and in apologetics.[4]

That Kierkegaard restricts his use of this term to the *Fragments* and the *Postscript* ought not lead us to conclude that he therefore is not dealing with the issues of apologetics in his own way. His restricted use of the concept more likely reflects his awareness that most of his audience operated with an understanding of apologetics that he opposed.

The fullest discussions of the concept of apologetics in Kierkegaard's books appear in *The Book on Adler* (rewritten multiple times in the 1840s) and in *The Point of View for My Work as an Author* ("as good as finished" by April, 1848)—books that were only published after his death. In the Adler book orthodox apologetics is depicted as really being engaged in the same enterprise as that of the atheists, with the aim "to make *Christianity probable*," for making it probable is the same as falsifying it.[5] Being successful at making Christianity probable at the same time would rob Christian faith of its substantial content, so that what began as a defense of the faith would turn into an attack on the faith. Theologians and pastors are operating in ignorance, employing the latest speculative thought in an effort to make Christianity probable or comprehensible by taking it out of the God-language of the paradox and into the language of speculative thinking or the Enlightenment.[6] The proper defense of Christianity must do precisely the opposite and "assert the *improbability* of Christianity."[7] He continues, "Such an introductory scholarship would develop the dialectic of the improbable and its scope, together with the existence-category (faith) that corresponds to it";[8] it would take on the features of a "qualitatively altered method" as shaped by the paradox "that God once came into existence in time," which is "the offense" and "also the point of departure" that as "eternally concluded" provides the beginning for every Christian.[9] In that way apologetics would actually become an asset, unlike contemporary orthodox apologetics that thinks of itself as the Good Samaritan when in reality it has done as much harm as the robbers.[10]

---

[3]   See *Pap.* V B 7 / *PF*, Supplement, 217.
[4]   *SKS* 7, 24 / *CUP1*, 15.
[5]   *SKS* 15, 159 / *BA*, 39.
[6]   *SKS* 15, 159–60 / *BA*, 40.
[7]   *SKS* 15, 160 / *BA*, 40.
[8]   Ibid.
[9]   *SKS* 15, 159–60 / *BA*, 40–1.
[10]   *SKS* 15, 160 / *BA*, 40.

In *The Point of View for My Work as an Author* Kierkegaard introduces apologetics into his discussion of how one can compel another to be aware. In the process he refers to apologetics as "a science of arms [*Vaabenlære*]." In Christendom, "the entire old science of arms, all the apologetics and everything belonging to it, serves…to betray the cause of Christianity."[11] He contends that what is called for "is a totally new science of arms…that is completely permeated by reflection," and in his books he provides the crucial elements of this new science, whose "method must become indirect" in order to expose the delusion of Christendom.[12] The strategy of the new apologetics must be constituted on the basis of having to contend with the delusion that people are already existing in genuine Christian faith; only when that delusion has been dealt with will it be possible for people to be moved into a proper relation to the Christian message.[13] Furthermore, the one employing this new science of arms must begin as an esthetic author before moving to the religious, all along remembering that the appropriate dialectical interaction of these two will maintain the religious as the crucial and the esthetic as the incognito.[14]

In August 1848 the Danish Socrates penned at the beginning of a section of his journal the stark words: "Why Has Christianity Come into the World?" and the response: "The Opposite of an Apologetic."[15] His point is that Christianity is about the becoming of human existence, and apologetics in its customary form addresses how Christianity is to be grasped by thought. A century-and-a-half before the appearance of the Liberation Theology movement he gave expression to its basic insight that orthopraxy or right action holds a certain priority over orthodoxy or right belief in considering the truth and truthfulness of Christianity. Kierkegaard charges that with all their defending of Christianity, the pastors and the scholars nevertheless do not believe in Christianity at all. In three notebook entries of 1848 and 1849 he makes use of the analogy of the lover to show how inappropriate is the whole business of identifying reasons to establish that the Christian experience is the highest and most blessed reality. The lover separated from the beloved hopes intently that the reunion will happen soon, just as the Christian expects Christ's second coming to happen soon.[16] The lover day-in and day-out can extol the virtues and gloriousness of the beloved; but if someone demands that he prove his love or defend it with three reasons, he would regard this as a crazy suggestion and tell the person making the request that he or she does not know what it is to be in love.[17] To suggest to a person in love that he could have fallen in love with another girl cannot be met with a proper reply because the lover knows only that he is in love with his beloved.[18] In the same way, the objections to Christianity cannot be taken seriously by "the person who in truth is conscious of being a sinner and in truth has

---

[11]   *SKS* 16, 34 / *PV*, 52–3.
[12]   *SKS* 16, 34 / *PV*, 52.
[13]   *SKS* 16, 34 / *PV*, 52–3.
[14]   *SKS* 16, 34 / *PV*, 53.
[15]   *SKS* 21, 74, NB7:2 / *KJN* 5, 76–7.
[16]   *SKS* 22, 85–6, NB11:147 / *JP* 1, 340.
[17]   *SKS* 20, 370–1, NB5:2 / *KJN* 4, 371.
[18]   *SKS* 22, 84, NB11:143 / *JP* 1, 502.

experienced belief in the forgiveness of sins in this name and in this faith is saved from his former sin."[19] A discursive attempt to prove the veracity of faith is merely a "masterful anticlimax," and the person who honors such attempts can no longer be considered a person of faith.[20]

The concept of apologetics has become problematic since it has lost its intimate connection to the Christian life and been reduced to discourse. An 1851 journal entry reports that this reduction has come with Christianity's slackening: first there is Christ, then the apostles, then the martyrs, and then the apologists; but "now there are only apologists," and "Christianity essentially comes to a standstill," and "science, scholarship and the theory of the Church begin."[21] At the beginning of Christianity Christians used apologetics, but these defensive efforts were directed explicitly to people who were not Christians and who had no interest in becoming Christians; the scene in the Christendom of Kierkegaard's day is quite the opposite, for now "all are Christians":

> The basic lie is in the dastardly irresponsibility with which we have seen to it that all become Christians—all the time conscious that this is a lie, and now approach it as if they were pagans but without first and foremost demanding that they give up the name Christian.
> To "defend" Christianity to *Christians* is abysmal nonsense.[22]

Apologetics, possibly with every good intention to make sense of the Christian religion, has nevertheless become nonsensical. Apologetics has assumed a form that necessitates differentiating it from an apology. Contemporary apologetics is now a science that deviates from what used to be the writing of apologies: "Everything gets farther removed from the existential. In former days they wrote apologies; this was in the situation of actuality against the pagans. Nowadays we have a scientific scholarship which is called apologetics, a science of writing apologies."[23] This is yet one further example of a more concrete first-order reality of actual, existential engagement in life giving way to a more abstract second-order reality of disengaged, speculative thinking about life.

Kierkegaard writes in 1849: "There is only one, and quite rightly pathological, proof of the truth of Christianity—when the anxiety of sin and the burdened conscience constrain a man to cross the narrow line between despair into madness—and Christianity."[24] Savonarola understood long ago what a true apologetic for Christianity is all about: "He proves the truth and divinity of Christianity by the transformation which occurs in those who become Christians—the proud become humble, the voluptuous chaste, etc."[25] This transformation takes place in faith, which is the greatest emphasis a person can put upon himself or herself; requiring

19	Ibid.
20	*SKS* 20, 370–1, NB5:2 / *KJN* 4, 371.
21	*SKS* 24, 258–9, NB23:106 / *JP* 3, 2662.
22	*SKS* 24, 230, NB22:48 / *JP* 6, 6708.
23	*SKS* 24, 338, NB24:36 / *JP* 4, 19.
24	*SKS* 22, 99, NB11:166 / *JP* 1, 503.
25	*SKS* 24, 338, NB24:35 / *JP* 4, 3842.

faith of oneself means that one must contend with reason and not succumb to "the intellectual approach [that] wants to put everything into a direct relation," "wants to have direct recognizability," "wants to have the most absolute harmony throughout Scripture," and therefore "wants to abolish faith."[26] The speculative theologians know nothing about what it means to require faith, and these "apologists are just as stupid as the free-thinkers" in the way they "are always shifting the viewpoint of Christianity."[27] Modern atheists attack Christianity, calling it mythology, but the apologetic official preachers, the defenders functioning as the rescue squad, are little better as they assure one and all that Christianity is anything but mythology, for in their sermons they completely leave out imitation, and in their lives one finds just about the opposite of the imitation of Christ; therefore, "Christianity is for them, in spite of all their protests, mythology."[28] To focus on transformation the apologists must realize that "the only form of polemic one can use against objections is to fall upon the objector from behind."[29] This means employing an indirect form of communication. Kierkegaard's entire authorship gives articulation to such a new form of apologetics.

See also Communication/Indirect Communication; Existence/Existential; Faith; Love; Offense; Paradox; Protestantism/Reformation; Speculation/Science/Scholarship.

---

[26] *SKS* 24, 450, NB25:19 / *JP* 2, 1144.
[27] Ibid.
[28] *SKS* 25, 78, NB26:74 / *JP* 2, 1915.
[29] *SKS* 22, 86, NB11:147 / *JP* 1, 340.

Apostle

Steven M. Emmanuel

Apostle (*Apostel*—noun; *apostolsk*—adjective)

The Danish word *Apostel* derives from the Greek ἀπόστολος, meaning "messenger" or "emissary."[1] In the New Testament the word refers mainly to the twelve disciples and to Paul—men who were called and sent forth by God on a divine mission.[2] While Kierkegaard sometimes uses "apostle" in a non-theological sense (as when Socrates is described as an "apostle of finitude"[3] and "the unhappiest one" of *Either/Or* is described as an "apostle of grief"[4]), he is chiefly concerned to elucidate the theological meaning of the term noted above and to draw out the implications of that meaning for understanding other key concepts, such as divine authority. Kierkegaard's reflections on apostleship also shed light on the requirements of Christian discipleship. The most important discussions of the concept are found in his unpublished papers and in the pseudonymously published essay entitled "The Difference between a Genius and an Apostle." The meaning of apostleship articulated in these writings is operative in the upbuilding discourses and reaffirmed by various pseudonyms.

In a journal entry dated 1845, Kierkegaard sharply criticizes those who entertain a romanticized view of the apostle as one who is blessed with good fortune. Such people, he says, have an "extraordinary conception of an apostle's sufferings,"[5] meaning that they completely ignore the fact that an apostle's fate is to be "laughed at, mocked, persecuted, poor, jailed, and slain."[6]

Kierkegaard detects a false modesty in the way many of his contemporaries seek to express humility by disavowing any claim to being an apostle. It is false modesty precisely because it is based on a retrospective assessment of the apostle's supposed honor and glory—an assessment that would hardly have been recognizable to the living apostle, who did not know honor, respect, or earthly advantage of any kind. To

---

[1]   *Ordbog over det danske Sprog*, vols. 1–28, published by the Society for Danish Language and Literature, Copenhagen: Gyldendal 1918–56, vol. 1, columns 774–6.

[2]   A single exception to this pattern occurs in Hebrews 3:1, where Jesus is referred to as "the apostle and high priest of the faith we profess."

[3]   *SKS* 1, 178 / *CI*, 127.

[4]   *SKS* 2, 222 / *EO1*, 202.

[5]   *SKS* 18, 235, JJ:302 / *KJN* 2, 216.

[6]   *SKS* 23, 283, NB18:50 / *JP* 1, 106.

be an apostle, Kierkegaard declares, is "sheer earthly suffering."[7] Indeed, nothing in the world makes it so impossible to enjoy life, he says, as being an apostle.[8]

Kierkegaard views this confused conception of what it means to be an apostle as a dangerous illusion. It not only takes the apostle in vain but looks away from what is most important about him as a teacher and a model of Christian discipleship. The apostle embodies the highest ethical demands of Christian faith: dying to the world, renouncing self-interest, suffering for the truth. By calling attention to the correct conception of an apostolic life, Kierkegaard wants to remind the age that human beings not only have a right to order their lives according to the apostle's ethical example, but that they *ought* to do this.[9]

Kierkegaard recognizes that to follow the ethical example of an apostle is not the same thing as being one, since the apostle is qualitatively distinguished from all other human beings by virtue of having divine authority. However, the question of whether or not a contemporary individual might actually be an apostle became a live one for Kierkegaard in the matter of Adolph Peter Adler.

In 1843, Adler, a pastor from the Danish island of Bornholm, published a collection of sermons. The work was unremarkable except in one respect: in the preface to the volume Adler claimed that he had received a divine revelation; indeed, that this had been dictated to him directly from Christ. With this claim, Adler had in effect cast himself in the role of a modern-day apostle with the divine authority to proclaim a new doctrine. He was eventually dismissed from his pastoral duties following an official investigation, in which he failed to provide satisfactory answers to direct questions concerning the alleged revelation.

Adler's case posed an interesting problem for Kierkegaard: "By his statement about himself, he is for the time being placed higher than every other human being, who, if he is to relate himself to him, *either* must submit…to his divine authority, *or* must with skeptical reserve refrain from every affirmation and every negation."[10] Kierkegaard chose the latter option, confining the scope of his analysis to the conceptual consistency of Adler's own account, as revealed in his deposition and other statements he made in subsequent published writings.

One feature of Adler's account stood out: as soon as he met with skeptical resistance, he began to retreat from his original claim. At first, Adler attempted to re-describe his "revelation" as a profoundly moving religious experience in which he was emotionally seized and awakened. Later he would claim that the content of his alleged revelation was actually the combined product of divine inspiration and intellectual achievement, and that his contribution was really a work of genius.

The problem, from Kierkegaard's perspective, was not that Adler wanted to revise his claim—he was certainly entitled to do that—but that "when a man unabashedly wants to reinterpret an intended apostolic life as being genius without revoking the first," he is guilty of confusing what is essentially a religious claim with an aesthetic one.

---

7   *SKS* 23, 284, NB18:50 / *JP* 1, 106.
8   *SKS* 24, 429, NB24:165 / *JP* 1, 110.
9   *SKS* 23, 409, NB18:135 / *JP* 1, 108.
10   *Pap.* VIII–2 B 7:5, 21–2 / *BA*, 51.

Believing that Adler's confusion was emblematic of the religious confusion of the age, Kierkegaard was keen to address it, and he worked on multiple drafts of a manuscript intended for publication.[11] However, for personal reasons, he published only a portion of that manuscript under the title "On the Difference between a Genius and an Apostle."[12] This essay, written ostensibly for a theological audience, appeared in 1849 under the pseudonym H.H. and contained no reference to Adler.

In the essay, H.H. explains that an apostle is not born, but rather "a man who is called and appointed by God and sent by him on a mission."[13] Unlike a genius, who is distinguished from others by having some innate gift or talent, an apostle is what he is by virtue of being invested with divine authority. The authority is the decisive thing. It is what makes the apostle absolutely qualitatively different from all other human beings. Because this authority has a transcendent source, it is outside the class of natural human attributes. The apostle himself stands in a paradoxical relation to this fact: "The apostolic calling is a paradoxical fact that in the first and the last moment of his life stands paradoxically outside his personal identity as the specific person he is."[14]

The person called to be an apostle does not therefore relate to other human beings *qua* human being, or in terms of having acquired some merely quantitative advantage. Indeed, his apostolic authority marks a decisive break with all quantitative thinking. The apostle's power does not lie in being more intelligent, imaginative, or discerning than others. The justification for his authority rests exclusively on the transcendent revelation he has received.

The message an apostle brings, being a transcendent revelation, is paradoxically new, meaning that it can neither be anticipated nor assimilated in the history of the race. It is therefore impossible to determine whether or not someone is an apostle on the basis of an aesthetic or philosophical appraisal of his doctrine. Properly understood, the apostle presents human beings with an unconditional either/or: will you or will you not obey? There is no middle ground, no room for argumentation: "I am not to listen to Paul because he is brilliant or matchlessly brilliant, but I am to submit to Paul because he has divine authority; and in any case it must become Paul's responsibility to see to it that he produces this impression, whether anyone submits to his authority or not."[15] The apostle produces this impression solely through the power of his conviction, his willingness to sacrifice "life and everything." In this way, the apostle does not compel others to obey, but rather addresses himself directly to the conscience of every human being.[16]

Everything is different in the case of the genius. While the apostle belongs essentially to the sphere of transcendence and the "paradoxical-religious," the genius belongs essentially to the sphere of immanence. Thus, even though the genius brings something new, "this in turn vanishes in the human race's general assimilation, just

---

[11]   This manuscript was eventually published posthumously.
[12]   *SKS* 11, 7–111 / *WA*, 93–108.
[13]   *SKS* 11, 99 / *WA*, 95.
[14]   Ibid.
[15]   *SKS* 11, 100 / *WA*, 96.
[16]   *SKS* 11, 100–1 / *WA*, 97.

as the difference 'genius' vanishes as soon as one thinks of eternity."[17] In the light
of these clarifications, we can more easily appreciate the depth of Adler's religious
confusion. He grasps neither the Christian meaning of revelation, nor the concepts
of apostleship and authority. He does not understand what it means to be called by
a divine revelation.

Like those who mistake the apostle's suffering for glory and honor, and thereby
praise him on purely aesthetic grounds, Adler's confusion once again shifts the focus
from the religious to the aesthetic. The danger of this confusion is that decisive
Christian categories become volatilized, so that no one any longer possesses the
correct understanding of the ethical requirements of the Christian life.

As the highest example of Christian discipleship, the apostle underscores a
crucial feature of Kierkegaard's elucidation of Christian faith, namely, that faith is
not an objective, intellectual relation to a doctrine or to a teacher with a doctrine,
but rather the existential striving to embody the ethical-religious requirements of
Christianity. These requirements are revealed in the life of the Teacher, who is the
living embodiment of the truth. Confronted by Christ's example in the situation of
contemporaneity, the true disciple does not demand evidence or proofs, does not
equivocate and temporize, but rather sees that the matter is quite simple: will you or
will you not obey, will you or will you not follow Christ's example, renouncing all
self-interest and all reliance on the things of this world, fully prepared to sacrifice
everything for the sake of the truth?[18] To the extent that the apostle embodies these
requirements, he is not only a disciple but a teacher by example.

As noted earlier, the meaning of apostleship presented above is operative
throughout Kierkegaard's writings. The upbuilding discourses contain extensive
reflections on the writings of the apostle Paul. These reflections are not only
illustrative of the nature of the apostolic calling but shed light on the life of faith. For
example, reflecting on Paul's letter to the Ephesians, Kierkegaard observes that both
prosperity and adversity can serve for "strengthening in the inner being."[19] However,
the most important point is that the condition for this strengthening is a gift of grace:
"Paul also reminds us of this in our text, because the witness itself is a gift from God,
from whom comes every good and perfect gift, the most glorious gift of all, a gift
from the Father in heaven...."[20] As a man, the apostle is weak. But he is "mightily
strengthened by God's spirit in his inner being."[21]

In the upbuilding literature, there is a constant emphasis on suffering as the true
mark of the apostle. But Kierkegaard makes a qualitative distinction between the
myriad forms of hardship that a person may experience in life—all of which the
apostle has tried—and what Paul enigmatically refers to as the "thorn in the flesh."[22]
While the thorn itself is not named, Kierkegaard explains that it is not merely

---

[17]   *SKS* 11, 98 / *WA*, 94.
[18]   *Pap.* VIII–2 B 15, 66–7 / *BA*, 34.
[19]   *SKS* 5, 104 / *EUD*, 98.
[20]   Ibid.
[21]   *SKS* 5, 91 / *EUD*, 83.
[22]   See, for example, "The Thorn in the Flesh" (*SKS* 5, 317–34 / *EUD*, 327–46).

suffering in an external sense;[23] it is rather the deepest expression of the existential pathos of the apostle.

For Kierkegaard, the idea of the "thorn in the flesh" provides the right perspective for all discussions of glory and honor in connection with being an apostle. There is clearly much to admire in Paul, whose achievements in the life of the spirit Kierkegaard describes as being akin to the miraculous: "To transform hardships into a witness for the truth of a teaching, to transform disgrace into glory for oneself and for the believing congregation, to transform the lost cause into a matter of honor that has all the inspiring force of a witness—is this not like making the cripples walk and the mute speak!"[24] Kierkegaard also notes that the apostle's activities "harvested many, many happy recollections for him."[25] Moreover, in 2 Corinthians 12:1–10, where Paul describes his ecstatic vision of God, he speaks of the ineffable bliss that is "being caught up into the third heaven." It would indeed seem that the apostle is blessed with good fortune. However, as Paul himself is quick to note, it is precisely his thorn in the flesh that prevents him from becoming proud. Kierkegaard seizes on this point in order to remind the reader that the apostle's life is essentially qualified by suffering: "As soon as the suffering is perceived and the thorn festers, the apostle has only himself to deal with. The beatitude has vanished, vanishes more and more—alas, it was inexpressible to have it; the pain is inexpressible since it cannot even express the loss, and recollection is unable to do anything but languish in powerlessness."[26]

Whatever satisfaction, joy, or ineffable bliss the apostle is capable of experiencing, he is nevertheless tethered to the world of immanence, to the frailty and fragility of his own humanness, separated from God. As high as the apostle rises, he must pay an equal price in suffering. Kierkegaard can only exclaim:

> To have been caught up into the third heaven, to have been hidden in the bosom of beatitude, to have been expanded in God, and now to be tethered by the thorn in the flesh to the thralldom of temporality! To have been made rich in God, inexpressibly so, and now to be broken down to flesh and blood, to dust and corruption![27]

The discourse concludes with a stern warning against those who would light-mindedly omit the danger associated with all spiritual striving: the more deeply one experiences the presence of God in this moment, the more keenly one suffers the absence of God in the next. Even the highest spiritual life, as exemplified by the apostle, has suffering; indeed, it has the hardest suffering of all.[28]

Finally, Climacus offers a brief but noteworthy discussion of the Apostles' Creed in the *Concluding Unscientific Postscript*. His comments are framed by a consideration of Nicolai Frederik Severin Grundtvig's vision of a Christian community based on the "Living Word." Grundtvig wanted to move the focus of

---

23   *SKS* 5, 321–3 / *EUD*, 332–3.
24   *SKS* 5, 90 / *EUD*, 83.
25   *SKS* 5, 329 / *EUD*, 340.
26   *SKS* 5, 325 / *EUD*, 336–7.
27   *SKS* 5, 325–6 / *EUD*, 337.
28   *SKS* 5, 334 / *EUD*, 346.

faith away from a reliance on the written word of the Bible. But as every religious community must organize itself around some authoritative teaching, Grundtvig pointed to the Apostles' Creed to serve this function: *"The Apostles' Creed* [is] the exclusive condition for incorporation into the society [that] attributes a redemptive power to the means of Grace—*baptism and Holy Communion."*[29] According to Grundtvig, the Creed represents the authority of the Living Word because it "is really what was orally present in the Christian Church from the first time it spoke."[30]

Climacus is sympathetic with Grundtvig's desire to move away from the "Biblical View," and for much the same reason: it inevitably leads to exegetical debates, questions about historical accuracy—in short, a scholarly engagement with the scriptural text that has nothing to do with the life of the spirit; or as Climacus would say, an endless "approximation-process" that leads away from inwardness and subjectivity, where the truth of Christianity is to be found.

Climacus' criticism of Grundtvig is that the attempt to substitute the Creed for the New Testament simply recreates the problem:

> If the historical aspect of the Creed (that it is from the apostles etc.) is to be decisive, then every iota must be infinitely insisted upon, and since this can be attained only *approximando* [by approximation], the individual finds himself in the contradiction of…wanting to tie his eternal happiness to it and not being able to do so because the approximation is never finished.[31]

If the Apostles' Creed contains any religious truth, it is a truth that can only be appropriated existentially, in the manner that the apostles themselves demonstrated by their living example as suffering witnesses to the truth of Christianity.

See also Authority; Genius; Martyrdom/Persecution; Witness.

---

[29]   See Bruce H. Kirmmse, *Kierkegaard in Golden Age Denmark*, Bloomington: Indiana University Press 1990, p. 213.

[30]   Ibid.

[31]   *SKS* 7, 49 / *CUP1*, 43.

Appropriation

Sean Anthony Turchin

Appropriation (*Tilegnelse*—noun; *tilegne*—verb)

The verb *tilegne* derives from the Old Danish *til eynath*, meaning to make (something) one's own. *Tilegnelse* corresponds to the Latin *appropriatio* and is best translated as either "acquisition" or "appropriation."[1] Kierkegaard's 1833 edition of Molbech's *Danish Dictionary* defines *Tilegnelse* as the acquiring of something for oneself.[2]

The concept of appropriation extends almost throughout Kierkegaard's *corpus*, beginning in 1841 with *The Concept of Irony* through to 1850 with *Practice in Christianity*. Although the term is found in numerous other works in this period, such as in *Either/Or*, *Philosophical Fragments*, *The Concept of Anxiety*, the various upbuilding discourses, *Stages on Life's Way*, and *Works of Love*, it appears most often in the *Concluding Unscientific Postscript*. Overwhelmingly, "appropriation" is used to denote the way in which the human subject ought to relate to ethical-religious truth. Kierkegaard maintains that "if inwardness is truth…[then] truth is the self-activity of appropriation."[3] If the individual is to make this truth his or her own, then it must be appropriated with subjective passion rather than being related to in some abstract fashion.

For the most part, Kierkegaard uses this concept to distinguish between one who is immersed in Christianity from one who merely observes Christianity objectively, from the outside. Thus the pseudonym Johannes Climacus uses "appropriation" to indicate the way in which the individual is supposed to relate to the objective uncertainties of the purported Christian truths. However, Climacus also uses "appropriation" with regard to truth, generally speaking. Therefore, "appropriation" has a slightly different meaning depending on the context in which it is found. In a general sense the concept of appropriation may signify that existential truth is only that truth which is appropriated by the individual. In other words, the act of appropriation discloses what the individual believes to be true by means of his or her existing in truth, by incorporating that truth as part of his or her existence. As an existential act, "appropriation" is often used to imply a sense of "inwardness." However, when "appropriation" is used in its predominantly Christian context, it is

---

[1]   *Ordbog over det danske Sprog*, vols. 1–28, published by the Society for Danish Language and Literature, Copenhagen: Gyldendal 1918–56, vol. 23, columns 1242–4.

[2]   Christian Molbech, *Dansk Ordbog. Indeholdende det Danske Sprogs Stammeord*, vols. 1–2, Copenhagen: Gyldendalske Boghandlings Forlag 1833, vol. 2, p. 502.

[3]   *SKS* 7, 220 / *CUP1*, 242.

defined as follows: "Appropriation is the paradoxical inwardness that is specifically different from all other inwardness."[4] This difference rests in that which is being considered for appropriation. However, this will be discussed in turn.

With its first use in *The Concept of Irony*, Kierkegaard describes the concept of appropriation or "acquisition" (*Erhvervelse*) as "manifestly the sole relation of knowledge to the known."[5] This relation is one that Kierkegaard takes seriously given his understanding of our capacity for epistemological certainty. Kierkegaard believed that the intellectuals of his day exhibited an unhealthy obsession with, and allegiance to, scientific scholarship. He criticized these intellectuals for thinking that science could make everything eminently clear to human understanding not only in the domain of the physical, but also with regard to questions about the human race, God, and Christianity.[6] However, Kierkegaard states: "In our joy over the achievement in our age, we have forgotten that an achievement is worthless if it is not made one's own."[7] For Kierkegaard, the challenge to his generation would be "to translate the achievement of scientific scholarship into personal life, to appropriate [*tilegne*] it personally."[8]

It is apparent that two usages emerge for "appropriation": (1) as found both in *The Concept of Irony* and the *Concluding Unscientific Postscript*, Kierkegaard's concern is with how the individual will come to appropriate (*tilegne*) the conclusions of scientific scholarship into one's own existence; (2) in *Philosophical Fragments*, the upbuilding discourses, *Stages on Life's Way*, *Works of Love*, the *Concluding Unscientific Postscript*, and *Practice in Christianity*, "appropriation" is used predominantly to indicate how the individual should relate to the objective uncertainties of Christian truths. With respect to the latter, the reader is faced with a choice either to appropriate the objective uncertainty or continue, fruitlessly, to seek objective certainty.

Kierkegaard believed that modern speculative thought had almost reduced Christianity to paganism.[9] Against the backdrop of what he thought inherently problematic with the mingling of speculative philosophy and theology (that Christianity ends in being equal in certainty to that of any other science and is therefore to be approached like any other science, with disinterest—culminating in "approximate" knowledge), Kierkegaard believed the Christianity of Christendom to be an "enormous illusion."[10] The self-deceptive tendency of the Christian culture dominant in the time of Kierkegaard extended into its attempt to secure a surer foundation for Christian truths by means of historical investigation and speculative philosophy. With these means, Kierkegaard thought that the result would not be a true representation of Christianity but rather something quite different. Since

---

4   *SKS* 7, 554–5 / *CUP1*, 610–11.
5   *SKS* 1, 107 / *CI*, 46.
6   *SKS* 1, 356 / *CI*, 327.
7   Ibid.
8   *SKS* 1, 356 / *CI*, 328.
9   *SKS* 7, 329 / *CUP1*, 361.
10   *SKS* 16, 23–7 / *PV*, 41–4.

Christian truths are inaccessible by such investigation or assessment, attempting to provide a greater amount of objective certainty for Christian faith is utterly futile.

At best, historical knowledge is for Kierkegaard an approximation (*Tilnærmelse*); we cannot have absolute certainty of past events.[11] Christian history, unlike human history, is a sacred history, a history whose events are not conditioned in the same way as natural history. With regard to our knowledge of the historicity of Christianity, a special case presents itself. Christianity's history has at its center an absurdity, a paradox; in fact it is an "absolute paradox." The inherent absurdity of Christian faith "is that the eternal truth has come into existence in time, that God has come into existence, has been born, has grown up, etc., has come into existence exactly as an individual human being, indistinguishable from any other human being."[12]

To those who would seek to prove the Incarnation by historical means, Kierkegaard responds that, at best, history can conclude that Christ "was a great man, perhaps the greatest of all."[13] And yet, Kierkegaard is appalled that "history is the very thing that people have wanted to use to demonstrate that Christ was God."[14] Therefore there are two fundamental problems concerning our seeking to provide ourselves with a surer relation to Christianity. The first is, as stated above, that historical knowledge is at best an approximation. Second, inasmuch as the very foundation of Christianity rests on the belief that God became a human being within history, human reason is unable to confirm such a belief when left to its own resources.

Kierkegaard's distinction between history and sacred history points to the supernatural element within Christianity, specifically, the incarnation of God. Although Kierkegaard believed Christianity is open to historical investigation, Christianity's essence is inaccessible to a mere historical observer.[15] Stated differently, accumulating a higher degree of historical objectivity in order to provide a more secure foundation for Christian truth is not what Christianity demands. Instead, given the objective uncertainty of Christian truths, Christianity demands that the individual exist in the truth of its teachings rather than speculate as to whether it is true.

In sum, "Christianity is spirit; spirit is inwardness; inwardness is subjectivity,"[16] according to Kierkegaard. "When the matter is treated objectively, the subject cannot impassionedly relate himself to the decision, can least of all be impassionedly, infinitely interested."[17] Therefore, Christianity is not an objective issue but rather is a subjective one; it asks about "the individual's relation to Christianity."[18] Thus, the "inquiring, speculating, knowing subject accordingly asks about the truth but not about the subjective truth, the truth of appropriation."[19]

---

11   *SKS* 7, 522 / *CUP1*, 574.
12   *SKS* 7, 192 / *CUP1*, 210.
13   *SKS* 12, 41 / *PC*, 27.
14   *SKS* 12, 45 / *PC*, 31.
15   *SKS* 7, 36 / *CUP1*, 29.
16   *SKS* 7, 40 / *CUP1*, 33.
17   *SKS* 7, 38 / *CUP1*, 31.
18   *SKS* 7, 26 / *CUP1*, 17.
19   *SKS* 7, 29 / *CUP1*, 21.

Discerning the difference between objective affirmations of the truth from that of existing in truth, Johannes Climacus offers his definition of what it means for the individual to be in relation to truth. He states, "Here is a definition of truth: An objective uncertainty held fast through appropriation with the most passionate inwardness, is the truth, the highest truth there is for an existing person."[20] Johannes Climacus' understanding of truth, and what it means to relate to that truth, is one that will later parallel the understanding of another of Kierkegaard's pseudonyms, the author of *Practice in Christianity*, Anti-Climacus. In 1850, Anti-Climacus writes: "Only then do I in truth know the truth when it becomes a life in me. Therefore, Christ compares truth to food and *appropriating* to eating, for just as, physically, food by being appropriated (assimilated) becomes the life sustenance, so also, spiritually, truth is both the giver of life and the sustenance of life, is life."[21]

Both Johannes Climacus and Anti-Climacus teach that being a Christian does not consist in mere adherence to Christian doctrine as had become the predominant view in Denmark. In fact, drawing on Luther's context as an analogy for the problems facing nineteenth-century Danish Christianity, Kierkegaard's pseudonym Johannes Climacus describes pre-Reformation Catholicism as one characterized by a surfeit of objectivity: "Did not the papacy have objectivity and objective definitions and the objective, more of the objective, the objective in superabundance? What did it lack? Appropriation, inwardness."[22] The only outcome of a solely objective reflection of, or adherence to, Christianity is to treat it disinterestedly as a mere object; with this approach subjectivity is disregarded, yet to "subjective reflection, truth becomes appropriation, inwardness, subjectivity, and the point is to immerse oneself, existing, in subjectivity."[23]

In seeking to emphasize that truth is not to be treated dispassionately but passionately in the individual's participation in the truth, the concept of appropriation is consistently used in relation to other concepts such as "inwardness" (*Inderlighed*) and "subjectivity" (*Subjektivitet*). According to Johannes Climacus, the truth of Christianity is both eternal and subjective.[24] Yet Christian truths can only be realized by the existing individual. This is partly because some Christian truths are paradoxical and are inaccessible to reason. These include the paradox of the Incarnation and the paradox of the forgiveness of sins.[25] Both are paradoxical by virtue of an eternal truth purportedly being related in time to an existing individual human being. Only faith can dissolve these paradoxes, and faith is a passion.[26] Passions are felt only by subjectivity. The other reason Christian truth is subjective is that "for an existing individual" objective truth can only be an approximation[27]—because existing

---

[20]   *SKS* 7, 186 / *CUP1*, 203.
[21]   *SKS* 12, 203 / *PC*, 206.
[22]   *SKS* 7, 333 / *CUP1*, 366.
[23]   *SKS* 7, 176 / *CUP1*, 192.
[24]   *SKS* 7, 205 / *CUP1*, 224.
[25]   Ibid.
[26]   *SKS* 4, 261 / *PF*, 59.
[27]   *SKS* 7, 205 / *CUP1*, 224.

individuals are temporal and finite and can never finish accumulating all the evidence that would amount to absolute truth.

To this point, truth "is the self-activity of appropriation."[28] Christian truth, to be the truth for an individual, must be appropriated. As stated, because the Christian faith has its basis in the belief that God and man were both manifested in Christ, human reason comes to an impenetrable barrier in its ability to accept this claim. Johannes Climacus maintains that reason can only be offended at Christ's claim to be God.[29] Intellectual assimilation of Christ can only result in either an empty objective adherence or an understanding of Christ merely as the ideal moral archetype. If either approach is detected in an individual or the Christian culture at large, it shows that the category of offense has not arisen. Offense indicates that the individual has confronted that which cannot be understood by reason—that is, that God had appeared in human flesh—and clears the way for faith. But faith, for Kierkegaard, allows for the "triumphant breakthrough" whereby the offense is overcome.[30] "Without faith one remains in the offense."[31]

The concept of faith, too, is often associated with inwardness, subjectivity, and appropriation. However, faith is distinguished as a form of appropriation by its intentional object. Faith appropriates, as the object of its most passionate belief, the paradoxical union of God and man in Christ.[32] Appropriating this objective uncertainty intensifies risk, and thus it also intensifies the inwardness and the appropriation of its object.

In conclusion, Kierkegaard believes that genuine Christianity primarily depends upon appropriation. One must appropriate and hold fast to this doctrine in a way entirely different from the way one holds to anything else. One ought to live and die in it, even risk one's life for it. For Kierkegaard, the very mark of being a Christian is appropriation.[33]

See also Approximation; Certainty; Decision/Resolve; Existence/Existential; Faith; Individual; Leap; Objectivity/Subjectivity; Offense; Passion/Pathos; Personality; Self; Spirit; Speculation/Science/Scholarship; Truth.

---

[28]   *SKS* 7, 220 / *CUP1*, 242.
[29]   *SKS* 12, 91 / *PC*, 81.
[30]   *SKS* 12, 127 / *PC*, 120.
[31]   Ibid.
[32]   *SKS* 7, 554–5 / *CUP1*, 610–11.
[33]   *SKS*, 7, 553 / *CUP1*, 608–9.

Approximation

Sean Anthony Turchin

Approximation (*Tilnærmelse*—noun; *Approximation*—noun)

The Danish word *Tilnærmelse* means approximation or approach. Throughout his *corpus*, Kierkegaard uses both *Tilnærmelse* and *Approximation* in order to convey either the idea of an epistemological estimation (knowledge that is limited in accuracy or that is possibly inexact in its representation) or the idea of an individual approaching another in nearness of relation.[1] Kierkegaard's own 1833 edition of Molbech's *Danish Dictionary*, under the entry for *Tilnærmelse*, includes the word *Approximation* in parentheses.[2] The word *Tilnærmelse* is a combination of the prefix *til* meaning "toward," and the word *Nærmelse* meaning proximity.

The infinitive form *at tilnærme* can mean either to come closer or to approach a place or a point as well as denoting a similarity between two things or people.[3] And herein, with *Tilnærmelse* also conveying an approach in relation to someone (to the point of ingratiation), rests the significance for Kierkegaard's use of both concepts. A careful examination of Kierkegaard's texts reveals that there is a slight nuance between his uses of *Approximation* and *Tilnærmelse*, with *Approximation* denoting an impossibility of convergence and *Tilnærmelse* denoting the opposite.

When *Tilnærmelse* is used, it is often in a relational sense with regard to two individuals or objects. Pertaining to individuals, the idea is one of an individual approaching in relation to another, in the sense of making advances toward another. Generally, *Tilnærmelse* conveys the idea of approximation as the possibility of approach or relation and thus seems more positive in meaning.

On the other hand, *Approximation* is predominately used in relation to Kierkegaard's discussions of both sensate knowledge and historical knowledge. Kierkegaard believes that such knowledge fails to deliver absolute certainty. Furthermore, this mode of knowledge is also often deceptive in nature in light of the primacy of the individual in this act of knowing. With historical knowledge, *Approximation* denotes that such knowledge is an estimate, limited in accuracy, or not necessarily exact in nature. Thus this sense conveys an understanding of our inability, or the impossibility, of attaining a perfectly accurate account of past events.

---

[1]   *Ordbog over det danske Sprog*, vols. 1–28, published by the Society for Danish Language and Literature, Copenhagen: Gyldendal 1918–56, vol. 23, columns 1358–9.

[2]   Christian Molbech, *Dansk Ordbog*, vols. 1–2, Copenhagen: Den Gyldendalske Boghandlings Forlag 1833, vol. 2, p. 708.

[3]   *Ordbog over det danske Sprog*, vol. 23, columns 1358–9.

Although Kierkegaard's conception of historical knowledge as an approximation is not negative in and of itself, it is negative within the context of the individual's desire to secure an absolute relation to Christianity via historical knowledge. This discussion takes place largely in the *Concluding Unscientific Postscript*. Each of these connotations will be discussed in turn.

In descending order of frequency, the term *Approximation* is found in the *Concluding Unscientific Postscript*, *The Concept of Anxiety*, *The Concept of Irony*, the notebooks and journals, *Either/Or*, and *Practice in Christianity*; for *Tilnærmelse* the order is the notebooks and journals, *Either/Or*, *The Concept of Irony*, the *Concluding Unscientific Postscript*, and *A Literary Review of Two Ages*.

In the earlier period of Kierkegaard's *corpus* from *The Concept of Irony* to *Either/Or*, *Tilnærmelse* is largely used to define the type of relation existing between two individuals in terms of comparison, emulation, and intention. For example, in *The Concept of Irony*, Kierkegaard discusses Socrates' ironic statements regarding the Sophists' lack of approach (*Tilnærmelse*) to the idea.[4] Later, when discussing Aristophanes' view of Socrates, Kierkegaard offers a comparison between Socrates and the clouds from which he concludes that Socrates is like the clouds whose "objective power…cannot find an abiding place on earth, whose approach [*Tilnærmelse*] to the earth is always at a distance."[5]

In two places in *Either/Or*, Part One, *Tilnærmelse* denotes the desire of one individual to draw close to another, to approach, or at least initiate a move toward another.[6] However, the most common use of *Tilnærmelse* is found within the context of Kierkegaard's relation to Regine.[7] In a journal entry from 1849 about Regine, Kierkegaard uses the word *Tilnærmelse* when contemplating how he should, or even would approach her. Here, the approximation conveys Kierkegaard's uncertainty over whether he should literally approach her. The situation was that Regine's father had just passed away, and Kierkegaard thus thought that Regine would expect him to face her. In the end, he did not approach her, but approached her husband, Schlegel, instead. He explains his reason as follows: "I take the risk of her completely misinterpreting my approach before I get the chance to explain what I want."[8] In another journal entry from 1849, Kierkegaard ponders the possible outcomes of approaching Regine, depending on whether or not she has essentially changed.[9] *Tilnærmelse* is also used in the context of Kierkegaard's discussions of his desire to come into closer proximity to God and/or Christianity as seen in his notebooks and journals. Here to come closer to God is, paradoxically to be further removed from God, which is "*really* drawing near."[10] This approach (*Tilnærmelse*) to God is *qualitative* and is a task for every individual. No quantity of striving by other

---

4   *SKS* 1, 166 / *CI*, 114.
5   *SKS* 1, 188 / *CI*, 138.
6   Cf. *SKS* 2, 296 / *EO1*, 307; *SKS* 2, 349 / *EO1*, 360.
7   *SKS* 22, 370, NB14:44 / *JP* 6, 6538.
8   Ibid.
9   *SKS* 22, 160, NB12:28 / *JP* 6, 6454.
10   *SKS* 24, 327, NB24:14.

individuals, or cumulative effort by generations of the race, can help the individual converge on the unconditioned.[11]

The context wherein *Approximation* assumes significance begins in *Philosophical Fragments*, where Climacus raises the question as to what extent the quest for historical certitude about Christianity can aid the individual in becoming a Christian. He asks, "How can an eternal happiness be built on historical knowledge?"[12] In sum, this question concerns itself with the "subjective individual's most passionate interest," namely immortality.[13]

The question of the relation between historical knowledge and eternal happiness is one that Kierkegaard had formulated in reaction to the climate of nineteenth-century theology whose methods sought to procure for Christianity a greater amount of rational accessibility via historical investigation and speculation. For Kierkegaard, such methods betray that the issue of Christianity is incorrectly treated in an objective manner.[14] These methods suggest, according to Kierkegaard, that if only the truth of Christianity could be given enough clarity and certainty, then it would surely become acceptable to the individual, as acceptable as other historical truths.[15] But Christianity does not demand a merely objective adherence whereby the subject, or individual, is ultimately disregarded.[16] Instead, Christianity requires the infinite interest of the individual:[17] that the individual exist in its truth with the utmost passion of subjectivity, namely, faith.[18] In contrast, "the way of objective reflection now leads to abstract thinking, to mathematics, to historical knowledge of various kinds and always leads away from the subjective individual...."[19]

Aside from pointing out that historical investigation fosters an objective approach to Christianity, Johannes Climacus notes that a problem faces the individual who seeks to base his or her Christian faith on historical knowledge.[20] This problem is "that with regard to the historical the greatest certainty is only an approximation, and an approximation is too little to build his happiness on."[21] An event that is historical is by nature an event in the past and therefore "has the ideality of recollection,"[22] which falls short of actuality. All historical knowledge, regardless of how thorough the investigation, is only an approximation.[23] Endeavoring to approximate historical certainty about the seemingly impossible event of the eternal God coming into existence in time is absurd, but absurd in a different sense from the absurd claim of Christian doctrine about the Incarnation. It is an attempt to render the absurd

---

[11]   *SKS* 24, 497, NB25:82.
[12]   Cf. *SKS* 7, 329 / *CUP1, 361.*
[13]   *SKS* 7, 161 / *CUP1,* 174.
[14]   *SKS* 7, 52 / *CUP1,* 46.
[15]   Ibid.
[16]   *SKS* 7, 176 / *CUP1,* 192.
[17]   *SKS* 7, 61 / *CUP1* 57.
[18]   *SKS* 7, 124 / *CUP1,* 132.
[19]   *SKS* 7, 177 / *CUP1,* 193.
[20]   *SKS* 7, 30 / *CUP1,* 23.
[21]   Ibid.
[22]   *SKS* 7, 522 / *CUP1,* 574.
[23]   *SKS* 7, 523 / *CUP1,* 575.

probable—thereby confusing "the absurd fact of coming into existence, which is the object of faith, with a simple historical fact."[24] For Johannes Climacus, the truths purported by Christianity exist therefore in a realm of uncertainty far more extreme than other historical events. This is because the absurdity of the Incarnation disqualifies it from all consideration by calculative reason, and therefore entirely beyond approximation and probability.

Pondering the idea of God's coming into existence, Johannes Climacus, in the *Fragments*, asks, "How is that changed which comes into existence or what is the change of coming into existence?"[25] The question concerns something even more radical than the certitude of historical knowledge. It questions the ontological basis of becoming and plumbs its modal implications. When something comes into existence a change is presupposed, namely, from non-existence to existence. If a certain object has come into being, then we assume, by this coming into being, that it did not previously exist and, as such, is not necessary. As an example Kierkegaard states, "If, in coming into existence, a plan is intrinsically changed, then it is not this plan that comes into existence; but if it comes into existence unchanged, what, then, is the change of coming into existence? This change, then, is not in essence but in being and is from not existing to existing."[26]

That something has come into existence is, for Kierkegaard, a movement from possibility to actuality.[27] But then Kierkegaard asks, "Can the necessary come into existence?"[28] When we refer to something as necessary, we are making a claim about the form of its existence, that is, that it necessarily exists. Anything that comes into existence has demonstrated that it is by definition not necessary: "For the only thing that cannot come into existence is the necessary, because the necessary is."[29] What Kierkegaard has in mind in regard to this discussion, beyond the remoteness of historical events in general, is the very central Christian claim of the Incarnation that the eternal, that is, the necessary, has come into existence. If God, as necessary, comes into existence, does this not prove that he is indeed not necessary since his coming into existence would prove that he did not exist?

The past, too, is sometimes regarded as necessary since it is the way it is and can no longer become something else. Historical knowledge can at best only approximate the past and cannot exhaust how it is. But this is quite different from the attempt to approximate knowledge of a supposedly necessary being in the process of becoming contingent.

Insofar as historical investigation presupposes an object or event open to human rationality, in the most empirical and rational sense, the notion "that an individual human being is God, that is, claims to be God, is indeed the offence (in an eminent sense),"[30] because, as Kierkegaard states, it "conflicts with all (human)

---

24   *SKS* 7, 193 / *CUP1*, 211.
25   *SKS* 4, 273 / *PF*, 73.
26   Ibid.
27   *SKS* 4, 274 / *PF*, 74.
28   Ibid.
29   Ibid.
30   *SKS* 12, 40 / *PC*, 26.

reason."[31] Thus, in proclaiming "itself to be the eternal, essential truth that has come into existence in time"[32] this paradox offers the individual one of two choices. Either the individual, in faith, is convinced of the truth of Christianity, or he remains in an objective relationship of observation.[33] Approximation can continue as long as it pleases.[34] Historical evidence may always be waiting to be discovered, waiting to be counted among the rest of the evidence in providing history greater clarity. Thus the historian, like all those before him, seeks to account for the exactness of the past with as much certainty as is possible."[35] But, as we have stated, Christian truths evade historical and critical investigation insofar as its truths have their ground outside of human history. Even if one admits, as does Climacus, "that the historicity of Christianity is true…it would still be impossible to establish more than an approximation."[36]

And yet, Kierkegaard posits that one's eternal happiness must be based "on something historical, of which the knowledge, at its maximum, is an approximation."[37] That Kierkegaard finds it objectionable for one to rest his or her eternal happiness on an approximation, and yet believes this is what is required of the individual in order to secure eternal happiness, appears contradictory. However, Climacus thinks that with regard to the historical there is no problem.[38] Rather, the problem arises when one seeks to base the utmost decision of one's eternal happiness on probability by means of historical investigation.

Even though "approximation" is used largely in relation to the uncertainty of historical knowledge, it is also used with regard to sensate knowledge. Kierkegaard writes, "Sensate certainty, to say nothing of historical certainty, is uncertainty, is only an approximation."[39] Therefore sensate knowledge is also inappropriate and inadequate as a basis for Christian faith.

In conclusion, sensate and historical knowledge offer only approximation, which is too shaky a foundation for one's eternal happiness. Therefore, the methods of historical investigation, empiricism, and speculation fall short. Christianity demands subjective passion and absolute commitment, rather than objective or historical probability (even when the latter approximate certainty).

See also Absurd; Appropriation; Certainty; Contingency/Possibility; Decision/ Resolve; Faith; History; Leap; Objectivity/Subjectivity; Speculation/Science/ Scholarship; Truth.

---

[31]   Ibid.
[32]   *SKS* 7, 195 / *CUP1*, 213.
[33]   *SKS* 7, 28 / *CUP1*, 21.
[34]   *SKS* 7, 39 / *CUP1*, 32.
[35]   Ibid.
[36]   *SKS* 7, 524 / *CUP1*, 576.
[37]   *SKS* 7, 524 / *CUP1*, 577.
[38]   *SKS* 7, 524 / *CUP1*, 576.
[39]   *SKS* 7, 44 / *CUP1*, 38.

Archimedean Point

Diego Giordano

Archimedean Point (*Archimediske Punkt*—noun)

Archimedes was a Syracusan mathematician, famous for discoveries in applied mechanics. To him is attributed the saying: "Give me a place to stand (a fulcrum), and I will move the world," hence the phrase *Archimedean Point*, used connotatively.[1] This expression frequently occurs in the works of Kierkegaard, who usually uses it as a philosophical notion designating something utopian, that is, something ultimately not achievable because it is "outside the world"[2] (*udenfor Verden*) and outside the "restrictions of time and space."[3]

The first time Kierkegaard makes use of the expression is in an early journal entry dated September 11, 1834, where it appears twice apropos his personal inability to enjoy nature, not realizing what he actually enjoys.[4] This is not an isolated case of Kierkegaard making this connection between the lever, as a simple mechanical device that changes the movement of a thing, and nature, considered from the point of view of the *natural sciences*.[5] It occurs again in a draft of a letter (June 1, 1835) addressed to the natural scientist Peter Wilhelm Lund,[6] where Kierkegaard says that

---

[1]   The most important ancient source of this anecdote, as well as of the figure of Archimedes, is in Plutarch's *Parallel Lives*, in the part devoted to comparing Pelopidas and Marcellus. Kierkegaard owned this work (*ASKB* 1197–1200). See, for example, Plutarch's "Marcellus" 14, *Lives*; *Plutark's Levnetsbeskrivelser*, vols. 1–4, trans. by Stephan Tetens, Copenhagen: Brummers Forlag 1800–11, vol. 3, p. 272, where it is written: "Archimedes, who was a kinsman and friend of King Hiero, wrote to him that with any given force it was possible to move any given weight; and emboldened, as we are told, by the strength of his demonstration, he declared that, if there were another world, and he could go to it, he could move this" (*Plutarch's Lives*, vols. 1–11, trans. by Berandotte Perrin, New York: Putnam 1914–26, vol. 5, p. 473).

[2]   *SKS* 17, 15, AA:6 / *KJN* 1, 10; *SKS* 20, 107–8, NB:171 / *KJN* 4, 107–8; *SKS* 20, 416, NB5:111 / *KJN* 4, 417; *SKS* 23, 482–3, NB20:168 / *JP* 2, 2089.

[3]   *SKS* 17, 15, AA:6 / *KJN* 1, 10.

[4]   *SKS* 27, 117, 96:1 / *JP* 1, 117: "A work of art, on the other hand, I can grasp. I can—if I may put it this way—find the Archimedean point, and as soon as I have found it, everything is readily clear for me."

[5]   *SKS* 17, 20–1, AA:12 / *KJN* 1, 16: "Including in this classification all those who seek to clarify and interpret the runic inscriptions of nature."

[6]   Emanuel Hirsch has considered this letter fictive and as part of the "Faustian letters." See Emanuel Hirsch, *Kierkegaard Studien*, vols. 1–2, Gutersloh: Bertelsmann 1933, vol. 2, pp. 490–2.

he thinks very highly of the "researchers who through their reflection have found or are trying to find that Archimedean point which is nowhere in the world."[7] But he continues writing that even though he has been and still is enthusiastic about the natural sciences, he does not think he will make them his principal study, since life, by virtue of reason and freedom, has always interested him most. Directly referring to this letter, Kierkegaard seems to disclose his need to seek *his* Archimedean Point ("from which one can lift the whole world"),[8] namely, the need he feels "to find a truth which is truth *for me*, to find *the idea for which to live and die*," as he writes two months later in the famous letter from Gilleleje (August 1, 1835).[9] Such identification is confirmed when, a few years later, he considers the "true Archimedean point" on a religious ground, defining it both as the point—not yet found—in which he would wish to rest,[10] and as the conception of divine love, which is the one single unshakable thing in life.[11] Kierkegaard alludes to this principle of physics in several journal entries, where he discusses God, love, inwardness, conscience, and the infinite. For example, when speaking about the responsibility before God, he writes "this phrase and this thought—*for the sake of conscience*—is a transformation of language, is the Archimedean point outside the world."[12] When he gives a more precise description of this "point outside the world," he calls it "a prayer chamber where a true man of prayer prays in all honesty—and he will move the earth."[13] Elsewhere, he explains that the infinite "in the guise of being nothing…is in the world the point outside of the world which can move all existence."[14]

Hitherto we have referred only to Kierkegaard's unpublished work,[15] but references to the "Archimedean Point" are present in the published works as well. These can be found in *Either/Or*, *Repetition*, and the *Concluding Unscientific Postscript*. In "Rotation of Crops" and "The Balance between the Esthetic and the Ethical in the Development of the Personality," both from *Either/Or*, Kierkegaard reasserts that the Archimedean Point is the point from which one can lift the whole world. In the first case the expression is connected to the Platonic notion of oblivion as an art through which "recollection" is guaranteed, since "forgetting and recollecting are identical," and when something is written "in the book of oblivion, we are indeed suggesting that it is forgotten and yet at the same time is preserved."[16] In the second case the principle of Archimedes, in its linguistic-metaphorical meaning, is used by Kierkegaard in order to describe "personality" as the consciousness of the single

---

7   *SKS* 17, 20–1, AA:12 / *KJN* 1, 16; cf. also: *B&A*, vol. 1, pp. 32ff. / *LD,* Letter 3, pp. 41ff.
8   *SKS* 17, 15, AA:6 / *KJN* 1, 10. See also: *Pap.* III B 122:10 / *EO1*, Supplement, 549.
9   *SKS* 17, 20–1, AA:12 / *KJN* 1, 16.
10   *SKS* 18, 24, EE:53.c / *KJN* 2, 20.
11   *SKS* 19, 200, Not6:24 / *KJN* 3, 196.
12   *SKS* 20, 107–8, NB:171 / *KJN* 4, 107–8.
13   *SKS* 20, 416, NB5:111 / *KJN* 4, 417.
14   *SKS* 23, 482–3, NB20:168 / *JP* 2, 2089.
15   See also *SKS* 18, 220, JJ:251 / *KJN* 2, 202 (on the figure of Archimedes); *SKS* 22, 322, NB13:79 / *JP* 6, 6519 (apropos the fulcrum).
16   *SKS* 2, 284 / *EO1*, 295.

individual of being the absolute.[17] In *Repetition*, again referring back to the Greek philosophical conception of recollection, Constantin Constantius talks about the notion of repetition as that "point" which remains transcendent both for himself and for modern philosophy in general.[18] Finally, in the *Concluding Unscientific Postscript*, this concept is mentioned several times. Two main references are in the section devoted to Lessing where Kierkegaard, expressing his gratitude to the German philosopher, says that the latter was the only one who has grasped "that Archimedean point of religiousness,"[19] because he actually understood that the religious concerned every human being isolated from the world. A little later in the text, talking of Jacobi and Lessing regarding the so-called "deadly leap" (or somersault), he goes along with Lessing in criticizing the leap as something objective, "something analogous to, for example, finding the Archimedean point."[20]

Insofar as the discovery of that physical principle can be used as a general philosophical notion (as it were, "on paper"), as a category for showing something extremely important, a true Archimedean Point always has a direct relationship with an existing person who, through this secure foothold which is to be found in inwardness, can "succeed in moving the whole world."[21]

See also Absolute; Faith; Immanence/Transcendence; Religious/Religiousness.

---

[17]   *SKS* 3, 253 / *EO2*, 265.

[18]   *SKS* 4, 57 / *R*, 186. On the doctrine of recollection, see David D. Possen, "*Meno*: Kierkegaard and the Doctrine of Recollection," in *Kierkegaard and the Greek World*, Tome I, *Socrates and Plato*, ed. by Katalin Nun and Jon Stewart, Aldershot: Ashgate 2010 (*Kierkegaard Research: Sources, Reception and Resources*, vol. 2), pp. 29–35.

[19]   *SKS* 7, 67 / *CUP1*, 65.

[20]   *SKS* 7, 100 / *CUP1*, 102.

[21]   *SKS* 7, 381 / *CUP1*, 419.

Art

Nathaniel Kramer

Art (*Kunst*—noun)

The Danish word for "art" (*Kunst*) derives from the German word *Kunst* with its roots in the verbs *kennen*, "to know," and *können*, "to know how, or to be able to." The lexical meaning of the Danish is therefore a broad understanding, study, or experience of a particular field of knowledge. Such an understanding and knowledge may be acquired through education, practice, or experience and often pertains to the development of certain skills or proficiencies. Because of this sense of technical and theoretical development, the term functions in opposition to a sense of natural endowment or innate ability or skill. Hence, the term refers to human activity as opposed to nature and its forces. Art also carries with it the sense of adroitness or dexterity in said skills. This sense of art as an acquired skill, whether technical or theoretical, further develops in the direction of a knowledge or work that requires specialized training and education. One might think of the artisan or the craftsman that creates products or goods that require a more specialized form of knowledge. Art then may also refer not only to the profession or craft itself but also to the objects produced by someone so trained. In this sense the emphasis in the term is often on the mechanical and industrial crafts or handiwork. As such, art comprises those works that demand a certain experience or practice. In a further development of this sense of a more specialized training and education, art may also be used to describe something inventive or ingenious and clever. Art may also refer to a trick or ploy, or even to something deceitful or cunning or crafty. The idea of art as a presentation of emotional and intellectual content in a visible form is a relatively late development in the meaning of the term, and was influenced by the German Romantics (Herder, Goethe, and Schiller). This more aesthetic sense of art emphasizes intellectual imagination and creativity, as opposed to a technical and theoretical proficiency, and is sometimes contrasted with science or the application of more scientific principles. While art in this aesthetic sense may refer broadly to any objects that fit the above description, there is particular emphasis placed on the plastic arts (drawing, painting, sculpture, and architecture). Art may also refer to music, song, and dance as well as acting.[1]

---

[1]   *Ordbog over det danske Sprog*, vols. 1–28, published by the Society for Danish Language and Literature, Copenhagen: Gyldendal 1918–56, vol. 11, columns 754–62.

The word for art and its different meanings are found throughout Kierkegaard's *corpus*, especially in the journals, notebooks, and loose papers. The sheer number of references to the term in these works suggests that art as an idea or a concept was important for him. If one turns to the published works, the most frequent occurrence of the term is to be found in the volumes of *Either/Or*, with the first volume being the most significant. As one would expect, the two volumes of *Either/Or* contain extensive references to art, especially since in Part One we are given a window into the world of the aesthete, and then in Part Two a critique by Judge William of that world. After *Either/Or*, the *Concluding Unscientific Postscript*, *The Concept of Irony*, *Works of Love* and *Stages on Life's Way*, in that order, either explore or use the term "art" extensively or develop Kierkegaard's particular valences of the term. The Christian discourse "The Lily in the Field" also utilizes the term significantly in its discussion of the Christian attitude of patience. *The Concept of Anxiety*, *A Literary Review of Two Ages*, *Practice in Christianity*, and references in several of the upbuilding discourses round out the most significant occurrences of the term "art" in Kierkegaard's *oeuvre*. It may be worth noting that "art" is used throughout the pseudonymous works as well as those published under Kierkegaard's own name.

Much, of course, has been made of the significance of art for Kierkegaard and his authorship. The term is often used by Kierkegaard not in its aesthetic sense but in terms of a learned skill or ability. Kierkegaard employs this definition of art as practiced skill or ability in a wide variety of contexts. For example, in one of A's papers entitled "Rotation of the Crops," A speaks at length on the art of forgetting and the art of remembering.[2] This idea of remembering and forgetting as an art, itself having roots in antiquity, is also echoed in *Stages on Life's Way*, where William Afham, in the preface to "In Vino Veritas," also makes a distinction between two kinds of remembering as an art.[3] Indeed there are numerous similar uses of such a genitive construction: the art of seduction,[4] the art of being mysterious to everybody,[5] the art of being a good reader,[6] the art of the inclosingly reserved person,[7] the art of the actor,[8] the art of being silent,[9] and the art of communication.[10] All of these accordingly suggest a practiced skill, one that develops over time and through education, training or experience (or all three).

As mentioned above, one of the important distinctions created in such a definition is the difference between a learned art and an innate skill or ability. Judge William, in his critique of the aesthete and in a defense of marriage, argues that "true art goes in the direction opposite to that of nature, without therefore annihilating it."[11] Kierkegaard also suggests this nuance of definition when the aesthete in "The

---

[2]   *SKS* 2, 282 / *EO1*, 293.
[3]   *SKS* 6, 20–1 / *SLW*, 10–11.
[4]   *SKS* 4, 232 / *PF*, 24.
[5]   *SKS* 3, 158 / *EO2*, 160.
[6]   *SKS* 4, 91 / *R*, 225.
[7]   *SKS* 6, 333 / *SLW*, 358.
[8]   *SKS* 6, 332 / *SLW*, 358.
[9]   *SKS* 11, 16 / *WA*, 16.
[10]   *SKS* 12, 137 / *PC*, 133.
[11]   *SKS* 3, 130 / *EO2*, 131.

Seducer's Diary" emphasizes that being in love is no art and requires no study, and hence is something natural or innate. Incidentally, in the Hong translation the word used here is "skill," even though the Danish is *Kunst*.[12] Likewise Kierkegaard, utilizing the example of the prophetess Anna from the New Testament, writes in "Two Upbuilding Discourses" that there is no art to praying.[13] Again, the implication is that praying does not require any training or skill.

This issue of what is untutored and untaught as distinct from what is, is a very important distinction for Kierkegaard. In true Kierkegaardian fashion though, the definition of art as an acquired skill and the more Romantic definition of art as implying a talent one is born with are often played off against each other. For example, in *Works of Love* Kierkegaard writes that "it is no 'art' to praise love, for just that reason to do it is a work. 'Art' pertains to the accident of talent, and work pertains to the universally human."[14] Though Kierkegaard defines art here as exclusively the province of a few and an accident of birth, Kierkegaard overturns this definition and insists on the idea of art as a work, or more specifically an effort having to do with skill. To do this, Kierkegaard refers to a Danish proverb, which reads in English "To say it is not art, but to do it is." Kierkegaard continues: "This is a proverbial remark that is quite true if one sensibly excludes the instances and situations in which the art actually is 'to say it.' "[15] Here, as well as in the following sentences and paragraphs, Kierkegaard exploits this ambiguity found in the term "art": art as a practiced and performed skill that requires work and the idea of art as an inborn poetic gift.

It may well be the case that any and all definitions of the term "art," including the idea of art as aesthetic representation, may be in play in any given instance when Kierkegaard uses the term. The use of the term "art" often appears in the context of selfhood, either in descriptions of various attitudes or comportments to what it means to be a self or in claims about what a self is. Perhaps one of the most recognizable uses of the term is Johannes Climacus' claim in the *Concluding Unscientific Postscript* that "the subjective thinker is not a scientist-scholar; he is an artist. To exist is an art."[16] The opposition established here between "science-scholarship" and art suggests a difference between particular fields of knowledge and/or expertise. This idea that art is its own branch or field of knowledge opposed to science is fairly conventional and reiterated throughout the *corpus*. Climacus thus spends time throughout this section of the *Postscript* developing the claim that existence requires its own specialized kind of knowledge and understanding, one that may well require practice and experience in addition to learning. However, one may also assert that the idea of existence as an art also implies a sense of creative and imaginative skill more in keeping with the definition of art as aesthetic representation. Hence existence well may be an aesthetic enterprise also.

---

[12]   *SKS* 2, 324 / *EO1*, 334.
[13]   *SKS* 5, 222 / *UD*, 222.
[14]   *SKS* 9, 353 / *WL*, 359.
[15]   Ibid.
[16]   *SKS* 7, 321 / *CUP1*, 351.

The sense of art as it relates to the idea of the self also leads to questions about the authenticity of such art and how to evaluate it as such. The distinction between technical and theoretical proficiency and that of natural or innate ability as suggested above intensifies in the direction of art as artifice. Art may indicate some subterfuge or deception and thus a ploy or trick. In the Christian discourse "The Lily in the Field" Kierkegaard takes up the idea of the Christian self in the context of such dissimulation: "This innocent child cannot dissemble, nor is it asked to, and its good fortune is that it cannot, because the art of being able to dissemble is indeed purchased at a high price."[17] The innocent child referred to here is like the lily and the bird, which silently suffer the pains of existence and do not pretend otherwise. Kierkegaard develops this sense of art as artifice more fully in the context of the definition of art as aesthetic representation, which will be addressed below.

The definition of art as the presentation of an emotional and aesthetic content—and thus the expression of imagination and creativity—is a relatively late development in the meaning of the term. Influenced by the German Romantics, Kierkegaard uses this broad meaning of the term as well as its various nuances throughout his *corpus*. Within this general definition of art, there is a specification in which art comes to refer not only generally to these kinds of objects (though Kierkegaard uses this more general definition of the term to demarcate a certain branch of objects in which creativity or imagination is used according to aesthetic principles), but more specifically to the visual arts: painting, drawing, sculpture and sometimes architecture. Kierkegaard often invokes art in this context by making a distinction between what he calls "art and literature" (*Kunst og Poesi*).[18] In the first part of *Either/Or*, for example, A makes a distinction between art and poetry or literature by claiming "art depicts repose, poetry motion,"[19] a view actually articulated first by Gotthold Lessing in his famous essay *Laocoön*.

Kierkegaard's references to actual works of visual art are relatively few. In a sermon entitled "Watch your Step when you go to the House of the Lord," for example, there is a probable reference to Bertel Thorvaldsen's sculpture *Christus*, as well as to the altar in front of the *Christus*.[20] In *Stages on Life's Way*, the "Married Man" refers to a painting of Romeo and Juliet by Ferdinand Piloty (1786–1844).[21] In *Repetition*, Constantius refers obliquely to what were called Nüremberg prints, these being rather crude depictions of religious scenes.[22] In *Either/Or,* the seducer writes in a letter to Cordelia of a certain painting depicting Ariadne tearfully watching a ship sail away.[23] Relatively speaking, however, Kierkegaard's use of, and references to, the visual arts are rather few and far between.

The sense of art as referring to the visual arts, however, is counterbalanced by the fact that it may also designate music, song, dance, as well as the theatrical arts. In

---

[17]   *SKS* 11, 21 / *WA*, 15.
[18]   *SKS* 3, 259 / *EO1*, 273.
[19]   *SKS* 2, 329 / *EO1*, 169.
[20]   *SKS* 10, 175 / *CD*, 163.
[21]   *SKS* 6, 156 / *SLW*, 167.
[22]   *SKS* 4, 33 / *R*, 158.
[23]   *SKS* 2, 391 / *EO1*, 403.

Either/Or, A claims simply that "music is an art," though in this case A is probably suggesting the development of the ability to play music. In *Repetition*, Constantius hypothesizes an individual who "perhaps...went frequently to the ballet and admired the art of the dancer."[24] In *From the Papers of One Still Living*, Kierkegaard refers to "Jubal's art," a reference to a descendant of Cain found in the Bible who played the harp and flute.[25]

One of the very important contexts in which Kierkegaard utilizes the term "art," and its more specific valence as referring to the visual arts, is the question about the nature of Christian art. In *Practice in Christianity*, Kierkegaard's characteristic ambivalence toward art and the artistic comes through quite clearly here as he calls Christian art "a new paganism."[26] The issue here is precisely the necessary falsification in the artist's attempts to depict or to represent Christ, which according to Kierkegaard must remain fundamentally unrepresentable. The sensuous nature of art runs contrary to the sacred nature of the object being depicted.

This issue of art's capacity to represent or depict as well as the concern that it necessarily fails to do so successfully is a major theme in Kierkegaard's writings. In *Works of Love*, Kierkegaard wonders how a painter might paint mercifulness and decides that it cannot be done.[27] Art, because it exists in the realm of sensual presentation, ultimately cannot portray the unrepresentable. Following this line of thinking in relation to the sense of art as a trick or a ploy, Kierkegaard often emphasizes the element of deception or deceit associated with the term "art." For example, in the *Concluding Unscientific Postscript* Johannes Climacus discourses on suffering and the sufferer in a long section titled "Pathos." In this particular section, Climacus suggests that "an actor, especially a comic actor, may likewise at times be suffering in existence, but he does not concentrate on the suffering; he seeks to escape from it and finds alleviation in the confusion that his art encourages."[28] A similar conception of art as associated with deception is expressed in *Works of Love*, where Kierkegaard reiterates the actor's art as one of deception. This sense of a trick or ploy being an inherent part of the actor's art is further explored in terms of the actor donning a certain disguise: "one must not be able and must not want to see the actor through the costume; therefore it is the pinnacle of art when the actor becomes one with what he represents, because this is the pinnacle of deception."[29] Elsewhere in *Works of Love*, Kierkegaard writes: "the theater of art is like a world under a magic spell. But just suppose that some evening all the actors became confused in a common absentmindedness so that they thought they actually were what they represented. Would this not be what we might call, in contrast to the spell of the dramatic arts, the spell of an evil spirit, a bewitchment?"[30] This idea that actors practicing their art might be deceived into actually believing that they are not just

---

[24]   *SKS* 4, 33 / *R*, 158.
[25]   *SKS* 1, 53 / *EPW*, 98.
[26]   *SKS* 12, 246 / *PC*, 254.
[27]   *SKS* 9, 321 / *WL*, 324.
[28]   *SKS* 7, 403 / *CUP1*, 444.
[29]   *SKS* 9, 92 / *WL*, 87–8.
[30]   *SKS* 9, 91 / *WL*, 87.

playing a part but living it, and hence are under some spell, speaks to a deep and abiding ambivalence about the value of art understood as aesthetic representation.

In summary, Kierkegaard uses the term "art" throughout his authorship to convey the idea of a learned skill or ability, as well as the relatively recent use of the term to designate creative and imaginative abilities and works. In these senses of the term, the distinction between an inborn talent and the product of education, practice, and experience becomes an important part of Kierkegaard's use of the term. Furthermore, "art" not only designates specialization through practice, experience, and education but also merges with a sense of deception, a trick or ploy. Kierkegaard is particularly keen on exploring the possibility that art, in whatever context it is used, may well be artifice.

See also Aesthetic/Aesthetics; Allegory; Classicism; Dance; Epic; Fairytale; Genius; Lyric; Music; Novel; Poetry; Romanticism; Satire; Story-Telling; Theater/Drama; Tragedy; Vaudeville/Farce; Writing.

Asceticism

David Coe

Asceticism (*Askese*—noun)

From the Greek ἄσκησις (originally just meaning "exercise" or "training"), the Danish word *Askese* denotes self-chastisement through strict abstinence from sensual enjoyment. Its goal is the spirit's mastery of the flesh.[1]

The great majority of Søren Kierkegaard's pseudonymous references to asceticism occur in Johannes Climacus' *Concluding Unscientific Postscript*. The pseudonym Judge William in *Either/Or* has a few references to asceticism. Of Kierkegaard's signed works, *For Self-Examination* and *Judge For Yourself!* treat asceticism in depth. Kierkegaard's pseudonymous and signed use of asceticism normally refers to the practice of asceticism in the monasticism of the Middle Ages.

Dialectically, Kierkegaard criticizes the negatives and lauds the positives of monastic asceticism. Negatively, both his pseudonymous and signed works criticize the conceit potentially accrued through asceticism. Kierkegaard's pseudonym Judge William proclaims, "In the Middle Ages it was thought that in choosing the monastery one chose the extraordinary and became an extraordinary person oneself; from the altitude of the monastery one looked down proudly, almost pityingly, on the ordinary people."[2] But to desire to be supposed a holy person, the pseudonym Johannes Climacus warns, is the most dreadful profanation of the holy.[3] It is an irony that the person who renounces vanity wants to be admired for renouncing it.[4]

But Kierkegaard cautions, "Let us not go too far; let us not make a previous age's error an excuse for a new error."[5] Kierkegaard lauds medieval monasticism in comparison to modern mediation, for the former at least had passion and respect for the absolute.[6] "In our day," writes Judge William, "the market value of the monastic life has fallen; we seldom see a person break altogether with existence, with the universally human."[7] Climacus claims monasticism at least attempted to relate itself to the absolute absolutely, that is, earnestly to permeate everything in existence with the thought of

---

[1]   *Ordbog over det danske Sprog*, vols. 1–28, published by the Society for Danish Language and Literature, Copenhagen: Gyldendal 1918–56, vol. 1, column 898.

[2]   *SKS* 3, 309 / *EO2*, 327.

[3]   *SKS* 7, 378 / *CUP1*, 416.

[4]   *SKS* 7, 513 / *CUP1*, 564.

[5]   *SKS* 13, 44 / *FSE*, 15.

[6]   *SKS* 7, 376 / *CUP1*, 414.

[7]   *SKS* 3, 309 / *EO2*, 328.

God.[8] Modern mediation, on the other hand, merely dabbles in the absolute, relating to the absolute relatively. For example, Climacus saw modern mediation mitigating the absolute in relative ends such as mundane vocational competence (e.g., "king, cabinetmaker, tightrope walker, etc."), thereby emancipating itself from the earnest thought of "God present every day in everything."[9] In comparison, Kierkegaard lauds the Middle Ages: "However great its errors were, its conception of Christianity has a decisive advantage over that of our time. The Middle Ages conceived of Christianity along the lines of action, life, existence-transformation."[10] For Climacus, "it behooves us to have respect for the monastic movement of the Middle Ages,"[11] making "a powerful attempt to think God and the finite together."[12]

While lauding this attempt, Kierkegaard simultaneously criticizes the medieval presumption that thought this could actually be done and "that this could be done only in the monastery":[13]

> It is another matter that some of the actions they hit upon were strange, that it could think that in itself fasting was Christianity, that entering the monastery, giving everything to the poor, not to mention what we can scarcely mention without smiling—scourging oneself, crawling on one's knees, standing on one leg, etc.—that this was supposed to be true imitation. This was an error.[14]

Climacus explains that monasticism's distinct separate outward form is only relatively different from all other outward forms: "The Middle Ages wanted a little cubbyhole in order to be able to occupy itself properly with the absolute, but it was precisely by this that the absolute lost, because it still became something outward."[15] Hence, the medieval error was the belief that the outward form of asceticism directly corresponded to the interiority of the absolute.[16] "Precisely because there is the absolute difference between God and man, man expresses himself most perfectly when he absolutely expresses the difference."[17] As a corrective, Climacus counsels "to relate oneself absolutely to the absolute *telos* and relatively to relative ends," and even then, "humbly before God" and with "a certain sense of shame."[18]

For Kierkegaard's Lutheran convictions, an even bigger problem was the attachment of soteriological merit to the practice of monastic asceticism in the Middle Ages. Kierkegaard's critique is that "[s]omething worse than the first error did not fail to appear: they came up with the idea of meritoriousness, thought that they earned merit before God through their good works."[19] Climacus explains, "The

---

8	*SKS* 7, 368 / *CUP1*, 405.
9	*SKS* 7, 430 / *CUP1*, 474.
10	*SKS* 16, 238 / *JFY*, 192.
11	*SKS* 7, 381 / *CUP1*, 419.
12	*SKS* 7, 429 / *CUP1*, 473.
13	*SKS* 7, 430 / *CUP1*, 474.
14	*SKS* 16, 239 / *JFY*, 192.
15	*SKS* 7, 370 / *CUP1*, 408.
16	*SKS* 7, 378 / *CUP1*, 416.
17	*SKS* 7, 376 / *CUP1*, 412f.
18	*SKS* 7, 377 / *CUP1*, 414.
19	*SKS* 16, 239 / *JFY*, 192.

first true expression of relating oneself to the absolute *telos* is to renounce everything, but lest retrogression begin at once, one must truly understand that this renunciation of everything is nothing if it is supposed to merit the highest good."[20] Kierkegaard illustrates the wrong and the right approach to ascetic works:

> The approach to these works should indeed be, for example, like that of a militant youth who, in connection with a dangerous undertaking, voluntarily comes and pleads with his leader, saying: May I not be permitted to come along! If in the same way a person were to say to God: "May I not be permitted to give all I own to the poor—not that this should be meritorious, no, no, I am deeply and humbly aware that if I am ever saved I will be saved by grace, just as the robber on the cross, but may I not be permitted to do this so that I can work solely for the extension of God's kingdom among my fellow beings.[21]

For Kierkegaard, "The degeneration was not so much the monastic life as the meritoriousness it was presumed to have."[22] "Just as a beloved does not regard it as meritorious that she cannot at any moment do without the sight of her lover...so must the candidate for the monastery regard his relationship with God."[23]

As a corrective to the errors of monastic merit, Kierkegaard lauds the former monk Martin Luther as a prototype. Being a man of the Middle Ages, Luther anxiously attempted ascetic monasticism for the sake of meriting his salvation. But Luther was of such an exacting conscience that, after years of attempt, he felt his every good work for soteriological merit presumptuous, prideful, and even resentful of God. After years of despairing effort, Luther's scriptural discovery of justification by the full merit of Christ alone—given by grace alone, received by faith alone—without any merit of his own was a subjective and existential relief to Luther.[24] Given Luther's medieval context, Kierkegaard lauded Luther's timely message of grace to a works-ridden Middle Ages: "Since the Middle Ages had gone farther and farther astray...Luther came along and accentuated the other side, that he is a gift and this gift is to be received in faith."[25]

While lauding Luther's prescription of grace alone in Luther's medieval context, Kierkegaard diagnosed that modern Denmark was the opposite of the medieval Christianity of Luther's time. For three hundred years, Lutheranism had been the State Church of Denmark, but Danish Lutheran Christendom, generations removed, no longer possessed an anxious conscience like that of Luther or Luther's medieval audience. Instead, they assented objectively to the doctrine of justification and took it to such a one-sided extreme that the doctrine of justification by grace alone apart from works served as justification for ceasing to do works altogether.

As a corrective Kierkegaard dialectically presents Luther in *For Self-Examination* to his Lutheran public as a man of both faith and works, not someone who so stressed faith as to exclude works: "His life expressed works—let us never forget that—

20	*SKS* 7, 368 / *CUP1*, 404.
21	*SKS* 13, 45 / *FSE*, 15.
22	*SKS* 23, 152, NB16:86 / *JP* 3, 2513.
23	*SKS* 7, 377 / *CUP1*, 414.
24	*SKS* 16, 240 / *JFY*, 194.
25	*SKS* 21, 296, NB10:76 / *JP* 3, 2481.

but he said: A person is saved by faith alone."[26] Kierkegaard expressed the same in *Judge For Yourself!*:

> But let us not forget, Luther did not therefore abolish imitation, nor did he do away with the voluntary, as pampered sentimentality would like to have us think about Luther. He affirmed imitation in the direction of witnessing to the truth and voluntarily exposed himself there to dangers (yet without deluding himself that this was meritorious).[27]

With Luther, Kierkegaard reforms the outward expression of Christian works. No longer are Christian works ideally expressed via monastic asceticism but through good works that any Christian can express if he is willing to suffer for them:

> This is Christian piety: renouncing everything to serve God alone, to deny oneself in order to serve God alone—and then to have to suffer for it—to do good and then to have to suffer for it. It is this that the prototype expresses; it is also this, to mention a mere man, that Luther, the superb teacher of our Church, continually points out as belonging to true Christianity: to suffer for the doctrine, to do good and suffer for it, and that suffering in this world is inseparable from being a Christian in this world.[28]

To summarize, Kierkegaard dialectically lauds and criticizes the positives and negatives of monastic asceticism. In comparison to modern mediation, he lauds medieval monasticism's passionate attempt to find everything permeated with God. Yet he criticizes monastic asceticism as a source of personal conceit, as a presumptuous expression of the absolute, and, worst of all, as a source of soteriological merit. Kierkegaard sees in Luther a prototype. Correcting asceticism's errors, Luther reformed and affirmed Christian works, but did not regard them as a source of conceit or merit.

See also Absolute; Catholicism; Dying to/Renunciation; Earnestness; Humility; Imitation; Middle Ages; Monasticism; Passion/Pathos; Pride; Protestantism/ Reformation.

---

[26]   *SKS* 13, 45 / *FSE*, 16.
[27]   *SKS* 16, 239 / *JFY*, 193.
[28]   *SKS* 16, 218 / *JFY*, 169.

Atonement/Reconciliation

Lee C. Barrett

Atonement/Reconciliation (*Forsoning* or *Soning*—noun)

The lexical meaning of *forsoning* and *soning*, from the Old Danish *sone*,[1] includes atonement, expiation, propitiation, and reconciliation. In the Danish usage of Kierkegaard's era, both of these words were employed to refer to the removal of impediments to fellowship with God through the sacrificial rituals of the Old Testament, and to refer to the work of Christ in making possible a new saving relation to God.[2] Often the terms indicated the paying of the penalty for sin. To suggest reconciliation with God more broadly, without the nuance of an atoning sacrifice, Kierkegaard usually used *Forligelse*, which connoted an amicable settlement.

These concepts, and the imagery associated with them, appear most frequently in *The Concept of Anxiety*, *Works of Love*, *Christian Discourses*, *Two Ethical-Religious Essays*, and the various discourses for the Communion on Fridays. In all of these instances Kierkegaard used "atonement/reconciliation" in the context of God's act, through Christ, of forgiving the guilt of sin and overcoming sin's corruption.[3] Sometimes Kierkegaard pointedly contrasted this religious understanding of reconciliation (*Forsoning*) with its speculative philosophical meaning.[4]

The concept of the restoration of a right relation to God through the life, death, and resurrection of Christ was a recurring theme in Kierkegaard's authorship. He did not engage in any revision of the traditional Lutheran teachings, but sought to show how truly understanding them involves a transformation of the pathos of the believer. He basically assumed the validity of the inherited theological motifs and sought to clarify their often occluded meaning by displaying their appropriate use in the life of faith.

I. Kierkegaard's Main Use of the Concept of Atonement

Kierkegaard used the concept of atonement/reconciliation most frequently in articulating one of the four major ways of conceptualizing the soteriological work of Christ that had developed in the Christian tradition. This particular model of Christ's

---

[1] See Otto Kalkar, *Ordbog til det ældre danske Sprog*, vols. 1–4, Copenhagen: Universitets-Jubilæets danske Samfund 1881–1907, vol. 4, p. 42.

[2] See Christian Molbech, *Dansk Ordbog. Indeholdende det danske Sprogs Stammeord*, Copenhagen: Gyldendal 1833 (*ASKB* 1032), vol. 1, p. 294, vol. 2, p. 384.

[3] See, for example, *SKS* 4, 334 / *CA*, 28; *SKS* 4, 339 / *CA*, 33; *SKS* 4, 342 / *CA*, 36.

[4] See *SKS* 4, 318–20 / *CA*, 10–11.

saving work, which the historian of theology Gustaf Aulén would later designate the "Western" or "Latin" type, presents Jesus' life and death as the remedy for the problem of human sin and guilt.[5] This basic model assumed the form of different sub-varieties, with each variant utilizing a slightly different conceptuality. The metaphor of Christ as a "sacrifice" for sin suggested that a sin-offering, analogous to the sacrifices in the Old Testament to overcome defilement, cleanses those who have been stained by guilt. Alternatively, Anselm of Canterbury proposed that God's honor as lord of the cosmos had been offended by human sin, and then "satisfied" by Christ's offering of perfect respect and obedience unto death.[6] Yet another sub-variety, the "penal substitution" view, suggested that Jesus received the punishment for sin that sinful humanity deserved, and thereby fulfilled the demand of retributive justice. A more economically-oriented variant asserted that Christ paid the debt of righteousness that we impecunious sinners owed God. All of these views, although they relied upon different metaphoric domains, were "objective" in the sense that they implied that Christ's life, death, and resurrection have changed the actual relationship of God to humanity.

Kierkegaard was well aware of this general "Western/Latin" view of the atonement and its various sub-species from his general upbringing in the Lutheran heritage and his more technical seminary studies. Kierkegaard did not set out to analyze the intricacies of these diverse models of atonement, but rather borrowed their vocabulary and used their images to stimulate and shape the earnest self-concern of his readers. In so doing, he clarified the meaning of the various atonement models by exhibiting their rhetorical valences and pastoral purposes.

For Kierkegaard the most important thing about these theories was that they all directed attention to the dialectic of guilt and the forgiveness of sins;[7] they correctly recognized that anguish over guilt is a foundational presupposition of Christianity.[8] A primary virtue of these particular theories of atonement is their foregrounding of the fact that the forgiveness of sin is a gracious and unmerited act of God. Kierkegaard makes it clear that part of the rhetorical force of the Latin/Western doctrine of the atonement is to insist that forgiveness is due to the gracious agency of God, and is not a reward for the meritorious initiatives of individuals.[9] He further emphasizes the objectivity of the atonement and its independence from any human response by asserting that we are not even able to do anything to make ourselves receptive to the offer of forgiveness. For example, Kierkegaard warns, "If at the Communion table you want to be capable of the least little thing yourself, even merely to step forward yourself, you confuse everything, you prevent the reconciliation, make the satisfaction impossible."[10] Similarly, in the prayer that introduces *Judge for Yourself!*

---

5   Gustaf Aulén, *Christus Victor: A Study of the Three Main Types of the Idea of the Atonement*, trans. by A.G. Hebert, New York: Macmillan 1972, pp. 17–20; pp. 97–109. For a nuanced revision of Aulén's typology, see Peter Schmiechen, *Saving Power: Theories of the Atonement and Forms of the Church*, Grand Rapids, Michigan: Eerdmans 2005.

6   Aulén, *Christus Victor*, pp. 97–109.

7   *SKS* 12, 298 / *WA*, 184.

8   *SKS* 8, 129–36 / *UD*, 14–19.

9   *SKS* 10, 273–4 / *CD*, 260.

10   *SKS* 10, 313–14 / *CD*, 298–9.

Kierkegaard intones, "O Redeemer, by your holy suffering and death you have made satisfaction for everyone and everything; no eternal salvation either can or shall be earned—it has been earned."[11]

Most aptly, these Latin/Western models of atonement also link the forgiveness of sins to the sufferings of Christ and highlight the shockingly high cost of Christ's fulfillment of his role as Redeemer. Kierkegaard announced that the purpose of Christ was to suffer and die for the lost.[12] These various atonement models, using sacrificial, legal, and economic metaphors, all point to the fact that forgiveness necessarily involves the pain of God, for the suffering experienced by the human nature of Christ is attributable to the incarnate Second Person of the Trinity. Reconciliation with God comes at a price to God, which signals that this new fellowship must never be taken lightly.

In elaborating these Christological themes Kierkegaard promiscuously borrowed vocabulary from all of the varieties of Western/Latin atonement theories, without worrying about the mixing of metaphors or the conflation of conceptual domains. In spite of this sometimes indiscriminate latitude, he did tend to use the language of "satisfaction" and "sacrifice" more frequently than "penal substitution." In fact, "the Sacrifice" is one of his more common designations of Christ.[13] Elsewhere Kierkegaard explains that, contrary to human sentimental notions of love and reconciliation, atonement involves a sacrificial death.[14] But Kierkegaard also employed language associated with the "satisfaction" model to portray the atoning work of Christ, observing that Christ as the atonement makes restitution for sin, a process to which the believer contributes absolutely nothing.[15] He even adopted the venerable financial metaphor and described Christ's work as a "repayment" for the sins of the world.[16] Moreover, the rhetoric of penal substitution was by no means totally absent from his pages. Kierkegaard asserted that Christ paid the penalty for our sins,[17] and suffered the punishment for sin in our place.[18] In general Kierkegaard was drawn to all of these articulations of the Western/Latin view of the atonement because they highlighted the continuing importance of striving to lead a life of obedience to God's law of love, and the horrendous consequences of failing to pursue this ultimate *telos* that God had ordained. Kierkegaard praised Anselm's satisfaction view of the atonement because it made it clear that God's intention in creating human beings must be respected, and that God's standard for human life must be applied.

According to Kierkegaard, another virtue of the doctrine is that it points to the divine resolution of our predicament. Kierkegaard observed that Anselm rightly realized that God's commitment to the lofty standard of human righteousness and

---

[11]   *SKS* 16, 199 / *JFY*, 147.
[12]   *SKS* 12, 18 / *PC*, 10.
[13]   *SKS* 11, 93 / *WA*, 88; *SKS* 26, 23–4, NB31:30 / *JP* 1, 83.
[14]   *SKS* 9, 116 / *WL*, 110.
[15]   *SKS* 22, 368, NB14:42 / *JP* 1, 983.
[16]   *SKS* 10, 300 / *CD*, 280.
[17]   *SKS* 12, 300 / *WA*, 186.
[18]   *SKS* 11, 258–9 / *WA*, 123.

God's desire for reconciliation with those who fail to approximate it generated a "conflict of divine passion with itself."[19] God could not simply forgive sin, for such an irresponsible course of action would suggest that God is a lenient and somewhat negligent grandparent who simply allows the children to misbehave. If God were not to require satisfaction, we complacent and spiritually lethargic creatures would begin to suspect that God was not seriously interested in our pursuit of the lofty goal established by God. According to Kierkegaard, the beauty of Anselm's account of the atonement is that it articulated this tension between God's commitment to human growth and God's passion for mercy, and saw the tension resolved in the satisfaction of God's honor by Christ.

Even as he borrowed the language of these Western/Latin atonement theories, Kierkegaard insisted that the purpose of these doctrinal formulae was not to promote a grasp of the metaphysics of divine/human interaction, but to nurture piety. The doctrines make no sense without passionate appropriation.[20] Often Kierkegaard attempted to elicit the necessary pathos in the reader by encouraging a sense of contemporaneity with the shocking reality of the crucifixion.[21] The crucifixion is not a mere past event to be treated as an object of historical curiosity, nor is it an intriguing metaphysical puzzle that requires explanation.[22] A critical dimension of the proper way to passionally engage the doctrine of the atonement is to feel horror at the extent of one's culpability and frustration over one's impotence to heal the motivational roots of sin.[23] Often Kierkegaard employed the story of the crucifixion itself as a mirror in which the reader will discover the depths of his or her own depravity.[24] Kierkegaard encouraged the reader to regard the crucifixion as a contemporary event at which the reader is present as a participant; the reader should imagine himself or herself as one of the crowd conspiring to eliminate Jesus.[25]

Of course, as employed by Kierkegaard, the purpose of the Western/Latin view of the atonement is not merely to afflict, offend, and convict. More importantly, the doctrine of Christ's atoning death is intended to comfort and relieve the anguished conscience, and should awaken in us the most blessed comfort.[26] Appropriately, Kierkegaard often encourages this pathos in his readers by exhibiting it himself and inviting the reader to share his joy. In many of his authorial voices he enthuses about the comforts and delights of reconciliation with God, often waxing quite lyrical.[27] In fact, he exults that ascribing all power and glory to God in the matter of our salvation

---

[19]   *SKS* 24, 302–3, NB23:205 / *JP* 1, 532.
[20]   *SKS* 10, 290–1 / *CD*, 272.
[21]   *SKS* 12, 177–80 / *PC*, 174–9.
[22]   *SKS* 10, 292–3 / *CD*, 274.
[23]   *SKS* 21, 119, NB7:28 / *JP* 4, 4016.
[24]   *SKS* 11, 61–93 / *WA*, 55–89.
[25]   *SKS* 10, 184–6 / *CD*, 172–4; *SKS* 10, 273 / *CD*, 259–60; *SKS* 10, 299 / *CD*, 278; *SKS* 13, 86 / *FSE*, 64; *SKS* 10, 300 / *CD*, 280.
[26]   *SKS* 12, 272–3 / *WA*, 158–9; *SKS* 11, 258 / *WA*, 123; *SKS* 13, 44 / *FSE*, 15; *SKS* 11, 65 / *WA*, 58.
[27]   *SKS* 5, 65–86 / *EUD*, 55–78; *SKS* 10, 287 / *CD*, 268; *SKS* 13, 44 / *FSE*, 15.

from sin is an intimation of an eternity of joy.[28] The principal mood in which the Western/Latin view of the atonement should be considered is doxological.

II. Three Other Understandings of the Atoning Work of Christ

Sometimes using the word "atonement" and sometimes not mentioning it at all, Kierkegaard did present three other historic understandings of the work of Christ, all very different from the Latin view. His notes from the theology lectures of Henrik Nicolai Clausen show that he was aware that these could all be called theories of atonement.[29] By juggling all four motifs, Kierkegaard was either suffering from a profound internal theological conflict or giving expression to the complex multi-dimensionality of his religious heritage.

Occasionally the atonement is construed by Kierkegaard as the defeat of sin conceived as an enemy power, a view that Aulén referred to as the "classic" model.[30] For example, Anti-Climacus claimed that Christianity "by means of the Atonement wants to eliminate sin as if it were drowned in the sea."[31] Here sin is hypostasized as a force that can be extracted from humanity and destroyed. At times Kierkegaard does write about being protected from sin by Christ "our safe refuge," as if sin were an enemy assaulting us.[32] In Kierkegaard's pages the proper context for appropriating the rhetoric of the classical view of the atonement is the earnest struggle to follow Christ, for pilgrims who falter on the way need encouragement. Only those who have striven can sincerely appreciate the reassurance that Christ has defeated all opposition. According to Kierkegaard, the true purpose of the classical view of the atonement is to give hope to those who are heavy-laden, and not to give further comfort to those who already feel triumphant and secure.

Kierkegaard also relied upon a third interpretation of the work of Christ as a revelation of God's suffering love so dramatic that it has the power to move the sinner's heart to love God in return, a view often linked with Peter Abelard. Aulén hailed this as the "subjective" theory, for it focused on the interior transformation of individuals.[33] Kierkegaard frequently claimed that Christ's voluntary suffering reveals the extreme depths to which God was willing to go in order to be in relationship with humanity. Kierkegaard appreciatively marveled that Christ "performs love's miracle, so that—without doing anything—by suffering he moves every person who has a heart."[34] The most dramatic aspect of this manifestation of love is the fact that Jesus accepted his destiny of being killed by a hateful, hostile humanity in order to be in fellowship with that same humanity.[35] When stressing this theme, Kierkegaard exuberantly lauds the attractive beauty of such a potent self-sacrificial love.

---

[28]   *SKS* 11, 48 / *WA*, 44.
[29]   *SKS* 19, 45–58, Not1:8 / *KJN* 3, 40–53.
[30]   Aulén, *Christus Victor*, pp. 20–3 ; pp. 32–76.
[31]   *SKS* 11, 214 / *SUD*, 100.
[32]   *SKS* 12, 299–300 / *WA* 185–6.
[33]   Aulén, *Christus Victor*, p. 19; pp. 149–59.
[34]   *SKS* 10, 300 / *CD*, 280; *SKS* 12, 178 / *PC*, 176.
[35]   *SKS* 9, 114–16 / *WL*, 110–11; *SKS* 13, 83 / *FSE*, 60.

Finally, Kierkegaard often associated Christ's redemption of humanity with the provision of his own life as a rigorous prototype to be imitated.[36] This, too, is a "subjective" theory of atonement, for in it Christ saves individuals only insofar as he inspires and guides a monumental change in their way of life. By describing Christ as the prototype whose path must be followed, Kierkegaard was elaborating themes associated with the "moral influence" or "exemplary" view of the work of Christ. Here Kierkegaard avoided using the concept "atonement," for he did not want to imply that any such *imitatio Christi* could be meritorious. But the furnishing of the prototype is clearly part of Christ's saving work for Kierkegaard. Mixing pedagogical and juridical imagery, he claimed that Christ's life was an examination in obedience, showing what sort of test we all must go through.[37] That ideal is the pattern of self-giving love, lowliness, and self-denial which is now presented as the revelation of genuine human nature rather than as the disclosure of the nature of God.[38] This narrow way certainly involves the likelihood of being misunderstood and even vilified and persecuted by the very people one loves.[39] The example of Christ's life of suffering love can and should stir up such a yearning to be sacrificed for the truth even as Christ was.[40]

As we have seen, Kierkegaard's writings contain strong echoes of these four very different historic views of the work of Christ, usually referred to as theories of the atonement. In Kierkegaard's pages the first three views correspond to his musings about Christ as the Redeemer, and the last variety is linked to his valorization of Christ as the prototype. Significantly, he did not integrate these understandings of the saving work of Christ into a grand theological meta-theory. Rather, in Kierkegaard's authorship the atonement motifs are related in a variety of *ad hoc* complementary relationships. Sometimes Kierkegaard suggests the standard Lutheran pattern of convicting the sinner with the law in order to then comfort the penitent with the promise of grace. For example, he proposes, " 'The prototype' must be presented as the requirement, and then it crushes you. 'The prototype,' which is Christ, then changes to something else, to grace and compassion, and it is he himself who reaches out to support you."[41] At other times Kierkegaard suggests that reconciliation effected by Christ inspires further striving. For example, in the prayer at the beginning of *Judge for Yourself!* Kierkegaard claims that after one "droops under the prototype, crushed, almost despairing, the Redeemer raises him up again; but at the same moment you [Christ] are again the prototype so that he may be kept in the striving."[42] However, at other times Kierkegaard asserts that all our striving will be shown to be mere paltriness at the final Judgment, suggesting that our faith must finally rest in the Redeemer.[43] Every ostensible step forward is really a step backward, for as the ideal

---

[36]   *SKS* 12, 183–4 / *PC*, 183–4.
[37]   *SKS* 12, 174 / *PC*, 171; *SKS*, 16, 199 / *JFY*, 147.
[38]   *SKS* 8, 323–5 / *UD*, 221–3.
[39]   *SKS* 10, 194–5 / *CD*, 183–5; *SKS* 12, 115 / *PC*, 106.
[40]   *SKS* 11, 74 / *WA*, 72.
[41]   *SKS* 22, 346, NB14:7 / *JP* 1, 349.
[42]   *SKS* 16, 199 / *JFY*, 147. See also *SKS* 21, 362–3, NB10:198 / *JP* 1, 334.
[43]   *SKS* 24, 483–4, NB25:67 / *JP* 2, 1909.

becomes clearer so also does the magnitude of the vast gap between the individual and the prototype.[44]

In general, Kierkegaard sought to keep in play both the view of atonement as God's gift of reconciliation and the atonement as God's empowering of human striving in such a way that neither one jeopardized the integrity of the other. His fear was that the Lutheran emphasis of the grace of the Redeemer had undermined the sense of the continuing seriousness of pursuing the task of growing in Christ-likeness.[45] Luther's message of salvation by grace had been appropriated by the present age as a justification for indolence.[46] According to Kierkegaard, in his current context of spiritual complacency the empowerment aspect of redemption should be accentuated in order to serve as a corrective to the misuse of the justification aspect.[47]

Kierkegaard's seemingly unsystematic juggling of all these views of the atonement had deep roots in his general understanding of the Christian hope for redemption. For Kierkegaard, redemption had at least two very different aspects. One aspect, emphasized by Lutheranism, was the present assurance of being loved and forgiven by God, quite apart from any question of merit or spiritual accomplishment. The other aspect, more typical of Catholicism, was the hope of actual progress toward the goal of Christ-likeness. Kierkegaard's authorship affirms both views. Rather than constructing a theological system, he set out to exhibit in his writing the particular passional circumstances and edifying purposes appropriate to each doctrine of the atonement. When trying to inspire his readers to identify with Christ's extreme love, he employed the language of the Abelardian view. When urging individuals to push themselves to enact that love, he used the conceptuality of the exemplary view. When comforting those who were keenly aware of their failings, he brought forth the imagery of the Western/Latin view. Finally, when reassuring those who were in danger of faltering, he relied on the imagery of the classical view. Different upbuilding authorial interventions in the lives of his readers required different atonement vocabularies. For Kierkegaard, the key that potentially integrates them all is not the symmetry of a theological system, but the coherence of the passions that constitute the Christian life. As the individual learns to strive without taking credit for anything, and to be grateful without becoming complacent, he may grasp the possibility of harmonizing the contrapuntal understandings of the atonement that the Christian tradition has generated.

See also Christ; Confession; Contemporaneity; Dying to/Renunciation; Faith; Grace; Holy Spirit; Imitation; Sacrifice; Salvation.

---

[44]   *SKS* 24, 47, NB21:67 / *JP* 2, 1789.
[45]   *SKS* 21, 296–7, NB10:76 / *JP* 3, 2481.
[46]   *SKS* 13, 52–3 / *FSE*, 24.
[47]   *SKS* 22, 241, NB12:162 / *JP* 3, 2503; *SKS* 13, 52–3 / *FSE*, 24.

Authority

Sean Anthony Turchin

Authority (*Autoritet*—noun; *Myndighed*—noun; *myndig*—adjective)

Derived from the old French *auctorité* (authority, prestige, right, permission) and thirteenth-century French *autorite* (book or quotation that settles an argument), and originally the Latin *auctoritas* (influence, advice, command), *Autoritet* in Danish denotes the right to demand and the ability to obtain obedience. It can also signify the ability to influence the actions or understanding of others, which confers authority (*Myndighed*) by dint of character. It can also refer to those persons or institutions that possess authority. *Myndig* can mean influential, powerful, respectable, commanding, and, in the context of having come of age in a legal sense, mature.[1] In Kierkegaard's 1833 edition of Molbech's *Danish Dictionary*, *Myndighed* signifies several things. First, it can refer to qualities that connote authority such as power or prestige. It can also refer to behavior or to speech that seems to presuppose authority, as demonstrated in the Gospels by Christ and the apostles.[2]

The concept of authority is found most often in "The Difference between a Genius and an Apostle," contained in the work *Two Ethical-Religious Essays*, as well as in the journals and notebooks. In addition, the concept is scattered throughout various other works including *The Concept of Irony*, the upbuilding discourses, *Three Discourses on Imagined Occasions* (especially "On the Occasion of a Wedding"), the *Concluding Unscientific Postscript*, *Upbuilding Discourses in Various Spirits* (especially "The Gospel of Suffering"), *Works of Love*, and *Practice in Christianity*. Kierkegaard uses *Myndighed* much more frequently than *Autoritet*, sometimes synonymously and sometimes in distinct contexts. *Myndighed* is usually used in relation to divine authority (*guddommelig Myndighed*). It is also used in reference to the authority of the apostles and Scripture[3] or in the context of the Greek gods. For example, in *The Concept of Irony* Kierkegaard mentions the Delphic oracle's pronouncement about Socrates which was given "with divine authority" (*guddommelig Myndighed*).[4] However, it is in the Christian context that this concept predominates.

---

[1]   *Ordbog over det danske Sprog*, vols. 1–28, published by the Society for Danish Language and Literature, Copenhagen: Gyldendal 1918–56, vol. 1, columns 958–9 (*Autoritet*), vol. 14, columns 597–600 (*Myndighed*).

[2]   Christian Molbech, *Dansk Ordbog. Indeholdende det danske Sprogs Stammeord*, vols. 1–2, Copenhagen: Gyldendalske Boghandlings Forlag 1833, vol. 2, p. 61.

[3]   *SKS* 26, 103, NB31:139 / *JP* 4, 4483. Cf. *SKS* 12, 250 / *PC*, 259; *SKS* 9, 22 / *WL*, 14.

[4]   *SKS* 1, 220 / *CI*, 172.

Autoritet is usually used within the context of civic, social, political, or personal authority, which Kierkegaard classifies as aesthetic authority. It is seen in *The Concept of Irony*, *Either/Or*, *Philosophical Fragments*, and the *Concluding Unscientific Postscript*. Here, "authority" carries a sense of one who has mastery in a certain field; for example, Climacus refers to Lessing's "psychological authority in poetically making something manifest."[5] But mere practical mastery of a field is not always enough to confer authority: Jean Paul, who was able to express irony, humor and moods as an aesthetician, failed to wield "any philosophic or genuinely esthetic authority" because he failed to give "grounds for his esthetic position."[6]

In *Philosophical Fragments*, Johannes Climacus voices his disgust that "every second person is an authority (*Autoritet*)" with regard to learning the truth, which leads to everything becoming confused in "a common lunacy and in a *commune naufragium* [common shipwreck]…since no human being has ever truly been an authority."[7] Climacus' complaint is that people confuse the Socratic sense of authority (*Autoritet*)—in which self-knowledge *is* God-knowledge[8]—with God's authority (*Myndighed*). Elsewhere, the concept of authority denotes the right of a person or establishment to exert power over another.[9] In this sense, the authority is, whether acknowledged or ignored, imposed on others.[10]

Christian authority, for Kierkegaard, is quite heterogeneous to the authority of reason. It has an existential basis, and therefore Luther was wrong to inveigh against "the faith that looks to the person instead of to the Word."[11] Christian faith is based on the person of Jesus Christ, and his authority is rooted in his life. Ethical-religious truth lies in the imitation of Christ's life, which is taken as authoritative: "perhaps the most important ethical-religious concept [is] authority."[12] This is in contrast with philosophy, for which "authority is nonsense. For a philosopher extends no further than his teachings. If I can show that his teachings are self-contradictory, faulty, etc., he has no significance."[13]

Those who fail to accept Christianity solely on its divine authority, and instead seek to make Christianity acceptable by means of the genius of its content, make a sort of category mistake in which they render the paradoxical-religious merely aesthetic.[14] This is a problem insofar as the content of Christianity has nothing that approximates genius. Rather, Christianity is offensive and far from anything which would be praised by humanity. For Kierkegaard, Christianity came into the world with divine authority. Kierkegaard thinks that there is something amiss for those who "seek on rational grounds to demonstrate, to substantiate the authority."[15] Such

---

[5]   *SKS* 7, 66 / *CUP1*, 64.
[6]   *SKS* 1, 284 / *CI*, 244–5.
[7]   *SKS* 4, 220 / *PF*, 11–12.
[8]   *SKS* 4, 220 / *PF*, 11.
[9]   *SKS* 1, 317 / *CI*, 276. Cf. *SKS* 1, 232 / *CI*, 185; *SKS* 2, 100 / *EO1*, 95.
[10]   *SKS* 1, 183 / *CI*, 132.
[11]   *SKS* 22, 421, NB14:134 / *JP* 3, 3218.
[12]   *SKS* 22, 152, NB12:12 / *JP* 6, 6447.
[13]   *SKS* 22, 421, NB14:134 / *JP* 3, 3218.
[14]   *SKS* 11, 97 / *WA*, 93.
[15]   *SKS* 26, 74, NB31:100 / *JP* 1, 191.

demonstration indirectly belies that Christianity is not an authority.[16] Even more, such demonstrations reveal that authority can also be abused. Such abuse is made manifest in those biblical exegetes who misinterpret biblical passages to justify their own ends, whereby submission to the "divine authority of the Bible" (*Bibelens guddommelige Autoritet*) "becomes a cunning way to derive advantage from the authority."[17]

Nevertheless the crucial mistake, in which the category of divine authority is replaced with that of rational or poetic appeal, is one of shifting "the sphere of the paradoxical-religious back into the esthetic."[18] With this shift the paradoxical essence of Christianity, which offends rationality, is translated into a work of literary genius and thereby is accepted for the wrong reason. A further consequence of this shift is that the qualitative difference between the apostle and the genius is lost, assimilated to the aesthetic.[19] In his work *Two Ethical-Religious Essays*, Kierkegaard seeks to maintain the difference between an apostle and a genius by means of identifying the difference in their authority. If one ignores that Christianity "has never repudiated its divine authority,"[20] then it appears that the apostle's authority must rest elsewhere, perhaps in his brilliance or philosophical fervor to make sense of metaphysics.[21] But neglecting the basis from which Christianity presents itself as authoritative does not lessen its paradoxical nature.

The difference between the apostle and the genius is a qualitative difference. The genius is what he is from birth, "is what he is in himself."[22] His authority is purely aesthetic in that it exists based upon the brilliance of who he is and what he has mastered. This means his authority exists within the spheres of the "political, civic, social, domestic, and the disciplinary realms or of the exercise of authority."[23] These temporal spheres betray a specific quality concerning their authority. What is revealed is that all such expression of authority is transitory in nature—it vanishes with time.[24] But could such an authority, which has no real existence outside of its own historical or situational confines, be truly authoritative? Kierkegaard does not think so.

For him, an authority that is truly authoritative is transcendent in nature. This is in order to separate the authority of the human from that of God. At the center of this distinction is the question of the power and gravity of each authority. Which is more binding, an authority whose ground is changing or one whose ground is unchanging? *"In the sphere of immanence, authority is utterly unthinkable, or it can be thought of only as transitory."*[25] This is why Kierkegaard is suspicious of the Kantian concept of autonomy (construed as "a human being is his own law"), which he thinks

---

16   *SKS* 26, 75, NB31:100 / *JP* 1, 191.
17   *SKS* 7, 548 / *CUP1*, 603.
18   Ibid.
19   *SKS* 11, 98 / *WA*, 94.
20   *SKS* 18, 64, EE:190 / *KJN* 2, 59.
21   *SKS* 11, 100 / *WA*, 96.
22   *SKS* 11, 98 / *WA*, 94.
23   *SKS* 11, 103 / *WA*, 99.
24   Ibid.
25   Ibid.

ultimately lends itself to "lawlessness or experimentation."[26] Kantian autonomy and
human authority are transitory and changeable; furthermore, they are not capable of
transforming the subject of authority. Christian authority, by contrast, can transform
the human being when he or she acts decisively—to obey. Then Governance can
bring him or her up under the authority of faith, free of the illusion of autonomy.[27]

But wherein lies the authority of the apostle? From a rational or empirical vantage
point, the apostle does not differ from the genius in any respect. The difference
between the two is that "a genius is evaluated purely esthetically according to
what his content, his specific gravity, is found to be; an apostle is what he is by
having divine authority (*guddommelig Myndighed*)."[28] Whereas the genius is born
a genius, the apostle is not born as an apostle. Rather he is an apostle by divine
calling.[29] In this context of divine calling, "divine authority is what is qualitatively
decisive" in distinguishing the apostle from the genius. The apostle and the genius
differ qualitatively from each other with regard to their authority; the apostle derives
divine authority categorically within the realm of transcendence and the genius,
merely humanly, within the category of immanence.[30]

Therefore, against the efforts of speculative thinking in making the authority
of Christianity amenable to human constructs of thinking, Kierkegaard maintains
that the apostle Paul is not to be heard because of his matchless brilliance but rather
because he has divine authority.[31] The transcendent nature of this authority rests in
the manner in which Paul received his authority—by revelation.[32] But, the eminence
of the apostle's authority pertains not only to the manner in which he has attained it
but also to the immutability of the revelation he has received.

Unlike the transient authority of the world, the apostle's message continually
abides beyond "a general assimilation by the human race."[33] And yet there is
something troubling about an authority of this kind. If revelation is indiscernible
to human reason then an authority that has its basis in revelation is in the same
condition. The apostolic calling wherein the authority rests is essentially paradoxical
and is beyond any assimilation in time.[34] The apostle's authority is thus wholly
unrecognizable to human understanding. His paradoxical existence as one with
divine authority is therefore far beyond the scope of what constitutes a genius.[35]
Both his message and his authority are beyond proof—as is the objective existence
of God, who is not object but is spirit.[36]

By virtue of the apostle's authority being grounded in God, the paradoxical
manifestation of his existence consists of his being equal to every other human being,

---

[26]   *SKS* 23, 45, NB15:66 / *JP* 1, 188.
[27]   Ibid.
[28]   *SKS* 11, 100 / *WA*, 96.
[29]   *SKS* 11, 99 / *WA*, 95.
[30]   *SKS* 11, 98 / *WA*, 94.
[31]   *SKS* 11, 100 / *WA*, 96.
[32]   Ibid.
[33]   *SKS* 11, 98 / *WA*, 94.
[34]   *SKS* 11, 100 / *WA*, 95.
[35]   *SKS* 11, 97 / *WA*, 94. Cf. *SKS* 24, 259, NB23:107 / *JP* 4, 3861.
[36]   *SKS* 11, 102 / *WA*, 98.

and yet he exists in a special relation to the divine. This relation is the paradoxical-religious, which consists in God's bestowing his authority on one who has no right to have it. All things considered, Kierkegaard asks, "What, then, is authority?"[37] He answers, "Authority is a specific quality that enters from somewhere else and qualitatively asserts itself precisely when the content of the statement or the act is made a matter of indifference esthetically."[38]

What this conveys is that even though two messages may be the same with regard to content, the difference resides in which of the two messengers has authority.[39] And with this development in the nature of divine authority as being necessarily paradoxical, Kierkegaard expounds another component of true authority. Although Kierkegaard does not give much time to this other component within his discussion of the apostle and genius, he does elsewhere throughout his journals and notebooks.

This other qualifier of true authority is what he calls "existential authority." Existential authority exists in a *voluntary* relation between word and deed: "Voluntariness is the precise form for qualitatively being spirit."[40] For example, if someone speaks about the issues surrounding poverty and yet is wealthy, it is easy to dismiss the words given the incongruity between what is said and what has never been experienced.[41] However, if one "voluntarily gave up wealth and is poor, only he has authority."[42] So an existential authority, in this case the authority to teach, is bestowed upon one who teaches what he himself has voluntarily experienced or experiences. The apostle indeed meets this second criterion for what constitutes true authority insofar as he gave up everything to follow Christ, even to the point of martyrdom.

In accordance with this existential motif within the category of authority, "authority" contains the element of risk, of being willing to venture.[43] It is this existential qualifier that accounts for the frequent appearance of the concept of authority in Kierkegaard's thinking about Christianity in relation to Christendom. He believed his task was to make room in Christendom for true Christianity. But this task of proclaiming the Christianity of the New Testament "is in one sense beyond man's powers; divine authority is required for this, or, more correctly, a divine absorption in the unconditioned."[44]

Approaching an issue, whatever it may be, with absolute authority signifies the absolute or ideal existence of the one who exercises authority. And since Kierkegaard considered himself as one far from embodying true Christianity, his approach to the problem of Christendom was poetic rather than authoritative.[45] In sum, he felt that his own life did not reflect Christianity and thus was existentially without authority.[46]

---

37   Ibid.
38   Ibid.
39   Ibid.
40   *SKS* 22, 332–3, NB13:89 / *JP* 2, 1258.
41   Ibid.
42   Ibid.
43   *SKS* 26, 321, NB34:10 / *JP* 3, 2995.
44   *SKS* 26, 213, NB32:126 / *JP* 6, 6924.
45   *SKS* 24, 298, NB23:197 / *JP* 6, 6753.
46   *SKS* 24, 433, NB24:170 / *JP* 6, 6746. Cf. *SKS* 23, 101, NB16:8 / *JP* 6, 6587.

In conclusion, the concept of authority in Kierkegaard's work is largely theological. It serves to highlight the significance in Christian faith of a divine power paradoxically manifested in the recipients of revelation, that is, the apostles. This concept also has temporal significance with regard to its gravity, which is only recognized in a correlation between word and action. But most importantly, the concept of authority is distinguishable from that of transitory nature as a power rooted solely in the eternal, transcendent God.

See also Apostle; Certainty; Dialectic; Faith; God; Immanence/Transcendence; Paradox; Passion/Pathos; Qualitative Difference; Reason; Revelation; Speculation/ Science/Scholarship; Truth.

Authorship

Joseph Westfall

Authorship (*Forfatterskab*—noun; *Forfatter-Virksomhed*—noun)

The Danish word *Forfatter* (author) comes from the German *Verfasser*.[1] *Forfatterskab* refers in Danish primarily to the quality, property, or state of being an author, customarily in the sense of a producer of written works. In its secondary sense, it refers to a body of works produced by an author or authors, ascribable in a literary if not also a legal sense exclusively to them. In this sense, *Forfatterskab* is used synonymously with the compound, *Forfattervirksomhed* (or, in Kierkegaard, *Forfatter-Virksomhed*). Thus, "authorship" can refer both to that property, quality, or activity which makes an individual an author, and to the body of works produced by that individual insofar as he or she is an author.[2]

The most frequent occurrence of the words "author" or "authorship" is in *The Book on Adler*, followed by *Prefaces*, then *The Point of View for My Work as an Author*. Multiple references significant to Kierkegaard's use of the terms also occur in *From the Papers of One Still Living*, the *Concluding Unscientific Postscript to Philosophical Fragments*, and *A Literary Review of Two Ages*. The passages dealing with authorship are split between considerations of authorship in the primary sense of "author-being," and considerations of authorship in the secondary sense of "author-work." The former are further divided into (A) authorship as a social role and livelihood, (B) authorship as a personal identity, and (C) authorship as an aesthetic or literary phenomenon. Authorship as author-work is treated most extensively in *The Point of View* and *On My Work as an Author*; authorship as author-being appears in the sense of (a) primarily in *Prefaces*; in the sense of (b) primarily in *The Book on Adler*, and in the sense of (c) in *From the Papers of One Still Living*, *A Literary Review*, and "A First and Last Explanation" from the *Concluding Unscientific Postscript*.

---

[1]   Although the Latinate *Autor* and *Autorskab* (English derived *author* and *authorship*) also appear in the Danish lexicon, they are not the terms customarily used by Kierkegaard.

[2]   *Ordbog over det danske Sprog*, vols. 1–28, published by the Society for Danish Language and Literature, Copenhagen: Gyldendal 1918–56, vol. 5, column 442.

I. Authorship as Author-Being

A. Authorship as Profession

Although the earliest references to authorship as a profession appear in the first volume of *Either/Or*,[3] most of the passages in Kierkegaard's *corpus* treating authorship as this sort of author-being appear in *Prefaces*. There, "Preface II" is devoted in large part to outlining Notabene's understanding of what it is to be an author in Denmark in a way that mirrors the earlier *Either/Or* references and can be associated with the depiction of authorship in the unpublished *Writing Sampler*, as well.[4] In all of these texts and passages, the situation of the author is presented as entirely dependent—especially financially—upon critics and readers: critics insofar as they determine public opinion, and readers insofar as they fund the author's professional (and personal) endeavors by way of purchasing copies of the author's books.

Despite the frequent humor of these sorts of references, taken together they present the most direct articulation of the notion of practical authorship—the practice of working as an author in Denmark in the mid-nineteenth century—that we find in Kierkegaard. To be an author is, at least in part, to work in one's society as an author. In Kierkegaard's society, according to Kierkegaard's pseudonyms, commercial and popular success required appealing to the interests (and vanity) of the reading public. This use of the concept of authorship in Kierkegaard reaches the apex of irony in *Writing Sampler*, where the pseudonymous author, A.B.C.D.E.F. Godthaab, asks his readers to tell him exactly what it is they want, so that he might provide it for them. He grants them full power and authority over his writings, claiming that it is they, not he, who can make him an author—that he is, as he writes, "a nobody, nothing."[5] While the dominant treatments of authorship in Kierkegaard shift away from the idea of practical authorship and toward a more idealized view, Godthaab's and Notabene's skepticism of popularity and readers remains, finding its most eloquent—and angry—expression in Kierkegaard's published and unpublished comments on his treatment as an author and a human being during and after his very public conflict with the satirical newspaper, the *Corsair*.

B. Authorship as Identity

The second sense in which Kierkegaard treats the concept of authorship as author-being is authorship as a kind of personal identity. In contrast to the social sense of being an author prevalent in *Prefaces* and *Writing Sampler*, this is a notion of authorship that identifies the author as a certain sort of human being—or, at least, as a human being engaged in a specifically personal sort of productive activity. Whereas *Prefaces* and *Writing Sampler* look to the external facts of an individual's existence to identify him or her as an author, this second notion—one that is presented

---

[3]   *SKS* 2, 20 / *EO1*, 13; *SKS* 2, 28 / *EO1*, 20.
[4]   *Pap.* VII–2 B 274:5, p. 318 / *P*, 74.
[5]   Ibid.

specifically and at some length in *The Book on Adler*—looks inward. It does so by making a distinction between authentic authors and spurious authors, or what Petrus Minor calls "essential authors" and "premise-authors" respectively.

According to Petrus, a premise-author (*Præmisse-Forfatter*) is "not an author, even though he produces."[6] He continues: "Here is not a poet, who poetically rounds out the whole; not a psychologist, who orders the particular and the individual in a total view; not a dialectician, who points out the place within the life-view at his disposal."[7] We thus learn two interesting things about authorship in Petrus' insistence that premise-authors are "not really"[8] authors: first, that what the premise-author lacks has everything to do with the desire, intention, or ability to unify his or her writings into a whole of some sort; and second, that Petrus can conceive of at least three distinct sorts of legitimate—or what he calls "essential"—authors, namely, the poet, the psychologist, and the dialectician. In all three cases, again, the element that enables us to identify the author as an essential author (*væsentlig Forfatter*) is the unified, holistic nature of the authorial production. This is reminiscent of the Kierkegaardian notion of the "life-view," the fundamental criterion used for distinguishing between good and bad poets in *From the Papers of One Still Living* and *A Literary Review*, and in fact the notion of a life-view recurs here in the brief description of the essentially authorial work of the dialectician.

Critical of an author such as Godthaab, Petrus notes that they "not only need the public's money and honors but even need the public in order, if possible, to arrive at understanding and meaning—then this is transferred as a matter of course to every author. But the very one who needs the public or discussion in order to find understanding is not an author."[9] An ingratiating or purely reactive public authorship is thus, for Petrus, not really authorship at all, and an author who is really an author must produce works that contain something more than what is expected, requested, or demanded by readers. We see here in *The Book on Adler* a serious analog to the playful irony of *Prefaces* and *Writing Sampler*, but in service of the same point: authorship, if it is to mean anything, must mean something more than writing for the public or at the public's behest.

An essential author is essentially an author not only because he or she writes, but because in what he or she writes it is evident that he or she has something coherent to say. On this version of the concept, then, to be an author requires that one be a certain sort of person, namely, one who has already achieved a high degree of certainty and coherence in his or her life. This leads Petrus to note that, "In his particular production the essential author is continually behind himself; he is certainly striving, but within a totality, not toward the totality."[10] Thus, although authorship in this sense is essentially a matter of identity and activity, it is nevertheless dependent upon a certain sort of productivity, as well. The essential author relates essentially to an idea (or a life-view), but is at the same time a producer of texts. Absent this productivity,

[6]   *SKS* 15, 93 / *BA*, 7.
[7]   Ibid.
[8]   *SKS* 15, 96 / *BA*, 10.
[9]   *SKS* 15, 100n. / *BA*, 14n.
[10] *SKS* 15, 99 / *BA*, 13.

it is not clear that Petrus (or Kierkegaard) would recognize the applicability of the term "author," but might substitute something like the terms "personality" or "self."

This insistence upon the conjunction of personal identity and productivity in the constitution of a "real" author is consistent throughout Kierkegaard's writings and is thus an essential component of any understanding of the Kierkegaardian concept of authorship. These elements alone, however, give only an incomplete picture of Kierkegaard's sense of the term, since the conjunction of identity and productivity gives us a notion of the author that remains essentially disconnected from the literary phenomenon of authorship to which readers have access. In addition to the social, personal, and productive aspects of authorship, then, we need to add the aesthetic-literary aspect—authorship from the reader's perspective.

C. Authorship as an Aesthetic Phenomenon

The third sense of authorship as author-being treats the author as a component of a written work, and thus brings the treatment of authorship closer to aesthetics and literary theory than any of the other senses of the term as used in the Kierkegaardian authorship. This use of the concept of authorship is also the earliest one evident in Kierkegaard's writings, appearing as early as 1838 in his first book, *From the Papers of One Still Living*. The work is a literary review of Hans Christian Andersen's third novel, *Only a Fiddler*, and is thus a useful resource for studies of writing and authorship in Kierkegaard. Nevertheless, despite the significance of what is written there for an understanding of his general concept of authorship, the primary term to describe Andersen's work as an author is not *Forfatter* but *Romandigter*, "novel writer" (although "*digter*" on its own means "poet") Insofar as the anonymous author of the review portion of *From the Papers of One Still Living* ("Andersen as a Novelist"—*Andersen som Romandigter*) employs the concept of authorship specifically, however, we can see that he is of one mind with Petrus Minor in *The Book on Adler*, written nearly a decade later. For both authors, the notion of the life-view is essential to the concept of authorship in the truest sense of the term. This demonstrates a remarkable consistency across the Kierkegaardian *corpus* with regard at least to this one concept.

For the anonymous reviewer (hereafter referred to as the One Still Living), a good novel must have at its foundation—both historically and aesthetically—what he calls a "life-view" (*Livs-Anskuelse*). The One Still Living restricts this requirement to novels and novellas, but Petrus will later extend its application to dialectical writings, as well, as we have already seen. The life-view is not just the "idea" of the novel, nor is it the "moral" of the story—it is the sole legitimate point of contact between the author and the work, and thus is something each of them must possess (the life-view in the work is, in the end, the author's life-view). That said, the One Still Living is particularly careful not to confuse this notion with the belief that the novel is an extension or expression of the author; by way of the life-view, rather, the novel is distanced absolutely from the author insofar as the author is a real person. Thus, the One Still Living writes, "A life-view frees [the novel] from being arbitrary and purposeless, since the purpose is immanently present everywhere in the work of art. But when such a life-view is lacking, the novel either seeks to insinuate some theory (dogmatic, doctrinaire short novels) at the expense of poetry or it makes a finite and incidental contact with the author's flesh and blood."[11] He goes on to describe in unflattering detail the situation characteristic of those novels which, in the absence of a life-view, rely altogether too fully on the personalities of their authors, noting "that in many otherwise fine novels there is to be found a residue, as it were, of the author's finite character, which, like an impudent third person, like a badly brought-up child, often joins in the conversation at unseemly places."[12]

Taken together, these passages in *From the Papers of One Still Living* indicate a very clear sense in the mind of the One Still Living that the author's personality has no business interfering with the works that author produces. In place of the author's actual personality, the life-view seems to serve as something of the author's representative in the work, a product of the author, and one the author must produce in order essentially to be an author. In order to function in this way, the author must do whatever he or she can to prevent himself or herself from becoming too thoroughly infused in or confused with the work he or she produces. This next point is reasserted and clarified by Kierkegaard in *A Literary Review*, where he writes: "An author certainly must have his private personality as everyone else has, but this must be his αδυτον [inner sanctum], and just as the entrance to a house is barred by stationing two soldiers with crossed bayonets, so by means of the dialectical cross of qualitative opposites the equality of ideality forms the barrier that prevents all access."[13] For Kierkegaard in *A Literary Review*, in order to be an author an individual must achieve distance from the matters about which he or she writes; otherwise, what is written is merely "chattering,"[14] better suited to the newspapers or feuilletons than to an aesthetic or dialectical authorship.

This distance between author and work is essential to the Kierkegaardian notion of authorship, but it is also specifically necessary for the existence of one mode of authorship unusually characteristic of many of Kierkegaard's works: pseudonymity. Without delving too deeply into Kierkegaard's concept of the pseudonym, it must be noted that the idea of authorship, for Kierkegaard, includes the idea of pseudonymous authorship—and, thus, everything that has been said of authors so far applies even in the case of the pseudonyms. Kierkegaard works through the aesthetic and literary consequences of this aspect of authorship most completely in his signed appendix to the *Concluding Unscientific Postscript*, "A First and Last Explanation." There, he not only carves out conceptual space for the pseudonyms to be understood legitimately as authors but also identifies yet another authorial possibility for himself, not as the author of the pseudonymous books, but as "the dialectically reduplicated author of the author or the authors."[15] Not only must the concept of authorship be able to apply in the case of pseudonymous authors, then, but also to the practice of an author who

---

11   *SKS* 1, 36–7 / *EPW*, 81.
12   *SKS* 1, 37 / *EPW*, 82.
13   *SKS* 8, 94 / *TA*, 99.
14   *SKS* 8, 95 / *TA*, 99.
15   *SKS* 7, 571 / *CUP1*, 627.

is "indeed not an author in the usual sense, but as one who has cooperated so that the pseudonyms could become authors."[16]

As aesthetic and literary phenomena, all instances of authorship occur for Kierkegaard in one of three modes: the straightforward authorship of works ascribed to the human beings who actually wrote those works, or what Kierkegaard calls authorship "in the usual sense"; pseudonymous authorship; and what we might call "author authorship," the "dialectically reduplicated" authorial work of "cooperating" to produce pseudonymous authors. This tripartite distinction might be understood to overlay any further distinctions between essential and premise-authors, such that we can imagine genuine and spurious examples of each of the three modes Kierkegaard identifies across his *corpus*.

II. Authorship as Author-Work

Kierkegaard uses the term "authorship" in the sense of one's work as an author (*Forfatterskab* as *Forfattervirksomhed*) almost exclusively in *On My Work as an Author* and *The Point of View for My Work as an Author*. Moreover, although there is some sense that one could legitimately apply the concept with reference to authorships other than Kierkegaard's, Kierkegaard does not generally do so. Reviewing Kierkegaard's comments on the Kierkegaardian authorship, we see that, beyond the bounds of the lexical definition of the term, Kierkegaard makes at least two interesting assertions about the nature of an authorship. First, his claims about the elements and structure of his own authorship indicate that he conceives of an authorship as at least potentially distinct from the sum total of an author's productivity. Thus, he can claim that a work he has written (*Two Ethical-Religious Essays*) "does not stand *in* the authorship as much as it relates totally *to* the authorship and for that reason also was anonymous, in order to be kept outside entirely."[17] In addition to the matter of what constitutes an authorship, Kierkegaard makes clear that he thinks an authorship can itself have a life-view or a point of view, such that one can reasonably read the total authorship as a single work (with a single author). As he notes in *The Point of View*, "this is an authorship [*Forfatter-Virksomhed*] of which the total thought is the task of becoming a Christian."[18] An authorship is thus not merely an aggregate of the works written by one individual; it is, rather, the deliberate arrangement of writings into a single coherent body of works. In this sense, the Kierkegaardian concept of an author is a necessary prerequisite for the Kierkegaardian concept of an authorship—and an authorship is the natural and necessary consequence of any true author's productive activity.

See also Aesthetic/Aesthetics; Chatter; Life-View; Novel/*Bildungsroman*; Personality; Poetry; Pseudonyms; Self; Writing.

---

[16]   *SKS* 7, 571–2 / *CUP1*, 628.
[17]   *SKS* 13, 12n. / *PV*, 6n.
[18]   *SKS* 16, 37 / *PV*, 55.

Baptism

David Coe

Baptism (*Daab*—noun; *døbe*—verb)

From the Old Danish *dob*, Old Saxon *dopi*. Its simplest lexical meaning in Danish is to immerse something in liquid. Normally, it refers to the sacrament of initiation and inclusion into the Christian community by pouring water on the head or (in Orthodox and Baptist churches) immersing the entire body in water. In the case of infant baptism, the bestowal of a name is often concurrent. It can also refer to an inauguration of any kind.[1]

The great majority of Kierkegaard's references to baptism occur in the *Concluding Unscientific Postscript* under the pseudonym "Johannes Climacus." The pseudonym "Anti-Climacus" in *Practice in Christianity* has a few references to baptism, while the pseudonym "Johannes" in "The Seducer's Diary" from *Either/Or* has one. In Kierkegaard's signed works, *Works of Love* contains a few references, and *Three Upbuilding Discourses* from 1844 and *The Moment* each have one. Kierkegaard's pseudonymous and signed use of the term "baptism" normally refers to the sacrament of initiation and inclusion into the Christian community.

Most often, Kierkegaard situates the sacrament of baptism under the existential categories of either approximation or appropriation. Under approximation, both his signed and pseudonymous works challenge the assumption that one's baptism is a final proof of one's Christianity. Under appropriation, both his signed and pseudonymous works laud a concerned remembrance of one's baptism as an ongoing practice in Christianity. Kierkegaard's critique of approximation stems from Gotthold Ephraim Lessing's "broad, ugly ditch" ("accidental truths of history can never become the proof of necessary truths of reason"),[2] portraying an ontological chasm between historical and eternal knowledge. Kierkegaard concurred with Lessing, granting that historical knowledge can, at best, result in an approximation and that an approximation is too little on which to build one's eternal happiness.[3] Thus, throughout his signed and pseudonymous *corpus*, Kierkegaard exhorted his

---

[1]   *Ordbog over det danske Sprog*, vols. 1–28, published by the Society for Danish Language and Literature, Copenhagen: Gyldendal 1918–56, vol. 3, columns 388–90 (*Daab*) and vol. 4, columns 1–3 (*døbe*).

[2]   Gotthold Lessing, *Lessing's Theological Writings*, ed. and trans. by Henry Chadwick, Stanford: Stanford University Press 1956, p. 55, p. 53 respectively.

[3]   *SKS* 7, 30 / *CUP1*, 23.

readers to leap from approximation to appropriation, from proving their Christianity with historical objectivity to practicing their Christianity with perpetual subjectivity.

Both Kierkegaard's pseudonymous and signed works abound with critiques of baptism as an historically objective proof of one's Christianity. Nineteenth-century Danish State Lutheranism baptized the majority of Danes as infants within a few weeks of being born. Kierkegaard himself was baptized on June 3, 1813, almost a month after his birth on May 5.[4] At a baptismal ceremony, the child was also officially named,[5] designated a citizen of Denmark, and given a baptismal certificate. Given this convention, the pseudonym Johannes Climacus parodies the notion of securing eternity in this historical act in the *Concluding Unscientific Postscript*: "My father has said so; it says so in the parish register; I have a certificate."[6] Likewise, he parodies the notion of securing eternity in geographical citizenship: "How can you not be a Christian? You are Danish, aren't you? Doesn't the geography book say that the predominant religion in Denmark is Lutheran-Christian?"[7] Kierkegaard's pseudonym Anti-Climacus parodies the same in *Practice in Christianity*: "It is certain that everyone who is baptized as a child and confirmed as a boy or girl is Christian—one can look it up in the parish register."[8] For Climacus, appealing to baptism is just like the Jews appealing "to circumcision and to their being Abraham's children as a decisive demonstration of the God-relationship."[9] It is an attempt "to find repose not in a spiritual relationship with God...but in an external event."[10] Climacus finds it ironic that orthodox Christianity teaches baptism as decisive, yet "continually complains that there are so few Christians among the baptized,"[11] suggesting that baptism cannot be the decisive factor. In the signed *Works of Love*, Kierkegaard similarly critiques the external sign of baptism as the sole certification of Christianity.[12] Climacus calls the appeal to any fixed point, whether baptism, a baptismal certificate, the parish register, or a geography book, "superstitious"[13] and "magical"[14] because it attempts to relieve an infinite anxiety with a finite fact. Such superstition shortcuts the God-relation because it does not attend to God but to one's actually having been baptized.[15] Climacus summarizes: "If being baptized is supposed to be the qualification, attention will immediately turn outward in deliberation on whether I actually have been baptized. Then begins the approximation with regard to a historical fact."[16]

---

[4]   *B&A*, vol. 1, p. 3 / *LD*, Document I, p. 3.
[5]   *SKS* 7, 339 / *CUP1*, 373.
[6]   *SKS* 7, 49 / *CUP1*, 44.
[7]   *SKS* 7, 55 / *CUP1*, 50.
[8]   *SKS* 12, 215 / *PC*, 219.
[9]   *SKS* 7, 50 / *CUP1*, 45.
[10]   Ibid.
[11]   *SKS* 7, 554 / *CUP1*, 610.
[12]   *SKS* 9, 147 / *WL*, 146.
[13]   *SKS* 7, 49 / *CUP1*, 44.
[14]   *SKS* 7, 50 / *CUP1*, 45.
[15]   Ibid.
[16]   *SKS* 7, 554 / *CUP1*, 610.

The state custom of infant baptism compounds the issue and serves as a prime example of the religious confusion of his day.[17] Climacus laments that to be born a human being and to become a Christian are almost identical: "Should this be understood to mean that everyone is a Christian as a matter of course by being baptized when he was a fortnight old?"[18] If one definitively becomes a Christian in infancy, then Christianity becomes only a sentimental recollection of the past.[19] Notwithstanding, Climacus and Anti-Climacus both defend infant baptism as a pious practice of parents who anticipate their child will become a Christian.[20] Pedagogically, parents bear the responsibility for rearing their children in the faith, and, psychologically, parents cannot bear the torment of experiencing an eternal happiness without their children.[21] But in the maturity of adulthood, one must decide for oneself to become a Christian or not.[22] Confirmation is the church's historical ceremony allowing the individual consciously to affirm her baptismal faith. But Kierkegaard argued that confirmation occurred too early in the Danish church, while the child was still "tender."[23] In a journal entry dated 1848, he wrote: "Infant baptism can very well stand, but confirmation ought to be postponed to the twenty-fifth year."[24] Nevertheless, Climacus does not advocate the Anabaptist position that baptism should occur in adulthood; instead, becoming a Christian "should occur quietly without any decisive external action."[25] Kierkegaard's journals demonstrate his awareness of the early church's practice of postponing baptism until one's deathbed, thereby ensuring that all of one's sins were forgiven from birth to death.[26] While Kierkegaard admired the ancient practice as a means of uniting baptism and earnestness, he did not advocate its supersession of infant baptism.

Behind the parodies and critique of infant baptism is Kierkegaard's concern that the passive custom inhibits the active appropriation and responsibility of adult Christianity. He does not advocate that baptism be abrogated but that baptism be appropriated. "What is Baptism without appropriation?"[27] Climacus forewarns that appropriation is not replacing an historical approximation with a learned understanding.[28] Instead, appropriation is the perpetual rigorousness of faith: "Being a Christian is defined not by the 'what' of Christianity but by the 'how' of the Christian."[29] Climacus compares appropriation to the immediate pathos of an erotic lover: "He will hold it fast and appropriate it in a way entirely different from the way

---

[17]   *SKS* 7, 380 / *CUP1*, 419.
[18]   *SKS* 7, 334 / *CUP1*, 367.
[19]   *SKS* 7, 547 / *CUP1*, 602.
[20]   *SKS* 7, 347 / *CUP1*, 381; *SKS* 12, 251 / *PC*, 260.
[21]   *SKS* 7, 546 / *CUP1*, 601.
[22]   *SKS* 7, 545 / *CUP1*, 601.
[23]   *SKS* 13, 299 / *M*, 244.
[24]   *SKS* 21, 181, NB8:86 / *KJN* 5, 189.
[25]   *SKS* 7, 331 / *CUP1*, 365.
[26]   *SKS* 25, 255, NB28:53 / *JP* 1, 543.
[27]   *SKS* 7, 333 / *CUP1*, 366.
[28]   *SKS* 7, 553 / *CUP1*, 609.
[29]   *SKS* 7, 554 / *CUP1*, 610.

he holds anything else, will live in it and die in it, risk everything for it."[30] Although Kierkegaard never mentions it directly, his desire for daily appropriation of baptism may stem from his Lutheran upbringing. Martin Luther's Small Catechism, the text historically used for Lutheran catechesis, asks the question,

> What then is the significance of such a baptism with water? Answer: It signifies that the old creature in us with all sins and evil desires is to be drowned and die through daily contrition and repentance, and on the other hand that daily a new person is to come forth and rise up to live before God in righteousness and purity forever. Where is this written? Answer: St. Paul says in Romans 6, "We were buried with Christ through baptism into death, so that, just as Christ was raised from the dead through the glory of the Father, we, too, are to walk in a new life."[31]

The pseudonym Johannes in "The Seducer's Diary" may suggest this influence when he briefly mentions a baptism by immersion whereby the "old man" is drowned and a new man arises.[32] Kierkegaard noted in a journal entry Christ's words from Mark 10:38, "Are you able to be baptized with the baptism with which I am baptized?" as a reference to Christ's suffering, not an *opus operatum*, which would confer grace irrespective of the recipient's faith.[33] Applying appropriation to baptism, Kierkegaard exhorts his reader to gain God's help at every moment to believe that he or she is saved by baptism instead of finding final certainty in the fact that he or she has been tangibly baptized.[34]

To summarize, Kierkegaard challenges the notion of baptism, especially infant baptism, as a once-and-for-all proof of one's Christianity, but lauds baptism as a daily practice in Christianity. While the former sidesteps the God-relationship by seeking security in a finite fact of the past, the latter daily seeks God's help to appropriate baptism's life-long significance.

See also Appropriation; Approximation; Communion; Leap; Objectivity/Subjectivity; Protestantism/Reformation; Salvation/Eternal Happiness/Highest Good.

---

[30]   *SKS* 7, 553 / *CUP1*, 609.

[31]   *The Book of Concord: The Confessions of the Evangelical Lutheran Church*, ed. by Robert Kolb and Timothy J. Wengert, trans. by Charles Arand et al., Minneapolis: Fortress Press 2000, p. 360.

[32]   *SKS* 2, 331 / *EO1*, 342.

[33]   *SKS* 26, 196, NB32:107 / *JP* 1, 368.

[34]   *SKS* 9, 372 / *WL*, 379.

Beginning

Sean Anthony Turchin

Beginning (*Begyndelse*—noun; *begynde*—verb; *begyndende*—participle)

Borrowed from the Middle Low German *beginnen*,[1] the Danish noun *Begyndelse* means the commencement or genesis of an action as seen, for example, at the start of a film, story, or speech. It further signifies that by which something begins, the first part of something, or its origin, source, or cause. It can also mean the first trace, first step, or first attempt. The verb *begynde* means to make the first step, to enter, to let something be the point of departure or serve as the introduction, to initiate or inaugurate.[2] Kierkegaard sometimes uses the nominalized present participle (*en Begyndende*) to mean a beginner.

The most frequent occurrences of the concept of beginning are in the *Concluding Unscientific Postscript* and *Johannes Climacus, or De Omnibus dubitandum est*, respectively. The next most frequent occurrences are in *The Concept of Irony*, *Upbuilding Discourses in Various Spirits*, *The Book on Adler*, the upbuilding discourses, and *Three Discourses on Imagined Occasions*, respectively. Whether in the context of the Hegelian notion of beginning philosophy without presuppositions, as seen in *From the Papers of One Still Living* and the *Concluding Unscientific Postscript*, or in terms of doubting in order to begin philosophizing, as seen in *De Omnibus*, or in the context of resolutely beginning the difficult road of life, as seen in *Three Discourses on Imagined Occasions*, the concept of beginning denotes a decisive starting point.

In the context of *From the Papers of One Still Living*, the concept of beginning emerges in light of Kierkegaard's questioning of the Hegelian claim to begin philosophy without presuppositions, beginning only with the concept of pure being. But for Kierkegaard this attempt fails to acknowledge the many inherited factors that shape our thinking. Kierkegaard writes, "Far from remembering with thankfulness the struggles and hardships the world has endured in order to become what it is, the whole newer development—in order to begin again from the beginning—has a great tendency even to forget, if possible, the results this development has gained in the sweat of its brow."[3] The attempt to begin philosophy from "pure being," abstracted from all content—and thereby equivalent to "nothing"—causes us to forget the

---

[1]   Niels Åge Nielsen, *Dansk etymologisk Ordbog*, Copenhagen: Gyldendal 1966, p. 24.

[2]   *Ordbog over det danske Sprog*, vols. 1–28, published by the Society for Danish Language and Literature, Copenhagen: Gyldendal 1918–56, vol. 2, columns 159–66.

[3]   *SKS* 1, 17 / *EPW*, 61.

very being we seek to explain. Moreover, it is a futile attempt since forgetting the concrete nature of being is simply a form of self-deception rather than a starting point without presuppositions. In particular, this attempt to find an absolute starting point for philosophy leaves out of account the concrete existence of the thinker who seeks the starting point for philosophy—and thereby omits the concrete relation between the thinker and that which is thought.

The willful forgetting of the history of being is not merely an error and an act of self-deception, but it also boosts self-importance and hubris about the present. Kierkegaard states:

> the development has a great tendency, on the one hand, to convince itself of its activity and significance and, on the other, to foist this acknowledgment upon posterity by making itself the true starting point of world history. It would like to do this by beginning, if it were possible, the positive era with itself and letting the previous existence, if one is still reasonable enough to presuppose such, be a life serfdom, a piece of subtraction on which one must only regret that it has been necessary to spend so long a time.[4]

The critique is aimed squarely at Hegelians, particularly Danish Hegelians, given that it opens Kierkegaard's review of Hans Christian Andersen's novel, *Only a Fiddler*. The review was originally intended for publication in Johan Ludvig Heiberg's journal *Perseus*, which was an organ of Danish Hegelianism.[5] Yet it is not immediately clear how far it is also an attack on Hegel himself, since Kierkegaard says that "this phenomenon...[finds its] most respectable form...in Hegel's great attempt to begin with nothing," and that "the beginning from nothing of which Hegel speaks was mastered by himself in the system and was by no means a failure to appreciate the great richness of actuality."[6] Instead, Kierkegaard implies that Hegel's genius has been hijacked by his followers and misused.[7] Yet he also claims that the whole idea of beginning with "pure being"—or nothing—is part of philosophy's drive to "reconsider continually its own premises" even if on this occasion "by a misunderstanding...[it] has also been directed at existence itself."[8]

Kierkegaard's questioning of the possibility for philosophy to begin without presuppositions continues in the *Concluding Unscientific Postscript*. Once again, this work reveals Kierkegaard's skepticism about the possibility for such a beginning. His pseudonym, Johannes Climacus, relates, "The system begins with the immediate and therefore without presuppositions and therefore absolutely, that is, the beginning of the system is the absolute beginning."[9] But Climacus betrays his frustration with this understanding of the "system" asking: "How does the system begin with the immediate, that is, does it begin with it immediately?"[10] To this question, Climacus answers that it does not. According to Climacus, the problem is that the immediate is

4   Ibid.
5   Cf. *EPW*, "Historical Introduction," p. xxxi.
6   *SKS* 1, 18 / *EPW*, 62.
7   *SKS* 1, 17–18 / *EPW*, 61–2.
8   *SKS* 1, 18 / *EPW*, 62.
9   *SKS* 7, 108 / *CUP1*, 111.
10   *SKS* 7, 108 / *CUP1*, 111–12.

only gained through reflection and abstraction.[11] But both reflection and abstraction are infinite.[12] So, only when reflection stops can the beginning occur.[13]

This being the case, Climacus asks, "How do I bring to a halt the reflection set in motion in order to reach that beginning?"[14] In sum, reflection and abstraction can only be stopped by a decision, and this decision presupposes a subject who makes it and thereby ends the potentially infinite process of reflection.[15] A beginning can be initiated only when the conscious decision of the subject puts a stop to reflection. But this is a matter of practical reason rather than pure reason, and belongs to being in the world rather than to "pure being."

In this practical context, the concept of beginning with the right resolution is illustrated by considering how one should enter a marriage. In "On the Occasion of a Wedding," found in *Three Discourses on Imagined Occasions*, Kierkegaard's use of the concept of beginning serves to emphasize that one's ability to weather the difficulties of life, in this case marriage, depends largely on how one begins the journey, and that depends on the resolution with which one begins—the extent to which the individual wills "to have a *true conception of life and of oneself*."[16] One should see life for what it is in all its hardships, sorrows, sufferings, and joys and yet resolve to face the challenge from the beginning. So, the beginning is the practical resolution, in full cognizance of the consequences (for better or for worse). This beginning does not start with nothing, or pure being, or without presuppositions. On the contrary, the resolution should take account of the nature of oneself and of one's betrothed and of the vicissitudes of life, in their concrete being, in order to be a *true* beginning. To illustrate this, Kierkegaard uses the picture of a wedding ceremony where the two lovers face each other ready to begin a journey together throughout this life. He asks, for those who would disagree with examining the idea of marriage in such rigorous and joy-depleting terms, "Would it be wiser, would it better stand the test in life if the two, without the resolution, rushed away with each other in the transitory moment of infatuation's dream, if they danced away the soundness and health of love on the wedding day?"[17]

The idea of beginning marriage with a resolution serves to highlight the importance of how one begins anything in life. In order to prevail against the hardships that lie ahead, one must make a "good beginning," by means of a resolution. The resolution is reinforced by faith that trial and tribulation will be overcome. Yet the resolution must also give earnest thanks to God in order to avoid the hubris that trial and tribulation have been overcome by merely human means.[18] Faith is an essential complement to resolution and is also the beginning of the overcoming of despair—even if, as we see in *The Sickness unto Death*, faith first leads to greater despair, since faith allows us

---

[11]   *SKS* 7, 108 / *CUP1*, 112.
[12]   Cf. *SKS* 7, 109 / *CUP1*, 112; *SKS* 7, 110 / *CUP1*, 114.
[13]   *SKS* 7, 110 / *CUP1*, 113.
[14]   *SKS* 7, 109 / *CUP1*, 112.
[15]   *SKS* 7, 112 / *CUP1*, 116.
[16]   *SKS* 5, 427 / *TD*, 52.
[17]   *SKS* 5, 439 / *TD*, 66.
[18]   *SKS* 5, 438 / *TD*, 65.

to apprehend the extent to which we are sinners. But despair over one's sins is also ultimately overcome by faith—faith in the forgiveness of sins.[19]

According to the first line of Genesis, "In the beginning God created the heavens and the earth" (Genesis 1:1). So God seems to have begun with creation. But according to the New Testament, "In the beginning was the Word, and the Word was with God, and the Word was God" (John 1:1). So it seems faith begins with the Word of God. Yet, paradoxically, although Christian faith requires that one believes John's word, it can only be understood in silence: "There is a beginning everywhere, and the good beginning is everywhere where you begin with God."[20] Yet this beginning must be approached backward. "The beginning is not that with which one begins but that to which one comes, and one comes to it backward."[21] In order to come to this beginning one must first become silent before God, which in turn

> is the beginning of the fear of God, because just as fear of God is the beginning of wisdom, so silence is the beginning of the fear of God. And just as the fear of God is more than the beginning of wisdom, is wisdom, so silence is more than the beginning of the fear of God, is the fear of God. In this silence the many thoughts of wishes and desires God-fearingly fall silent; in this silence the verbosity of thanksgiving God-fearingly becomes silent.[22]

The absolute beginning, contra Hegel, is not to begin with "pure being" or "nothing" in the abstract sense. Nor is it to begin with "immediacy" or one's unreflective, spontaneous nature. Rather, the absolute beginning lies in the resolution first to seek God's kingdom. Yet this seeking does not consist in positive self-assertion through willful resolution. It consists in making oneself nothing, becoming "nothing before God" by learning to be silent.[23] In this silence, in which one's immediate nature and reflective desires are muted, both egotistical pride and despair over sins become nothing—which is the true beginning, in faith, of a higher self.

See also Absolute; Concrete/Abstract; Consciousness; Decision/Resolve; Existence/ Existential; Faith; Immediacy/Reflection; Individual; Leap; Marriage; Objectivity/ Subjectivity; Silence; Will.

[19]   *SKS* 11, 221–36 / *SUD*, 109–24.
[20]   *SKS* 8, 237 / *UD*, 139.
[21]   *SKS* 11, 17 / *WA*, 11.
[22]   Ibid.
[23]   *SKS* 11, 16–17 / *WA*, 10–11.

Being/Becoming

Claudine Davidshofer

Being (*Væsen*—noun; *være*—verb); **Becoming** (*Vorden*—noun; *vorde*—verb; *Tilblivelse*—noun; *blive*—verb)

From Low German *wesen*, Danish derived *Væsen*. From Old Rune Danish *wæsa*, *wæra*, and Old Danish *wæræ*, Danish derived *være*. From the same sources Old English derived *wesan*, and modern English derived the preterite *was* (singular) and *were* (plural).[1] The lexical meaning of the noun *Væsen* in Danish is (1) an entity or individual, such as a thing, a human, another organism, or God; or (2) an individual's general character or natural disposition, as revealed through external behavior or internal spiritual life. Used as a verb, the lexical meaning is (1) to exist or to occur in reality; (2) to be in a settled state, condition, location, or position; or (3) to possess a certain predicate, such as a quality, condition, or function.[2]

The verb *vorde* is derived from old Danish *warthæ*, *worthæ*, meaning to turn or veer and is cognate with German *werden*.[3] The Danish noun *Vorden* means creation, coming into being, or development.[4]

The Danish verb *blive* derives from the Old Rune Danish *bliffue* and the Middle Low German *bliven*, as does the Old English *belifan*, whence *to become*.[5] Its lexical meaning in Danish is (1) to come into existence, to come into reality; (2) to change to another position, location, or situation; or (3) to undergo a change in quality, characteristic, state, or condition.[6]

Throughout his texts, Kierkegaard explores being, becoming, and the relation between the two. Being and becoming are discussed most explicitly in Kierkegaard's pseudonymous works. These texts include *Either/Or*, by Victor Eremita, *Fear and Trembling*, by Johannes de silentio, *The Concept of Anxiety*, by Vigilius Haufniensis, *Philosophical Fragments*, by Johannes Climacus, the *Concluding Unscientific Postscript*, by Johannes Climacus, and *The Sickness unto Death*, by Anti-Climacus.

---

1   Niels Åge Nielsen, *Dansk etymologisk ordbog*, Copenhagen: Gyldendal 1966, p. 467.
2   *Ordbog over det danske Sprog*, vols. 1–28, published by the Society for Danish Language and Literature, Copenhagen: Gyldendal 1918–56, vol. 27, columns 829–906 (*være*) and columns 984–94 (*Væsen*).
3   Nielsen, *Dansk etymologisk ordbog*, p. 462.
4   *Ordbog over det danske Sprog*, vol. 27, columns 457–63.
5   Nielsen, *Dansk etymologisk ordbog*, p. 34.
6   *Ordbog over det danske Sprog*, vol. 2, columns 820–831 (*blive*) and vol. 23, column 1224 (*Tilblivelse*).

For Kierkegaard, the metaphysical whole is split into two realms, the realm of eternal being (God) and the realm of temporal becoming (the earthly). God is transcendent, eternal, pure being. He is the only being that is full being and is not mixed with becoming. Temporal becoming is the immanent, concrete, earthly realm in which humans have their daily existence. Temporal becoming is unfinished and continually changing. The two realms are not completely separate, however. The Incarnation, the absolute paradox of Christianity, affirms that eternal being freely descended into temporal becoming in the form of a human being, Christ. Kierkegaard believes that the realms of eternal being and temporal becoming are connected through the composite nature of human being.

In *The Sickness unto Death*, Anti-Climacus explains that the human being is spirit and, as spirit, is a constant relating of "the temporal and the eternal,"[7] that is, of eternal being and temporal becoming. The human is a peculiar, intermediate being, for he has one foot in eternal being and one foot in temporal becoming, and he must balance solidly on both feet. Since he is both eternal and temporal, he is the midpoint of reality, the individual who can connect eternal being (God) and temporal becoming (the earthly). It is no wonder, then, that many individuals anxiously flee from their responsibility to become spirit. They overemphasize either temporal becoming or eternal being, living almost entirely in either the one or the other. It is only when the individual becomes a Christian and lives in faith that he is truly spirit and constantly relates eternal being and temporal becoming.

I. Temporal Becoming: The Aesthetic and Ethical Viewpoints

The aesthete lives primarily in temporal becoming. His goal is to avoid boredom, and he guards against all long-term commitments, such as official posts, friendships, and marriages, which eventually end in stagnation and boredom. He does not want to be a judge, a friend, a husband, or to be loyal, friendly, or respectable.[8] The aesthete avoids predicative being, because he does not want any stable function, quality, or characteristic predicated of him. For the aesthete, to be something is to be bored. Immersing himself in becoming, he hastens from amusement to amusement and enjoys only the "accidental," "arbitrary," and fleeting moments in life.[9] He becomes for the sheer sake of becoming, and he has no goal for his becoming. The aesthete never becomes anything, and even more gravely, he never becomes a self.

The ethical individual, however, believes long-term commitments give the individual a sense of stability and personal being. Judge William urges the aesthete to be something: be a judge, a husband, a friend; be loyal, friendly, respectable. For the Judge, a human being is based primarily in predicative being—on acquiring stable qualities, states, and functions that give the individual a character that persists throughout time.[10] But the ethical individual still lives primarily in temporal becoming, because he tries to carve out being within becoming, within the temporal

---

7   *SKS* 11, 130 / *SUD*, 13.
8   *SKS* 2, 284–7 / *EO1*, 295–8.
9   *SKS* 2, 288 / *EO1*, 299.
10   *SKS* 3, 213–17 / *EO2*, 222–6.

and earthly. Human being is not a sum total of predicates. If he is not spirit, then he lacks the essentially human being that gives meaning and being to all these lesser predicates. The ethical individual may take too much comfort in being something and forget that these things are not what make up the human being. Kierkegaard warns against this in a journal entry titled "Predicate-less Being," by saying, "Roguish, as everything related to humanity is, we express it in this way: earnestness is to be *something*...for example: I am Chancellor, Knight of Denmark, member of the Cavalry Purchasing Commission, Alderman, Director of the Club...But no doubt all these numerous predicates are actually diversions, distractions, which prevent a man from the deepest impression of this *to be*."[11] It is indeed easy to *be something*, but it is not so easy to *be a self*.

II. Eternal Being: The Philosophical Viewpoint

The abstract philosopher lives too much in eternal being. In the *Concluding Unscientific Postscript*, Johannes Climacus explains that the philosopher uses the abstract, metaphysical viewpoint, to analyze being *sub specie aeterni*. He thinks being as pure, eternal being, which is abstracted from the flux and particularity of concrete, temporal becoming. The eternal viewpoint seems advantageous, because it supposedly reveals the enduring truths of being as such. But this viewpoint is problematic, precisely because it abstracts from one entire side of reality—concrete, temporal becoming in which the human continually has his existence. Climacus cautions that the individual must "pay scrupulous attention to what is understood by being"[12] and what kind of being he seeks to study. There is a difference between abstract being and *human being*—being as it is specifically instantiated in and lived out by the human in concrete existence. The human is not himself abstract, eternal being. He assumes this guise only occasionally and temporarily, when he willingly abstracts from himself *qua* concrete existing individual and is "lured out into the indefinite and fantastically becomes something such as no existing human being has ever been or can be, a phantom with which the individual busies himself on occasion."[13] Once he returns to his natural standpoint within concrete being, his abstract reflections will likely have little significance for his daily existence.[14] Do his reflections on abstract being really relate to his life as a human being?

Kierkegaard sums up this point nicely in his journals and papers, by explaining that different methods should be used to study the different kinds of being. Ontology and existential science "accent being" in different ways, for they each examine different kinds and aspects of being.[15] Ontology uses the abstract, metaphysical viewpoint, and it looks for the eternal truths of being as such, abstracted from concrete, temporal being. Existential science (*Existential-Videnskab*) views being from a concrete, human standpoint, and focuses on human being, being that is individual, concrete,

---

[11]   *SKS* 25, 467–8, NB30:100 / *JP* 1, 200.
[12]   *SKS* 7, 174 / *CUP1*, 189.
[13]   Ibid.
[14]   *SKS* 7, 174–6 / *CUP1*, 189–91.
[15]   *SKS* 27, 271, Papir 281 / *JP* 1, 197.

temporal, and continually in flux. Climacus suggests that the existential viewpoint is the higher priority. The individual should be wary of spending too much energy analyzing abstract being, and should focus instead on concrete, human being, that is, on how to live as a human being. Presumably, however, there is a link between these two views on being: the individual should look at how the eternal truths of being as such, which are obtained from ontology, are instantiated by and expressed through the human being, through his own concrete existence.

Furthermore, the philosopher cannot adequately explain or experience becoming merely through abstract, metaphysical thought. In *The Concept of Anxiety*, Vigilius Haufniensis explains that since metaphysics looks at what eternally is, it must abstract from what becomes. It must abstract from all change, discontinuity, and newness in what is. He writes, "In logic, no movement must *come about*, for logic is, and whatever is logical only *is*…Every movement, if for the moment one wishes to use this expression, is an immanent movement, which in a profound sense is no movement at all."[16] Yet, becoming precisely is a break and an alteration in what is, a change from this to that, from here to there. It is strange that certain philosophers, such as Hegel, believe that metaphysical thought is suited to explain becoming when it purposely abstracts from all becoming. How curious it is to think that by setting aside and ignoring becoming, becoming is somehow thereby explained.[17] From the outset, it seems a futile and self-contradictory endeavor.

Any attempt to think becoming results in unsatisfying equivocations and insoluble paradoxes. According to Haufniensis, Plato rightly points out that becoming is too elusive and paradoxical a moment to be explained through metaphysics. Plato describes transition as a "strange entity…that lies between motion and rest without occupying any time, and into this and out from this that which is in motion changes to rest."[18] The precise moment of becoming—when one quality or thing turns into a new one and when motion turns to rest, that crucial turning point when something changes or comes into existence—is not open to thought. The moment of becoming seems to occupy no time and no space, and almost seems not to exist, but it must exist because the transition is certainly completed. How can thought capture this elusive point that is neither the first product nor the second product, is neither motion nor rest, and yet is that through which both are connected and the one turns into the other? Haufniensis agrees that the moment of becoming is opaque to metaphysical thought. Plato "deserves credit" for recognizing the paradoxical nature of becoming, even though he cannot get beyond the problem and has to let it go unsolved.[19]

Hegel foolishly ignores Plato's insight, and he simply assumes from the outset that metaphysical thought can explain becoming. While Hegel claims that no element may be employed within his metaphysical system that has not been established by a preceding stage of the dialectic, Haufniensis claims that his principles of transition (negation and mediation) are used throughout *The Science of Logic* without ever having been established within the system itself. He complains that "there is no

---

[16]   *SKS* 4, 320–1 / *CA*, 12–13. See also *SKS* 7, 106–7 / *CUP1*, 109–10.
[17]   *SKS* 7, 106–7 / *CUP1*, 109–10.
[18]   *SKS* 4, 385n. / *CA*, 83n.
[19]   Ibid.

embarrassment at all over the use in Hegelian thought of the terms 'transition,' 'negation,' 'mediation,' i.e., the principles of motion, in such a way that they do not find their place in the systematic progression. If this is not a presupposition, I do not know what a presupposition is."[20] Hegel's biggest presupposition of all is to believe that becoming belongs in metaphysics. Hegel employs these ambiguous and dubious principles to dupe the individual into thinking that becoming has been explained.

Negation and mediation are "disguised, suspicious and secret agents"[21] and "strange pixies and goblins"[22] that Hegel uses to obfuscate the paradoxical nature of becoming. Sublation—Hegel's famed *Aufhebung*—negates one term and simultaneously posits the next term in the dialectic. But sublation does not explain the crucial moment of becoming, which is neither the first term nor the second term, neither negating nor positing, and yet is that through which the one turns into the other. By using a principle that supposedly accomplishes both negating and positing, Hegel tries to trick the individual into believing that this principle somehow also captures and explains the pivotal moment of becoming. Perhaps negation captures the first product and the second product, negating and positing, but not the elusive moment of becoming itself, wherein the one turns into the other.

Haufniensis adds that mediation is likewise equivocal, "for it designates at once the relation between the two terms and the result of the relation...it designates movement, but at the same time rest."[23] By giving mediation the simultaneous functions of producing process and result, motion and rest, Hegel attempts to distract the thinker from the fact that mediation still does not explain that crucial in-between, the precise moment of becoming, which is neither motion nor rest, and yet connects them both. Mediation can perhaps explain what happens before and after the moment of becoming—it can capture the first and second, motion and rest—but it cannot seize the exact moment of becoming itself. Becoming in metaphysics remains a "clever turn," a prank, which Hegel plays on us all.[24]

The individual should not waste time trying to give becoming a home in metaphysics, when becoming so obviously belongs in concrete, existential experience. Diogenes does well to refute the Eleatics' metaphysical denial of motion by the comical and commonsensical response of simply walking up and down beside his tub. As Constantin Constantius reports in *Repetition*, "he did not say a word but merely paced and back and forth a few times, thereby assuming that he had sufficiently refuted them."[25] The quandaries of metaphysics are easily dissolved through the simplest of existential acts: walking. Becoming belongs to existence, so let the individual explain becoming through existence, by moving from here to there or changing this or that.

---

[20]   *SKS* 4, 384 / *CA*, 81.
[21]   *SKS* 4, 384 / *CA*, 82.
[22]   *SKS* 4, 320n. / *CA*, 12n.
[23]   *SKS* 4, 319 / *CA*, 11. See also *SKS* 4, 25–6 / *R*, 148–9.
[24]   *SKS* 4, 385 / *CA*, 82.
[25]   *SKS* 4, 9 / *R*, 131.

III. Instantiating Eternal Being in Temporal Becoming: The Religious Approach

Only when the individual becomes a Christian does he become spirit and constantly relate eternal being and temporal becoming. Johannes de silentio explains in *Fear and Trembling* that the knight of faith "has made and at every moment is making the movement of infinity."[26] He jumps up from the finite, reaches the infinite, and comes back down again to the finite. Put another way, he leaps up from temporal becoming, reaches eternal being, and comes back down again to temporal becoming. Faith is a double movement: it is a constantly repeated, two-directional becoming. The knight of faith brings the truths of eternal being (i.e., God) back down into temporal becoming (the earthly), thereby investing temporal becoming with the stability, importance, and divinity of eternal being. He concretizes pure, abstract, eternal being, by instantiating it in his own existential becoming. Ontological being and existential being meet in the knight of faith.

Becoming a Christian is an internal change. The individual executes the double movement of faith internally. The essence of human being, then, is that which makes a human truly a human—inwardness. Human being is not found in the external characteristics, qualities, and functions that others can predicate of the individual, but rather, is located in the most internal, invisible, secret, and individual part of the human. The moment wherein the individual becomes a Christian is a drastic and peculiar kind of becoming. In *Philosophical Fragments*, Climacus likens this moment of becoming to a rebirth, to the fundamental change of coming into existence, wherein something goes from not-being to being. He writes, "But this transition from 'not to be' to 'to be' is indeed the transition of birth...Let us call this transition *rebirth*, by which he enters the world a second time."[27] Inwardness comes into existence in the individual for the first time, and the individual becomes a fundamentally new self, a new creation.

Furthermore, Christianity is not a settled state, not something that the individual simply is once and for all. Being a Christian is always becoming a Christian. The individual must, at every moment, continually renew and repeat the double movement of Christianity. He does not become in the sense of moving on, of going beyond Christianity, but in the sense of continually re-enacting the decision and the task of being a Christian. It is a becoming as renewal and repetition. It is a movement that continually occurs within the same place.[28]

Now, the task of being spirit is difficult, even paradoxical and absurd. How can the individual do this? Kierkegaard suggests that the individual should imitate the example of Christ, for he, and perhaps he alone, was able to relate eternal being and temporal becoming. The Incarnation is a concrete, historical example of eternal being and temporal becoming meeting in and being expressed through an individual existing human. Christ continually made the double movement, and each moment he connected eternal being (God) and temporal becoming (the earthly). The human

---

26   *SKS* 4, 135 / *FT*, 40.
27   *SKS* 4, 227 / *PF*, 19.
28   *SKS* 7, 280 / *CUP1*, 308.

must strive to imitate Christ, and to express eternal being in temporal becoming, through his own individual human existence.

See also Christ; Double Movement; Existence/Existential; Faith; Inwardness/ Inward Deepening; Mediation/Sublation; Movement/Motion; Repetition; Time/ Temporality/Eternity; Transition.

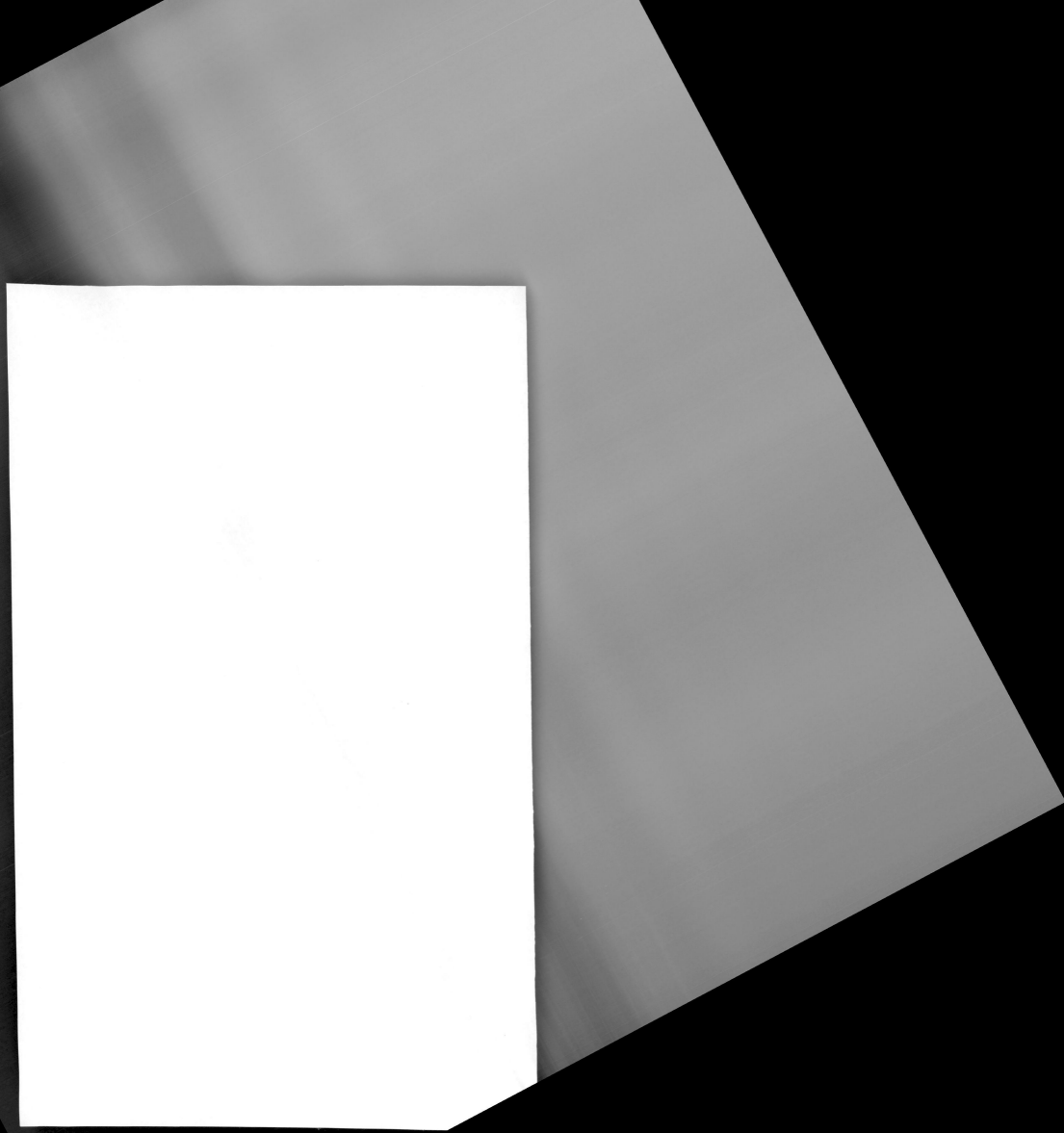

Calling

Robert B. Puchniak

Calling (*Kald*—noun; *kalde*—verb)

The lexical meaning of the Danish word is to be summoned into a vocation or mission, as from birth. The term connotes meaning with regard to a person's very life, that is, feeling a need to dedicate one's life to some duty or purpose. Christian Molbech's *Dansk Ordbog* cites several biblical examples of "calling." These include the experiences of Job, who "heard a voice" calling to him from silence, and Jeremiah, who chastised his people for not answering the Lord, although "I [God] spoke to you persistently."[1] In a more mundane sense, the verb *kalde* can be used to send for someone (with the preposition *på*), or to call someone by name. The term figures most prominently in the works, *Either/Or* and *The Book on Adler*, but is also found in *The Sickness unto Death*, the edifying discourse on "Purity of Heart," *For Self-Examination*, and with personal relevance to Kierkegaard in *The Point of View*.

Kierkegaard distinguishes between an earthly calling, such as an occupation, livelihood, or profession, and a divine calling, such as to become a Christian "apostle." As an ethical matter, a vocation is "to transmute one's talent into one's calling."[2] But an eternal calling requires much more than talent. This remains an important question for Kierkegaard—just how this worldly calling relates to religious obligations, presuming that one's livelihood impacts one's spiritual life. To Kierkegaard, religious concerns, however, will always trump the significance of a mere occupation.

In *Either/Or*, Part Two, "The Balance Between the Esthetic and the Ethical in the Development of the Personality," Kierkegaard's pseudonym Judge William includes an extended meditation on whether "it is every person's duty to work for a living."[3] "Our hero" in these deliberations, the imagined subject, desires work that is both pleasurable and meaningful.[4] He thinks "there is no abstract calling for all human beings," but rather "that each person has a particular calling."[5] While "the aesthete" thinks that some people are gifted with talent (and to this they are called) while others are not, "the ethicist" thinks everyone has a calling, even the most insignificant

---

[1]   Christian Molbech, *Dansk Ordbog*, vols. 1–2, Copenhagen: Den Gyldendalske Boghandlings Forlag 1833, vol. 1, p. 546. See Job 4:16 and Jeremiah 7:13 respectively.

[2]   *SKS* 18, 192, JJ:163 / *KJN* 2, 178.

[3]   *SKS* 3, 273ff. / *EO2*, 288ff.

[4]   *SKS* 3, 274 / *EO2*, 289. Judge William will later object to the title of "hero" for this person who is simply "a jobholder and a married man" (*SKS* 3, 283 / *EO2*, 298).

[5]   *SKS* 3, 276 / *EO2*, 291.

Robert B. Puchniak

person, regardless of talent. In the ethical view, then, "talent is not beautiful until it is transfigured into a calling, and existence is not beautiful until every person has a calling."[6] He continues, "When a person has a calling, he generally has a norm outside himself, which, without making him a slave, nevertheless gives him some indication of what he has to do, maps out his time for him, often provides him with an occasion to begin."[7] "Our hero," wants his work to relate to the work of other people; he wants to "*accomplish* something" in order to make his work his "occupation."[8] In contrast, the aesthete claims that "the satisfaction of the talent is the highest," whether or not he accomplishes something.[9] Behind this conflict lies the difference between what one *can* do and what one *should* do with one's life, and the dilemma of devoting oneself to artful beauty or to moral obligation.

The occasion of Pastor Adolf Peter Adler's private revelations in the early 1840s (Adler claimed that Jesus spoke directly to him and dictated some of his writings), prompted Kierkegaard to write "an ethical inquiry into the concept of a revelation, into what it means to be called by a revelation," and then claim exceptional authority because of that revelation.[10] Kierkegaard was wary of the "vacillating" person who might claim to be called by God yet want to "serve two masters," that is, to "be what the times demand," to use a claim of authority "to get a hearing in the noisy crowd."[11] He expected this could happen in an age such as his, when "the decisive religious categories have really been abolished."[12] In the essay, "The Difference Between a Genius and an Apostle," Kierkegaard writes, "An apostle is not born; an apostle is a man who is called and appointed by God and sent by him on a mission."[13] Every person is potentially equally close to being called in this fashion. The apostle, however, "does not become more intelligent, he does not acquire more imagination, greater discernment, etc."[14] He is "called for all eternity" and thus "made paradoxically different from all other human beings."[15] An apostle is not distinguished by "natural gifts" but rather by "divine authority"; this is what is "qualitatively decisive."[16] Kierkegaard listens to Paul not because he is brilliant, but because he has this divine authority, which originates in his call from God.

In the edifying discourse, "An Occasional Discourse," Kierkegaard focuses on "the awareness of being a single individual with eternal responsibility before God," and he asks the reader to consider how their "occupation" relates to this responsibility.[17] Kierkegaard cautions against "conformity" with the present generation and reminds others that God will "not reject the lowliest occupation

---

[6] *SKS* 3, 278 / *EO2*, 293.
[7] *SKS* 3, 278 / *EO2*, 294.
[8] Ibid.
[9] Ibid.
[10] *SKS* 15, 91 / *BA*, 3.
[11] *SKS* 15, 111 / *BA*, 24–5.
[12] *SKS* 15, 111 / *BA*, 25.
[13] *SKS* 11, 99 / *WA*, 95.
[14] *SKS* 11, 98 / *WA*, 95.
[15] Ibid.
[16] *SKS* 11, 100 / *WA*, 96.
[17] *SKS* 8, 236 / *UD*, 137–8.

if it has genuine integrity. There in eternity where he is, all petty diversities are forgotten...."[18] One should not be ashamed if one's occupation is "lowly," but rather, if one lacks integrity. Kierkegaard draws attention in this discourse not only to the importance of *what* a person does in their occupation, but also *how* one does it. Simply having the ability to execute an occupation will not necessarily mean that one is intended to do it. For example, if one is good at "cruelty" or "loathsome crime,"[19] this does not necessarily indicate this is one's "calling." "Favorable results" or "immediate success" should not determine if one has found the proper calling.[20] Being "in agreement with the crowd" means little in the face of being "eternally concerned."[21] A person's work, he thinks, must not conflict with willing "one thing." One must discern between his or her "temporal" obligations and "eternal responsibilities." The means to achieve the end (including one's occupation) must be in harmony with the desired eternal end, "to will one thing."[22]

In *The Sickness unto Death*, Kierkegaard's pseudonym Anti-Climacus laments the "profanation and prostitution of Christianity" prevalent in "Christendom," wherein understanding a true "call" becomes easily confused.[23] In this context, "in a little country, scarcely three poets are born in any one generation, but there are plenty of clergymen" who have merely passed an examination to be sufficiently qualified for the job.[24] Anti-Climacus remarks, "a true pastor is even more rare than a true poet"; however, being a pastor in Christendom is seen instead as "a way of making a living, devoid of the slightest mystery," something that is "an official appointment."[25] In these categories, a "calling" is quite different from a "career."

In the essay *For Self-Examination*, Kierkegaard considers how best to read the Scriptures in light of its invitation or "call" to the reader. He notes the critical difference between seeing the words on a page as something impersonal and objective, as a cultured intellectual might, or as something personal and subjective, as would an earnest Christian who seeks to relate to the divine Word. Especially poignant for Kierkegaard is the biblical story of King David and the prophet Nathan (2 Samuel 11:2–12:15), wherein the king does not recognize his guilt in coveting Bathsheba. In Nathan's exclamation, "Thou art the man," spoken after telling David a tale of great injustice, the reader witnesses what Kierkegaard calls "the transition to the subjective."[26] David was called to attention by the prophet out of his "impersonal" relation to the Word and into an immediate confrontation. Kierkegaard warns, "if you are to read God's Word in order to see yourself in the mirror, then during the reading you must incessantly say to yourself: It is I to whom it is speaking, it is I about whom it is speaking."[27] In order to discern authentically what Scripture

---

[18]   *SKS* 8, 237 / *UD*, 138.
[19]   *SKS* 8, 238 / *UD*, 139.
[20]   Ibid.
[21]   Ibid.
[22]   *SKS* 8, 239 / *UD*, 141–2.
[23]   *SKS* 11, 214 / *SUD*, 102.
[24]   Ibid.
[25]   Ibid.
[26]   *SKS* 13, 65 / *FSE*, 38.
[27]   *SKS* 13, 66 / *FSE*, 40.

calls the reader to, one "must not resort to quibbling, intermix irrelevancies," as the intellectual elites do, but instead "read a fear and trembling into your soul."[28] If the Bible amounts only to "a doctrine," contends Kierkegaard, then it cannot provide a mirror for subjective examination.

Kierkegaard was personally conscious of how "inwardness" weighed upon his own "proper task" in life, which for him amounted to becoming an author (and ultimately becoming a Christian).[29] Kierkegaard did think at one time of serving as a "rural pastor" and admitted confusion over discerning this calling, but in the end he could not accept a post "in the state as a teacher of religion," because, he rationalized, "I [would] obligate myself to be something other than I am."[30] In his own mind, his "intellectual gifts, abilities, and mental constitution" brought a "responsibility" to write, and this he could not refuse.[31] The road he walked was, in his words, not something self-inflicted, "for it was my calling [*mit Kald*], the whole of my constitution was meant for this."[32] Kierkegaard considered himself not well suited to be a rural pastor because he feared this vocation would "deify the existing order," as he thought Bishop Mynster had done.[33] As an independent author, owing nothing to other human beings and everything to God, he could act upon his calling without worldly restrictions.

In sum, Kierkegaard is attentive to the dilemma of being "called," in both his signed and his pseudonymous works. There is, in both, a strong understanding that one's vocation is about more than mere aesthetic satisfaction or the utilization of personal talents. Many of Kierkegaard's writings are fraught with a sense of responsibility before God (1) to properly discern one's calling, and (2) to act so as to fulfill that obligation. There is also keen awareness on Kierkegaard's part to avoid identifying one's "calling" with whatever "the crowd" might advise. Discerning one's "eternal" calling will be assisted, according to Kierkegaard, by reading Scripture—reading it with "fear and trembling" and with "subjectivity" in a mode of self-examination. In his journals, Kierkegaard wrote: "If there were a man who had achieved perfection in the art of always being able to discern the task, discern the task in everything and at all times, never without composure, never without courage…if there were such a man, then to see him related to God…this would be the most beautiful sight of all!"[34]

See also Being/Becoming; Conscience; Crowd; Self-Deception; Decision/Resolve; Duty; Ethics; Evil; Good; Freedom; Governance/Providence; Inwardness; Punctuation; Religious; Revelation; Witness.

---

28   *SKS* 13, 69 / *FSE*, 43.
29   *SKS* 18, 192, JJ:163 / *KJN* 2, 178.
30   *SKS* 20, 81, NB:107 / *KJN* 4, 80.
31   *SKS* 20, 82, NB:107 / *KJN* 4, 80.
32   *SKS* 20, 82, NB:107 / *KJN* 4, 81.
33   Ibid.
34   *SKS* 26, 89, NB31:120 / *JP* 4, 4480.

Care/Concern

Gerhard Thonhauser

Care/Concern (*Bekymring*—noun; *bekymre*—verb)

The Danish noun derives from the Middle Low German *bekummeringe*, also found in High German *Bekümmerung* (with the corresponding verb *bekümmern*). Two lexical meanings of *Bekymring* can be distinguished: first, a feeling of worry, anxiety, or concern, second, a feeling of responsibility, duty, or obligation. The first meaning has a tendency to merge into the latter. Accordingly, the verb *bekymre* means, first, to worry somebody or about somebody or something and, second, to take care of something or somebody.[1]

This article will only be concerned with the term *Bekymring*, which needs to be distinguished from several other Danish words with similar meanings. On the one hand, it should be demarcated from the Danish *Sorg*, which means a feeling of grief, sorrow, affliction, distress, or mourning, and the Danish *Kummer*, which is an even stronger term for grief, sorrow, affliction, distress, or anguish. On the other hand, it also needs to be distinguished from the Danish *Omhu*, which means care, loving care, or solicitude. *Sorg* appears in Kierkegaard's works approximately as many times as *Bekymring*, but it seems that there is no idiosyncratic use of the term. The term *Kummer* is hardly ever used, *Omhu* rather seldom.

The most frequent occurrence of the word *Bekymring* is in *Christian Discourses*, followed by *Upbuilding Discourses in Various Spirits*. The word appears more often in Kierkegaard's discourses than in the pseudonymous works. Likewise, the most significant discussion of the concept can be found in the aforementioned works and in some of the *Eighteen Upbuilding Discourses*. A major difficulty is that *Bekymring* often appears in colloquial, everyday usage in Kierkegaard's texts, many times in connection with one or more of the other terms mentioned. For instance, the expression *Sorger og Bekymringer* ("sorrows and troubles")[2]—sometimes in an enumeration with other expressions ("sorrows, anxieties, etc.")[3]—is commonly used by Kierkegaard. However, the following discussion will focus on his idiosyncratic use of the term.

In general, whenever Kierkegaard uses *Bekymring* in a conceptual way, he is occupied with the distinction between worldly, pagan, or everyday concern, and genuine Christian concern (the concern for an eternal happiness). However,

---

[1]   *Ordbog over det danske Sprog*, vols. 1–28, published by the Society for Danish Language and Literature, Copenhagen: Gyldendal 1918–56, vol. 2, columns 246–9.

[2]   *SKS* 3, 184 / *EO2*, 189.

[3]   *SKS* 1, 277 / *CI*, 236.

Kierkegaard has a tendency to use the same expression to denote both forms of concern. What this indicates is that these forms of concern are not strictly separate from each other but interconnected. Worldly concerns must be transformed into Christian concern. Christian concern can only be awakened in transition through the variety of worldly concerns.

I.

To begin with, the different uses of *Bekymring* will be traced by the example of *Eighteen Upbuilding Discourses*. In *Two Upbuilding Discourses* from 1843 Kierkegaard states: "The expectancy of faith, then, is victory."[4] In contrast to this "the troubled person [*Den Bekymrede*] expects no victory."[5] Similarly, the experienced person reminds us: "One ought to be prepared to have the troubles of life [*Livets Bekymringer*] visit also the home of the happy."[6] In the second discourse, Kierkegaard writes about the apostle Paul: "He raises the believer's mind above earthly and finite cares [*Bekymringer*], above worldly shrewdness and doubt, by means of a devout observation that we always ought to thank God."[7] In these passages, *Bekymring* signifies worldly concerns that need to be overcome in order for one to become a person of faith.

A shift takes place in the last of the *Three Upbuilding Discourses* from 1843, "Strengthening in the Inner Being," and a new use of the term *Bekymring* occurs:

> Not until the moment when there awakens in his soul a concern about what meaning the world has for him and he for the world, about what meaning everything within him by which he himself belongs to the world has for him and he therein for the world—only then does the inner being announce its presence in this *concern*.[8]

Now, *Bekymring* describes a development of the self—a form of awakening—that is a necessary precondition for faith: "In this concern, the inner being announces itself and craves an explanation, a witness that explains the meaning of everything for it and its own meaning by explaining it in the God."[9] In "Think about Your Creator in the Days of Your Youth," Kierkegaard writes accordingly that what matters are not bare truths, but "concerned truths,"[10] whose purpose is to "awaken you to concern about yourself."[11] A similar thought appears again in *The Sickness unto Death*: "All Christian knowing, however rigorous its form, ought to be concerned, but this concern is precisely the upbuilding. Concern constitutes the relation to life, to the actuality of the personality, and therefore earnestness from the Christian point of view."[12]

---

4   *SKS* 5, 29 / *EUD*, 19.
5   *SKS* 5, 29 / *EUD*, 20.
6   Ibid.
7   *SKS* 5, 50 / *EUD*, 42.
8   *SKS* 5, 93 / *EUD*, 86.
9   *SKS* 5, 94 / *EUD*, 87.
10   *SKS* 5, 233 / *EUD*, 233.
11   *SKS* 5, 234 / *EUD*, 234.
12   *SKS* 11, 117–18 / *SUD*, 5–6.

II.

Expressions for genuine Christian concern can be found throughout the authorship. *Fear and Trembling* speaks of the "concern for his soul."[13] In the *Concluding Unscientific Postscript* the crucial expression "concern for an eternal happiness"[14] makes its first appearance. In *Practice in Christianity* it is extended to the "infinite passion in his concern for an eternal happiness."[15] And in *The Moment* it is stated that the "concern for an eternal happiness" is clearly distinct from the striving for worldly comfort.[16]

Part One of *Upbuilding Discourses in Various Spirits* speaks of the "concern of inwardness" (*Inderlighedens Bekymring*), which is awakened and sharpened by repentance and regret.[17] It is further stated that repentance is a "quiet daily concern" (*stille daglig Bekymring*)[18] and that the single individual in repentance "learns earnestness in order to be concerned as a single individual about his eternal responsibility."[19] Thus, the single individual is defined by the steady *Bekymring* for one's eternal responsibility. A similar notion can be found in Part Four of *Christian Discourses*:

> Moreover, there is a concern, a deep, an eternal concern; it pertains not to externals, not to your fortunes, past or future; it pertains to your actions and, alas, it pertains to those very ones that a person would prefer to have forgotten, because it pertains to the actions, secret or open, by which you offended against God or against other persons. This concern is repentance.[20]

In Part Three of *Upbuilding Discourses in Various Spirits*, Kierkegaard talks about the "concern about oneself" (*Selvbekymring*).[21] The same expression is used again in several passages in Part Three of *Christian Discourses*, now translated as "self-concern."[22] In all these passages, the term *Bekymring* refers to a capacity of the self that is an integral part of what it means to be a person of faith; there can be no faith without this mode of concern.

III.

In addition to the two main categories of concern, there seem to be modes of *Bekymring* that do not characterize the person of faith, but cannot be classified as

---

13	*SKS* 4, 166 / *FT*, 75.
14	*SKS* 7, 523 / *CUP1*, 575.
15	*SKS* 12, 120 / *PC*, 112.
16	*SKS* 14, 151 / *M*, 109.
17	*SKS* 8, 130 / *UD*, 14.
18	*SKS* 8, 134 / *UD*, 19.
19	*SKS* 8, 233 / *UD*, 135.
20	*SKS* 10, 281 / *CD*, 264.
21	*SKS* 8, 363 / *UD*, 265.
22	*SKS* 10, 199–200 / *CD*, 189; *SKS* 10, 251 / *CD*, 244; *SKS* 10, 305 / *CD*, 284.

worldly concern either, but rather as the form of an intermediate step from worldly to Christian concern.

The first of these forms is *the care of doubt* (*Tvivlens Bekymring*). In the upbuilding discourse at the end of *Either/Or* a "more earnest doubt," a "deeper care" is introduced. This concern is about whether one has done what one could, or whether what one did—even though one did what one could—was still not enough. This concern cannot be calmed by any worldly security, since that would just set the doubt in motion and awaken the concern once again. Instead, the suggested solution is to think about how the point of view that in relation to God we are always in the wrong can be upbuilding.[23] According to the discourse, this thought is able to "calm the cares of doubt."[24] Similarly, it is stated in *Eighteen Upbuilding Discourses* that concern is related to doubt and that this care of doubt is a justified concern.[25] Finally, in *Christian Discourses* there is also a passage about "doubt that is the origin of self-concern."[26]

In "Does a Human Being Have the Right to Let Himself Be Put to Death for the Truth" a second intermediary form of *Bekymring* is discussed, one that is perhaps even closer to the person of faith's concern, namely, the *concern of responsibility*. This concern characterizes Christian love.[27] It involves "lovingly to *be concerned for the others*, for those who, if one is to be put to death, must become guilty of putting one to death. I am speaking of: with the courage to let oneself be put to death, in fear and trembling to be concerned about one's responsibility."[28] This responsibility for the others—who would become guilty of putting one to death—is—according to the text in question—the ultimate reason why one does not have the right to let oneself be put to death for the truth.

IV.

By far in most instances, *Bekymring* is used to describe the plurality of worldly concerns that need to be overcome in order to develop faith. In these instances, it is arguably impossible to draw a clear distinction between an everyday and an idiosyncratic use of the term. Still, it has become clear that overcoming these concerns does not mean to get rid of them once and for all. Rather it seems that Kierkegaard wants to indicate that the struggle with worldly concerns can never be left behind. On the contrary, it needs to be seen as an unavoidable part of the striving to become a person of faith.

In Part Two of *Upbuilding Discourses in Various Spirits*, Kierkegaard points out that the Gospel is

> not simply a joyful message; it has an essential quality that actually makes it into a Gospel—namely, it addresses itself to those who are worried [*Bekymrede*]. Indeed, in

---

[23]   *SKS* 3, 325–6 / *EO2*, 346–7.
[24]   *SKS* 3, 330 / *EO2*, 351.
[25]   See *SKS* 5, 135 / *EUD*, 132.
[26]   *SKS* 10, 202 / *CD*, 92.
[27]   See *SKS* 11, 80 / *WA*, 75.
[28]   *SKS* 11, 74 / *WA*, 69.

every line of this solicitous Gospel [*det bekymrede Evangelium*] it is clear that the words are being spoken not to the healthy, not to the strong, not to the happy, but to the worried [*Bekymrede*].[29]

Kierkegaard continues that the "solicitous Gospel" refers to the lilies in the field and the birds of the air as teachers, because with these teachers "no misapprehension is possible, because they are silent—out of solicitude for the worried person [*af Omsorg for den Bekymrede*]."[30] Moreover, "silence respects the worry" (*Taushed ærer Bekymringen*).[31] The first discourse about the lilies and the birds wants to consider how "the worried person [*den Bekymrede*] learns: to be contented with being a human being."[32] Only the first discourse will be considered here, because the following two present arguments that are analogously structured. The main argument is that the worried person should learn from the lily, which "is without worry."[33] It should learn that the worry stems from not being content with being what one is. Kierkegaard makes clear that "the discourse will respect his worry," and, therefore, he tells a metaphorical story about the "the worried lily"[34] and "the bird's worry."[35] What the stories attempt to show is that being contented with being a human being allows overcoming worldly worries; and this is achieved by not attempting to make comparisons with others.

In Part One of *Christian Discourses*, "The Cares of the Pagans" (*Hedningenes Bekymringer*), each discourse starts with the statement: "This care the bird does not have."[36] The purpose of the discourses is explained in the introduction: "Thus with the help of the lily and the bird we get to know the pagan's cares, what they are, namely, those that the bird and the lily do not have, although they have comparable necessities."[37] With this statement it also becomes clear that *Bekymring* does not refer to the objective conditions—the necessities—but to the way in which one relates to those conditions. Certain necessities cannot be overcome but are necessary parts of what it means to be a human being, and therefore, the possibility of *Bekymring* cannot be overcome but remains constantly present. As we will presently see, for Kierkegaard this is not at all a problem, but rather the precondition for reaching true Christian upbuilding.

In Part Two of *Christian Discourses* we can find the following statement, which is crucial for the understanding of Kierkegaard's discourses as a whole:

> But in order to find the upbuilding, one must first find the terrifying and thus take the time here to understand that in these words is contained the most somber view of life....

---

29   *SKS* 8, 260 / *UD*, 160.
30   Ibid.
31   *SKS* 8, 261 / *UD*, 161.
32   *SKS* 8, 261 / *UD*, 162.
33   *SKS* 8, 263 / *UD*, 164.
34   *SKS* 8, 266 / *UD*, 167.
35   *SKS* 8, 273 / *UD*, 174.
36   The only exception is discourse V, which starts with: "This care the lily and the bird do not have." *SKS* 10, 69 / *CD*, 60.
37   *SKS* 10, 23 / *CD*, 11.

See, now the upbuilding in the deepest sense begins. But earthly sagacity and impatience and worldly care that seek healing in a worldly way must not insist on the impossible, that one should be able to address them for upbuilding when one is to speak about the essentially Christian. Christianity really begins right there, or real Christianity begins right there where human impatience, whatever actual suffering it had to lament over, would find this to be infinitely increased—by the consolation—indeed, by consolation to the point of despair, because from the worldly point of view Christian consolation is much more to despair over than the hardest earthly suffering and the greatest temporal misfortune. *There* begins the upbuilding, the Christian upbuilding.[38]

For Kierkegaard, a message that is truly upbuilding must be terrifying in the first place. Thus, the upbuilding does not imply avoiding or denying the troubles and difficulties that are an integral part of being human, but rather requires confronting them and thereby getting involved with the concerns and worries caused by these conditions. Only through this procedure can the truly upbuilding arise—an upbuilding that is always at risk of despair given the unavoidable character of concern.

In *Practice in Christianity* Anti-Climacus expresses a more rigid point of view. He talks about "many tribulations…such as sickness, financial embarrassment, cares about the next year, what one is going to eat, or cares about 'what one ate last year but still has not paid for,' or about not having become what one wanted to become in the world, or other calamities."[39] According to Anti-Climacus, none of this has anything to do with the offense central to the requirement for becoming a Christian. Similarly, Kierkegaard asks in a journal entry, in a world dominated by Christianity, "how in the world is there any room for this concern: blessed is he who does not take offense at me."[40] It should also be noted that Kierkegaard shows no sympathy for any form of nationalism. The "concern of nationality" is one of the worldly worries that need to be overcome, since it is "politics to the point of despair."[41]

V.

Two further uses of the term *Bekymring* can be indicated that do not fit into the distinction of worldly and Christian concern. First, Climacus in the *Philosophical Fragments* talks about God's concern, when telling the story of the king who fell in love with a maiden of lowly station. A "concern" (*Bekymring*) was awakened in the king's soul, but at first he could not speak about it but had to keep "the sorrow" (*Sorgen*) in his own heart about whether it would make the girl happy.[42] The underlying problem is that true love requires equality and the king is concerned that equality with the maiden can never be achieved. In an analogy between God and the king, the text subsequently calls the concern "to bring about equality…God's concern."[43]

---

[38]   *SKS* 10, 109 / *CD*, 97.
[39]   *SKS* 12, 121 / *PC*, 113.
[40]   *SKS* 20, 300, NB4:29 / *KJN* 4, 301.
[41]   *SKS* 11, 67 / *WA*, 61.
[42]   *SKS* 4, 234 / *PF*, 26–7.
[43]   *SKS* 4, 235 / *PF*, 28.

Second, it should be mentioned that Kierkegaard from 1849 on regularly speaks about his "financial worries" (*oeconomiske Bekymringer*) in his journals.[44] This matter, however, is kept strictly apart from his published authorship.

VI.

To summarize, the term *Bekymring* is used in a multiplicity of ways in Kierkegaard's authorship, which is also indicated by the variety of translations to be found in the English edition of his works. In many cases the word is used in an everyday sense without conceptual significance, and especially in the case of worldly concern it is difficult, if not impossible, to determine when the colloquial use ends and where the idiosyncratic one starts. The distinguishing feature of Kierkegaard's conceptual use of the term, however, is his quest for a distinction of worldly concerns, on the one hand, and Christian concern, on the other. While this distinction is neither entirely selective—since we can also identify a variety of intermediary forms—nor covers all the uses of the term—since at least some of the uses cannot be categorized within this scheme—it is clearly a structural feature of Kierkegaard's conceptual use of the term. In this conception, worldly concern and Christian concern do not form two entirely separate spheres but have to be seen as interconnected. Even though Kierkegaard claims that overcoming of worldly concerns is the aim of Christian existence, he also points out that worldly concerns need to be taken very seriously, since they form an integral part of the human condition and that Christian concern can only be achieved in relation to worldly concerns; just as the upbuilding can only be reached by first finding and facing the terrifying.

See also Anxiety; Desire; Earnestness; Faith; Hope; Love; Passion/Pathos; Striving, Suffering.

---

[44]   See, for instance, *SKS* 22, 115, NB11:192 / *JP* 6, 6427; *SKS* 22, 232, NB12:143 / *JP* 6, 6489; *SKS* 22, 403, NB14:97 / *JP* 6, 6554; *SKS* 24, 500, NB25:84 / *JP* 6, 6795; *SKS* 25, 94, NB26:94 / *JP* 6, 6820; *SKS* 25, 227, NB28:16 / *JP* 6, 6840.

Category

Claudine Davidshofer

Category (*Kategori*, also *Kategorie, Categori, Categorie*—noun)

From the Greek κατηγορία, Danish derived *Kategori* and English derived *category*. The term has two main meanings in Danish: (1) the distinctly philosophical understanding of category, which originates with Aristotle, meaning the divisions in thought and/or being; and (2) the more common understanding of category as a group of people or things that are arranged together according to common features; definition or concept.[1]

Kierkegaard does not often use the term "category." It appears most explicitly in his journals and papers, under the entry "category," and in the *Concluding Unscientific Postscript*, published under the pseudonym Johannes Climacus. However, the task of properly understanding the main divisions in thought and being does occur in many of his texts. These texts include *Johannes Climacus, or De omnibus dubitandum est*, which Kierkegaard began writing under the pseudonym Johannes Climacus but did not complete, *The Concept of Anxiety*, published under the pseudonym *Vigilius Haufniensis*, and *The Sickness unto Death*, published under the pseudonym Anti-Climacus.

In the journals and papers, we find an entry titled "category," under which Kierkegaard lists only three basic questions. He asks, "What is the historical significance of the category? What is a category? Shall the category be derived from thought or from being?"[2] Providing some brief background information on these questions will help us to clarify Kierkegaard's own view of category.

Historically, the philosophical meaning of category originates with Aristotle. For Aristotle, generating a list of categories is the most fundamental task of metaphysics because the categories show the basic divisions in being as such. The categories answer the basic questions: What is this entity? What can be said of this entity? What entities are there in reality? Aristotle assumes a direct correspondence between thought and being. The categories he generates in thought correspond to the natural divisions in being.[3]

---

[1]   *Ordbog over det danske Sprog,* vols. 1–28, published by the Society for Danish Language and Literature, Copenhagen: Gyldendal 1918–56, vol. 10, columns 208–9.

[2]   *SKS* 27, 269, Papir 277:1 / *JP* 1, 240–1.

[3]   Aristotle, *Categories* in *Complete Works of Aristotle,* vols. 1–2, ed. by Jonathan Barnes, Princeton: Princeton University Press 1984, vol. 1, pp. 3–24.

Later philosophers continue the search for the categories, altering Aristotle's schema along the way. Immanuel Kant, for example, questions Aristotle's method for finding the categories, and questions whether Aristotle found all the essential categories. He also famously denies the correspondence between thought and being, claiming that the categories are merely divisions in our conceptual scheme, and not the natural divisions in being itself.[4] G.W.F. Hegel holds that if pure thought is left to its natural dialectic, it will produce its own self-enclosing system of categories, and the categories of thought do indeed correspond to the categories of being.[5] Empiricist philosophers, such as John Locke, think the category should not be generated first in thought, but directly from being itself, by abstracting from empirical being to the abstract divisions of being as such.[6]

Kierkegaard looks at the philosophical history of the category and raises quite different questions. In the *Postscript*, Johannes Climacus explains that, rather than worrying about the problematic relation between thought and being, we should first ask a more fundamental question about the significance of the category. We need to "pay scrupulous attention to what is understood by being."[7] What is meant by this term "being" to which the categories refer? What kind of "being" are we categorizing here? Traditionally, being is understood in the most abstract manner. Producing general divisions in being requires that we assume a general, abstract view of being as such. The categories apply to pure, eternal being. Climacus worries that this abstract view is not all that meaningful to the individual in his daily existence. The individual must willfully decide to assume this disinterested, eternal view of being, and he is "merely a fantast if he fancies himself to be *sub specie aeterni*" in everyday life.[8] This viewpoint is irrelevant to him once he returns to his more natural viewpoint, that of the existing individual who is immersed in temporal, existential being.[9]

Furthermore, worrying about the potentially problematic relation between thought and being is irrelevant for the existing individual because the coincidence between thought and being is never and can never be realized by him. Climacus explains, "existence separates thinking and being, holds them apart from each other."[10] The category loses the abstract, generalized form it has in thought, because it is particularized, concretized, and put into process by and according to the individual's own existential situation.[11]

In *Johannes Climacus, or De omnibus dubitandum est*, Climacus adds that the individual is necessarily "interested" in the categories. He is the "*inter-esse*," the

---

[4]   Immanuel Kant, *Critique of Pure Reason*, ed. and trans. by Paul Guyer and Allen W. Wood, New York: Cambridge University Press 1999, pp. 201–66.

[5]   G.W.F. Hegel, *Hegel's Science of Logic*, trans. by A.V. Miller, London: George Allen and Unwin 1989, pp. 25–79.

[6]   John Locke, *Essay Concerning Human Understanding*, ed. by Peter H. Nidditch, New York: Oxford University Press 1979, pp. 384–8.

[7]   *SKS* 7, 174 / *CUP1*, 189.

[8]   *SKS* 7, 176 / *CUP1*, 192.

[9]   *SKS* 7, 174–6, 299–307 / *CUP1*, 189–92, 328–35.

[10]   *SKS* 7, 303 / *CUP1*, 332.

[11]   *SKS* 7, 85–8 / *CUP1*, 84–8.

go-between, of the category.[12] He breaks up the relation between pure thought and pure being, but he realizes the relation between thought and concrete, existential being. The individual always views the category from his particular, existential circumstance. Thus, Climacus rethinks the structure of the category in a new way. Rather than seeing the category as a potentially problematic dichotomy between thought and being, he sees the category as having a "trichotomous" structure.[13] Thought and being are separated, and yet put back together, by the existing individual, according to his particular existential situation. The category is thought instantiated in existential being via the existing individual.[14]

In *The Concept of Anxiety*, Vigilius Haufniensis echoes Climacus' thoughts. He claims that abstract categories are not meaningful to the existing individual. He claims, "a person can hardly be inclined to apprehend essentially in the form of definition what must be understood differently, what he himself has understood differently."[15] The individual understands a category not in abstract terms, but always according to his own concrete existence. For example, if an individual intimately knows how "love" affects him personally in his daily life, then he need not waste time devising an abstract definition of "love." The abstract definition will add nothing to his already intimate and personal experience of love. Likewise, if an individual is passionately convinced that God exists, he need not cobble together some abstract definition of God, for this definition will add nothing to how he already experiences "God" in daily life. He says, "Whoever lives in daily and festive communion with the thought that there is a God could hardly wish to spoil this for himself, or see it spoiled, by piecing together a definition of what God is."[16] The category—whether it is being, modality, love, God, or anything else in between—is only meaningful according to the individual's own personal experience of it.[17]

Climacus and Haufniensis move the emphasis of the category away from the disinterested, abstract, and metaphysical, to the interested, concrete, and existential. They view the categories as existentially relevant and existentially dependent, for they necessarily involve the existing individual. The categories must be appropriated by the individual in his life. For abstract, metaphysical thought, the category tells us *what* something is. For Climacus, the category shows *how* something is for the individual.[18] It shows how the category affects him, how he lives within it, and how he gives it concrete meaning.

Climacus makes the existing individual essential to the categories. In *The Sickness unto Death*, Anti-Climacus agrees with Climacus, declaring outright that "the single individual" is the most important category.[19] For abstract thought, the single individual is a "disregarded and scorned category," precisely because the

12   *SKS* 15, 57 / *JC*, 170. Cf. also *SKS* 4, 25 / *R*, 149.
13   *SKS* 15, 56 / *JC*, 169.
14   *SKS* 15, 55–7 / *JC*, 169–71.
15   *SKS* 4, 447 / *CA*, 147.
16   Ibid.
17   Ibid.
18   *SKS* 7, 185–6 / *CUP1*, 202–3.
19   *SKS* 11, 231 / *SUD*, 120.

individual and the varying perspectives of individuals can never be reduced to abstract, general categories.[20] Climacus and Anti-Climacus, however, choose the category of the single individual as their most basic category. The existing individual is the category on which all other categories depend for their meaning, for they have meaning only when instantiated by the individual into his particular existential situation. Indeed, the category of the individual cannot be thought speculatively. The category of the individual must be lived and experienced by each individual according to his situation.

We end by briefly mentioning three general ways in which the individual can experience the categories (general principles or definitions) in his life: the aesthetic, the ethical, and the religious. The aesthetic individual is least "interested" in the categories. He remains uninterested in his own existence, viewing everything as accidental, fleeting, and merely amusing. The ethical individual is more invested in the categories, because he sees value in instantiating general principles—such as duty and love—in the particular situations of daily existence. Finally, the religious individual is most passionately invested in the categories, because he sees everything that he does in existence as being *before God*. For the religious individual, the categories have not only an earthly, temporal significance, but also an eternal and infinite significance.

See also Actuality; Appropriation; Concept; Concrete/Abstract; Existence/Existential; Experience; Objectivity/Subjectivity; Stages.

---

[20]   Ibid.

Catholicism

Christopher B. Barnett

Catholicism (*Katholicisme*—noun; *Katholik*—noun; *katholsk*—adjective)

From German *Katholizismus*, French *catholicisme*, corresponding to the English *Catholicism*. Kierkegaard largely adopts the spellings given above,[1] though, in recent usage, *katolicisme*, *katolik*, and *katolsk* are preferred. These terms are used of the Roman Catholic Church, with frequent reference to various aspects of Catholic life—for example, church doctrine, members, and rites—in contradistinction to those of other Christian bodies. Less commonly, it can signify the entire universal church, held together by what is considered right, orthodox doctrine.[2]

Kierkegaard does not often refer to "Catholicism" in his published writings, and most of these references are casual, lacking in sustained development and/or serious intention. For example, in *From the Papers of One Still Living*, Kierkegaard makes fun of Hans Christian Andersen, who, he suggests, is too superficial to understand the traditional motives for entering a monastery and so proffers a "new and very poetic motive for becoming a Catholic [*Catholik*]," namely, "fear otherwise of starving to death."[3] Three years later, Kierkegaard revisited Catholicism in *The Concept of Irony*. In fact, the Catholic motif turns up more in *The Concept of Irony* than in any other published work, albeit in illustrative—rather than substantive—fashion. In explaining that part of the "world process" involves negating and replacing the "given actuality" of a particular historical epoch, Kierkegaard cites the Protestant Reformation as a case in point: "Catholicism was the given actuality for the generation living at the time of the Reformation, and yet it was also the actuality that no longer had validity as such."[4] Also in *The Concept of Irony*, Kierkegaard mentions a popular tale by Johann Peter Hebel about an "argument between a Catholic and a Protestant that ended with their convincing each other, so that the Catholic turned Protestant and the Protestant turned Catholic."[5] Here again, though, this discussion does not concern Catholicism (or Protestantism) *per se*; rather, it puts these terms

---

[1] Where, on occasion, Kierkegaard uses an alternative spelling, the appropriate word will be given in brackets.

[2] *Ordbog over det danske Sprog*, vols. 1–28, published by the Society for Danish Language and Literature, Copenhagen: Gyldendal 1918–56, vol. 10, column 213. It is worth adding that, though not his typical usage, Kierkegaard does utilize the term, "catholicity" (*Catholicitæt*), in the sense of "universality." See *SKS* 1, 21 / *EPW*, 65.

[3] *SKS* 1, 55–6 / *EPW*, 101.

[4] *SKS* 1, 297–8 / *CI*, 260.

[5] *SKS* 1, 116–17 / *CI*, 56.

in service to another purpose—in this case, Kierkegaard's attempt to flesh out the outcome of irony in Plato's *Protagoras*.

This pattern of informal use is effectively repeated in a variety of early published writings, from *Either/Or*[6] to *Prefaces*[7] to *Stages on Life's Way*.[8] An arguable exception to this rule is *The Concept of Anxiety*, where Kierkegaard's pseudonym, Vigilius Haufniensis, mentions Catholicism on a few occasions and, in doing so, hints at a deeper engagement with the topic, particularly concerning dogmatic questions. Indeed, Haufniensis expresses misgivings about the veracity of Catholic teaching on original sin—even citing Thomas Aquinas in the process—but by no means takes on the issue of Catholicism writ large.[9] He also makes critical insinuations about the Catholicism's understanding of the Mass[10] and its ostensible promotion of works-righteousness.[11] But the end result here is no different: serious reflection is postponed in favor of fleeting allusion.

Indeed, for that reason, one of the last references to Catholicism in Kierkegaard's published authorship might have surprised his readers. After insisting that Protestantism has value only as a "correction," with the codicil that it becomes "a falsehood, a dishonesty…as soon as it is taken to be the principle of Christianity,"[12] he puts in the following elucidatory note: "Therefore, to join the Catholic Church would be a rashness of which I shall not be guilty, but which one perhaps will expect since in these times it seems to be utterly forgotten what Christianity is, and even the people who know Christianity best are still only ordinary seamen."[13] This comment was issued in the February 1855 issue of *Fædrelandet*. At that time, of course, Kierkegaard's censure of Protestantism would have shocked no one: his so-called "attack upon Christendom" had been going on for a year. But what might have seemed extraordinary—despite his dismissal of the idea—was Kierkegaard's apparent entertainment of the possibility of joining the Catholic Church. After all, Catholicism was not exactly a "live option" in nineteenth-century Denmark,[14] and

---

6   *SKS* 2, 55 / *EO1*, 47; *SKS* 3, 51 / *EO2*, 44.

7   *SKS* 4, 474 / *P*, 10.

8   *SKS* 6, 418 / *SLW*, 454. See also *SKS* 14, 70 / *COR*, 31.

9   *SKS* 4, 332ff. / *CA*, 25ff. See also *SKS* 18, 33, EE:86 / *KJN* 2, 28.

10   *SKS* 4, 406 / *CA*, 104.

11   *SKS* 4, 441 / *CA*, 139.

12   *SKS* 14, 173 / *M*, 41.

13   Ibid. See also *SKS* 13, 152 / *M*, 110, Kierkegaard's final (albeit minor) reference to Catholicism in his published *corpus*.

14   After the Protestant Reformation—with which the Danish crown sided—Catholicism was formally suppressed in Denmark until the liberal reforms of 1849. Thus Kierkegaard, who died in November 1855, only had about a five-year "window" in which he *could* have joined the Catholic Church. Further, there were "very few" Catholics in Denmark at that time. Kierkegaard himself alludes to the scarcity of Danish Catholics, when, in an 1853 journal entry, he notes that Danish Protestantism suffers from not having "the counterweight of Catholicism in the same country" (*Pap.* X–6 B 233 / *JP* 1, 825). In fact, there had not been a Catholic bishop in Copenhagen since 1536, and a new one would not be appointed until 1892. See James MacCaffrey, *History of the Catholic Church in the Nineteenth Century (1798–1908)*, vols. 1–2, 2nd ed., Dublin: M.H. Gill and Son, Ltd. 1910, vol. 1, pp. 411ff.

conversion hardly followed from Kierkegaard's dissatisfaction with the Danish State Church. Moreover, as has been seen, Kierkegaard's published writings do not betray a profound interest in Catholicism. Thus one might very well have wondered: why even raise the question?

A fuller view of Kierkegaard's *oeuvre*, however, would have answered this problem. Kierkegaard's journals and papers—first released to the public in 1869, some fourteen years after his death—reveal significant engagement with Catholicism. That is not to say, of course, that these "private" reflections on Catholicism yield a clear-cut conclusion. Rather, they demonstrate Kierkegaard's dialectical approach to the issue, indicating that he saw much good,[15] and some ill, in the Catholic approach to Christianity. Indeed, in the end, he appears to have adopted a posture of neutrality opposite Catholicism.

Kierkegaard's most positive appraisal of Catholicism centered on the issue of the imitation of Christ. His analysis is expressed bluntly in the following 1851 journal entry:

> There is more significance in Catholicism simply because "imitation" has not been relinquished completely.
>
> "Imitation" (properly understood, and therefore not leading to self-torturing or to hypocrisy and works-righteousness, etc.) really provides the guarantee that Christianity does not become poetry, mythology, and abstract idea—which it has almost become in Protestantism.
>
> "Imitation" places "the single individual," every one, in relationship to the ideal.[16]

An 1853 passage returns to this point: "[T]here is always present in Catholicism this element of good—namely, that imitation of Christ is demanded, imitation with all that this means remains firm."[17] To be sure, if anything, this entry has a more optimistic tone, for it says that *imitatio* is "always present" in Catholicism, while its 1851 predecessor merely states that it "has not been relinquished completely."

Kierkegaard's strong appreciation for the Catholic stress on imitation spilled over into a handful of related issues. In one 1854 note, he acknowledges that, as regards the veneration of the saints, "Catholicism has in a certain sense been right," for the saints represent a Christlike willingness "to be sacrificed for others."[18] Another 1854 entry argues that, unaided "by having Catholicism at its side, which was the case in Germany and other countries," the Danish church has made "apparent what nonsense, what dishonesty, and what corruption Protestantism is—if it is supposed

---

15   That is why some early commentators wondered if Kierkegaard would have become Catholic, had he only lived longer. See, for example, Harald Høffding, *Søren Kierkegaard som Filosof*, Copenhagen: Philipsens 1892, p. 158; Erich Przywara, *Das Geheimnis Kierkegaards*, Munich: Verlag von R. Oldenbourg 1929, p. 77, p. 102. Also compare with Heinrich Roos, S.J., *Søren Kierkegaard og Katolicismen*, Copenhagen: Munksgaards Forlag 1952 (*Søren Kierkegaard Selskabets Populære Skrifter*, vol. 3), pp. 7ff.

16   *SKS* 24, 384–5, NB24:105 / *JP* 2, 1904.

17   *SKS* 25, 251–2, NB28:48 / *JP* 2, 1923. For other similar comments, see *SKS* 27, 96, Papir 55:2 / *JP* 1, 273; *SKS* 25, 328–9, NB29:57 / *JP* 3, 3619; *SKS* 26, 287, NB33:48 / *JP* 4, 4814.

18   *SKS* 26, 24, NB31:30 / *JP* 1, 83.

to be religion, to be Christianity, rather than a necessary corrective at a given time."[19] Thus Kierkegaard recommends a patently Catholic response: "Back to the monastery, from which Luther broke away, is the first cause for Christianity to take up."[20] Though appearing quite late in Kierkegaard's authorship, these passages are hardly discontinuous with a much earlier 1837 journal entry, in which Kierkegaard expresses admiration for the Catholic "courage" to declare the Protestant Reformers "heretics."[21] He even adds that, inasmuch as the Protestants did not have the "courage to carry to their conclusion the premises which they have historically given themselves," the "*possibility* of the parties that have separated from the mother church returning to the same"[22] remains open.

In contrast to these positive views on Catholicism stand a number of negative ones, which tend to cluster around the problem of outward piety. An 1854 passage worries that Catholicism, no less than Protestantism, has misunderstood the role of Christianity in the world: the latter transposes "Christianity into hidden inwardness" and so sidesteps "the Christian collisions," even as the former makes "it into a kingdom of this world…whereby the Christian collisions vanish, and direct recognizability, which is pleasing to men, becomes the rule…."[23] To be directly recognizable, for Kierkegaard, is to be noticed—and *commended*—as a devout Christian. Such an emphasis on pious " 'works' suggests Catholicism," and, in this connection, Kierkegaard maintains that "everything Catholicism has thought up about the meritoriousness of works of course has to be rejected completely."[24] Related to this problem is the Catholic sacrament of Holy Orders, which, according to Kierkegaard, falsely introduces a "qualitative distinction"[25] between the clergy and lay persons, particularly with regard to marriage. Indeed, the "error in Catholicism is not that the priest is unmarried," but that, out of a "concession of weakness in the direction of numbers,"[26] the Catholic Church fails to apply this teaching across the board. "[A] Christian ought to be unmarried,"[27] notes Kierkegaard.

As mentioned above, Kierkegaard's dialectical back-and-forth on Catholicism ultimately characterizes his conception as neutral. That is to say, he makes no definitive declaration about it. Several other journal passages support this conclusion, albeit in different ways. An 1852 entry criticizes Catholicism for using mediatory figures such as the Virgin Mary as a means of putting " 'imitation' at a distance," though it immediately adds that the "hypocrisy of Protestantism is actually heightened and refined hypocrisy."[28] This statement is "neutral" in the sense that, although critical,

---

[19]   *SKS* 25, 403–5, NB30:26 / *JP* 3, 2763. See also footnote 14 above.
[20]   Ibid.
[21]   *SKS* 17, 214, DD:4 / *KJN* 1, 206.
[22]   Ibid.
[23]   *SKS* 26, 250, NB33:7 / *JP* 1, 614. See also *SKS* 24, 492, NB25:73 / *JP* 2, 1912.
[24]   *SKS* 27, 570–1, Papir 458 / *JP* 3, 2543.
[25]   *SKS* 26, 320–1, NB34:9 / *JP* 3, 2622. See also *SKS* 26, 138, NB32:30 / *JP* 3, 3182.
[26]   *SKS* 26, 320–1, NB34:9 / *JP* 3, 2622.
[27]   Ibid.
[28]   *SKS* 24, 508–9, NB25:92 / *JP* 2, 1913.

it does not "take sides."[29] Elsewhere, however, Kierkegaard's neutrality is of a more reportorial nature—a tendency that is especially common in the notes dating from his student days. An 1837 entry simply contrasts the role of the individual in Catholicism and in post-Reformation thinkers such as Johann Georg Hamann,[30] while one from 1838 observes that both Pietism ("separatism, conventicles, etc.") and Catholicism are complements to the "*Protestant* view of life," which underdevelops the "shared carrying of life's burdens in a social life."[31]

Indeed, there is also a sense in which Kierkegaard's neutrality might be seen as *ecumenical*. In an 1834 text, Kierkegaard wonders if the "Catholic-Protestant issue" could be brought "to a better understanding," if there were more dialogue on the question of how "man receives divine grace."[32] But the most salient example in this connection stems from 1853–54:

> Are not Catholicism and Protestantism actually related to one another as a building which cannot stand is related to buttresses which cannot stand alone, but the entire structure is able to stand, even very stable and secure, when the building and the buttresses together give it stability (this may seem a strange analogy, but this is the way it actually is in the physical world). In other words, is not Protestantism (or the Lutheran principle) really a corrective, and has not a great confusion been brought about by making this normative in Protestantism?[33]

Here Kierkegaard suggests that Catholicism and Protestantism should be seen as mutually supportive, rather than as mutually opposed. Each needs the other to stand— or, at least, to stand solidly. Without Protestantism, Catholicism risks degenerating into "surface sanctity," and, without Catholicism, Protestantism risks degenerating into "spiritless secularism."[34]

Of course, this is by no means a robust ecumenical theory. But it brings to mind a potential development of Kierkegaard's neutrality on the issue of Catholicism. Kierkegaard's untimely death, however, ensured that his views on the matter would remain distinguished by his famous dialectic, rather than by any single, unified conception.

See also Christ; Christendom; Church; Corrective; Courage; Dialectic; Grace; Holy Spirit; Imitation; Individual; Inwardness/Inward Deepening; Marriage; Monasticism; Pastorate; Protestantism/Reformation; Sacrifice; Sin.

---

[29] See also *SKS* 23, 398–9, NB20:14 / *JP* 3, 3153; *SKS* 26, 138, NB32:30 / *JP* 3, 3182; *SKS* 25, 399–401, NB30:22 / *JP* 3, 2550.
[30] *SKS* 17, 214, DD:3 / *KJN* 1, 206.
[31] *SKS* 17, 254, DD:108 / *KJN* 1, 245. See also *SKS* 17, 46, AA:28 / *KJN* 1, 39–40; *SKS* 17, 259–60, DD:132 / *KJN* 1, 250.
[32] *SKS* 27, 98, Papir 59 / *JP* 2, 1463.
[33] *SKS* 27, 563, Papir 455 / *JP* 3, 3617.
[34] Ibid.

Cause/Effect

Shannon M. Nason

Cause (*Aarsag*—noun); **Effect** (*Virkning*—noun)

Aarsag comes from the Old Danish *Orsagh* and the later *Orsaghe*. *Virkning* is similar to the German *Wirkung*. Lexically, *Aarsag* carries philosophical meaning. A cause produces some necessary effect or consequence. A cause may also refer to an explanation or reason for something. A cause is not always the temporal origin of something or some event (for example, the turning of the key causing the car to start), or the source of some motion, but may also refer to the metaphysical origin or reason for something, like an ultimate or sufficient reason for why there is anything at all, and also why some things are not.[1] The lexical meaning of *Virkning* is diverse. It ranges from personal and social actions and the impact of those actions to notions involving effects of causes in nature.[2]

Kierkegaard discusses cause and effect and associated concepts (like final causation) very briefly in a few places in his authorship, primarily within the context of his more developed account of motion (*Bevægelse*) and change (*Forandring*). His most sustained discussion of cause and effect is found in the "Interlude" of *Philosophical Fragments*, attributed to the pseudonym Johannes Climacus and published in 1844. In addition, Kierkegaard's other Climacean text, *Concluding Unscientific Postscript to Philosophical Fragments*, argues that movement and change *must* be aimed at a goal (*Maal*), without which there would be no motion.[3] Climacus identifies this goal as both the end and the criterion or measure of motion, and he associates this with the Aristotelian notion of final causation.[4] *The Concept of Anxiety* and *The Sickness unto Death* invoke similar notions of teleology.

Kierkegaard's account of cause and effect is fragmentary, and thus not systematic. However, in *Philosophical Fragments*, Johannes Climacus does offer readers a glimpse into his *metaphysical* and *epistemological* commitments involving cause and effect. First, Climacus' metaphysical commitments concerning cause and effect revolve around questions central both to cosmology and human action. In particular, without offering a cosmological argument *per se*, but appearing to issue a set of claims within the general vicinity of cosmological proofs, Climacus argues that not only is

---

[1]   *Ordbog over det danske Sprog*, vols. 1–28, published by the Society for Danish Language and Literature, Copenhagen: Gyldendal 1918–56, vol. 1, columns 72–3.
[2]   Ibid., vol. 27, columns 194–6.
[3]   *SKS* 7, 284 / *CUP1*, 312.
[4]   Ibid.

the sequence of efficient causes in the world contingent, their contingency points to, in all cases, an ultimate (divine) free cause, and, in some cases, a relative (human) free cause.[5] In this context, he argues that the relationship between free causation and the efficient causal series of the world amounts to only an apparent tension, concluding that free causality explains the existence of the causal series. Second, Climacus is interested in how knowledge of efficient causes is possible. He argues that human reason (particularly inductive reason) is met with obstacles when inferring a cause from an experienced effect. For him, beliefs about a particular cause on the basis of our experience of, or our having learned (for example, through historical testimony) about, some effect are uncertain. Consequently, Climacus argues that beliefs about the cause of an effect are not arrived at inferentially, but by a decision, or, what he is sometimes prone to call a "leap."[6] The following discussion develops the metaphysical commitments Kierkegaard and his pseudonyms have concerning cause and effect; first, by clarifying Climacus' understanding of the relationship between free causation and causal necessity in *Philosophical Fragments*; and second, by addressing the notion of final causation in the *Concluding Unscientific Postscript*, *The Concept of Anxiety*, and *The Sickness unto Death*.

Climacus stresses the free activity of divine and human causation. In the case of divine causation, he argues that the world is the result of an ultimate and free cause. In addition, throughout both his signed and pseudonymous writings, Kierkegaard appears to hold the view that God, as the ultimate cause, is also final cause, both of the natural world as well as human beings.[7] Furthermore, free human actions occur within and yet are not the same sort of events that make up the causal sequence of nature and history. In this context, Climacus shows that the difference between changes in nature and the changes that result from free human action is found in the notion of "redoubling" (*Fordobling*), which he defines as a "possibility of coming into existence within its own coming into existence."[8] The concept of redoubling emphasizes the unique freedom that human beings enjoy in self-consciously realizing possibilities. Thus, for Climacus (and Kierkegaard), the causal character of human action is distinct from the network of efficient causes in nature.

However, Climacus additionally argues, "*All* coming into existence occurs *in freedom*, not by way of necessity. Nothing coming into existence comes into existence by way of a ground, but everything by way of a cause. Every cause *ends*

---

[5]   *SKS* 4, 275 / *PF*, 75–6.

[6]   *SKS* 4, 282–3 / *PF*, 83–4. In the same year as the publication of *Philosophical Fragments*, Kierkegaard wrote in his journal that "by analogy and induction the conclusion can only be reached by a leap" (*SKS* 18, 225, JJ:266 / *KJN* 2, 206). Kierkegaard's concept of the leap and its implications for epistemological issues surrounding inductive knowledge will not be discussed here. However, it is important to note that in Kierkegaard's thought, the leap does occupy a central place in his understanding of belief, knowledge, and discursive reason.

[7]   It may seem surprising that Kierkegaard would argue that even nature strives toward God as its goal, especially due to his persistent emphasis on the unique subjectivity inherent in the God-relationship. However, as I will explain shortly, for Kierkegaard even the natural world (which we could call, for the sake of contrast, objectivity) strives in its own way for divine perfection.

[8]   *SKS* 4, 276 / *PF*, 76.

in a freely acting cause."[9] The central proposition Climacus issues here is that all causes of change are free in some way. At first glance, it is difficult to process the claim that *all* change is freely caused, considering that changes in nature (the coming into existence of plants and animals, geological movements, dramatic shifts in weather systems, etc.) are caught up in a network of efficient causes governed by laws of nature.

To answer the question as to how all change is freely caused, Climacus cannot deny that *some* changes are necessary. To do so would amount to a flat-out denial of the necessary causal connection between events within nature. Thus, to motivate a coherent theory of free causality, Climacus will need to show that freedom is in some way compatible with *causal* necessity, but incompatible with *absolute* or *logical* necessity. With some reconstruction of his fragmentary discussion, we see that Climacus correctly makes this move. Climacus writes:

> Every cause ends in a freely acting cause. The *intervening causes are misleading* in that *the coming into existence appears to be necessary*; the truth about them is that they, as having themselves come into existence, definitively point to a freely acting cause. As soon as coming into existence is definitively reflected upon, *even an inference from natural law is not evidence of the necessity of any coming into existence.* So also with manifestations of freedom, as soon as one refuses to be deceived by its manifestations but reflects on its coming into existence.[10]

Climacus here distinguishes between the first cause and the subsequent sequence of intermediate causes that are the effect of that first cause. He states that these intervening causes are misleading because they make it appear that the series of causes *itself* as well as each particular cause is necessary. Presumably, the reason the intervening causes present this ambiguity is because *they are in fact necessary*. Whatever the primary cause is of the cue stick striking the billiard ball, there is no mistaking the fact that hit (under regular conditions) at a certain velocity, the ball *will* move at a determinate speed, and that it will continue along its trajectory until it is obstructed.

There is no use multiplying examples. The point is that the intermediate causes (even if they result from a free act) *will* produce their appropriate effects. This seems to be why, then, they might mislead some into thinking that their having come into existence was determined. However, Climacus clearly states that neither an inference from laws of nature nor from the necessity of an efficient cause can establish that the coming into existence of the world itself or of some particular part of it is necessary. On the one hand, Climacus is correct to argue that just because particular causes in nature are necessary, it does not follow that the entire assemblage of causes is

---

[9]   *SKS* 4, 275 / *PF*, 75. Emphasis mine. Limited space will not allow me to discuss the full significance of this passage. By asserting that changes of coming into existence are not necessary and that they do not come about by way of a ground, Climacus is claiming that *all change is contingent and thus not absolutely necessary.* I address this passage in detail in my "Contingency, Necessity, and Causation in Kierkegaard's Theory of Change," *British Journal for the History of Philosophy*, vol. 20, no. 1, 2012, pp. 141–62.

[10]   *SKS* 4, 275 / *PF*, 75. Emphasis mine.

necessary. However, on the other hand, it seems incorrect to say that an inference from laws of nature cannot establish the conclusion that some particular event is determined to happen (as the billiard ball example shows).

To understand his position, it is crucial to see that Climacus is contrasting two kinds of necessity: *causal* necessity and *absolute* necessity. Briefly, that which is causally necessary is the determined consequence of a cause while the absolutely necessary is that the denial of which is impossible. The point is that causal necessity and absolute necessity are not correlative: what is causally necessary is not absolutely necessary and vice versa. We might wonder why anyone would think they were correlative, and why Climacus even brings up the point. One reason might be that Kierkegaard appears to think that Hegelian metaphysics endorses absolute necessitarianism, that all that exists and all that has come into existence (that is, every effect of a cause) is absolutely necessary because everything flows from the necessity of the divine nature.[11] Additionally, it would be poor reasoning indeed to believe that the coming into existence of the world or some part of it cannot have failed to happen (without contradiction) on the basis of what is causally necessary. Climacus tells us why. He argues that what is causally necessary (some effect of a cause) has come into existence, is the result of a change, while the absolutely necessary *simply* exists.

Two passages from *Philosophical Fragments* are helpful to consider in this context: first, "Nothing whatever exists [*er til*] because it is necessary, but the necessary exists because it is necessary or because the necessary is."[12] Secondly,

> Coming into existence is a change, but since the necessary is always related to itself and is related to itself in the same way, it cannot be changed at all. All coming into existence is a suffering [*Liden*], and the necessary cannot suffer the suffering of actuality—namely, that the possible...turns out to be nothing the moment it becomes actual, for possibility is annihilated by actuality. Precisely by coming into existence, everything that comes into existence demonstrates that it is not necessary, for the only thing that cannot come into existence is the necessary, because the necessary *is*.[13]

The contrasting features of causal necessity and logical necessity are made quite explicit in these passages. The first passage stresses the contingency of changes that are causally necessary. Since some effect of a cause is a change, is an event whereby something comes into existence, it is contingent. Climacus seems to understand the contingency of efficient causes in two ways: (1) causal events *depend* for their occurrences on prior causes. In other words, unlike the "self-relatedness" of what Climacus calls "the necessary," effects are dependently related to their causes. (2) Unlike the necessary, effects of causes are able not to exist: they come into existence from a state of non-existence and they can go out of existence. On the other hand, "the necessary" does not exist because it has come into existence, but because it cannot have failed to exist. To invoke Climacus' modal concepts of

---

[11]   For a detailed discussion of Kierkegaard's critique of Hegelian necessitarianism, see my "Contingency, Necessity, and Causation in Kierkegaard's Theory of Change."
[12]   *SKS* 4, 274 / *PF*, 75.
[13]   *SKS* 4, 274 / *PF*, 74.

possibility, actuality, and necessity, this means that the absolutely necessary does not undergo a change from possibility to actuality, as if what is necessary in this sense (for example, that a triangle is a three-sided figure) once was possibly so and now is actually so. On the contrary, Climacus suggests that something is absolutely necessary if and only if it cannot possibly fail to be actual, cannot not exist.[14]

If the series of efficient causes in the world is causally and, thus, not absolutely necessary, then it is contingent, in the double sense of dependently relating to a prior cause or causes and being able to not exist. It is this metaphysical commitment concerning the contingency of efficient causes that renders more palatable Climacus' additional claim that all change points back to a free cause. Even though not every efficient cause is the *immediate* result of some free act, Climacus argues that free causation is the only viably probable explanation for the actual series of the world. Because everything that comes into existence is contingent, then nothing can come into existence by necessity—and if not by necessity, then through some free act. While Climacus does not offer a strict cosmological-style argument (in the tradition of Aquinas and Leibniz) to the effect that the world came into existence by means of an ultimately free cause, it is clear that his conclusion that all change points back to a free cause is motivated by his denial that the existence of the world is absolutely necessary. Climacus' argument may be reconstructed as follows:

1. The world is contingent.
2. If the world is contingent, then the world came into existence.
3. Anything that comes into existence comes into existence either by necessity or through a free causal act.
4. What is contingent could not have come about by necessity.
∴ 5. The world did not come into existence by necessity.
∴ 6. The world came into existence through a free causal act.

As reconstructed, Climacus' argument is valid. However, premise 3 ignores another possibility, namely, that the coming into existence of the world may be an accident, a result of blind chance, and thus without any explanation at all; it is just a brute fact. Climacus does not explicitly consider this option in *Philosophical Fragments*. However, if his metaphysical commitments concerning the contingency of efficient causes and the laws of nature that govern changes in the world are correct, then what follows from Climacus' reasoning is that the individual who harbors the brute fact view of the world strangely ends up committed to absolute necessitarianism.

This is due in large part to the overhasty arbitrariness of (a) correctly believing that everything that occurs in the world is the result of a cause and thus that everything that occurs has a reason for its occurring other than itself (that is, that everything that has come into existence in the world is contingent); but (b) that this is not true of the causal series of the world itself. As far as Climacus' argument for free causality goes, to believe (b) is to commit to absolute necessitarianism, because

---

[14]   Climacus does not provide a list, but it is probably safe to include rules of logic (like modus tollens), geometrical and mathematical truths, and, perhaps, the existence of God as absolutely necessary.

(b) denies that the world is contingent. However, as was shown above, if the world is absolutely necessary, then everything in the world is absolutely necessary, and thus every change, every event, every cause, could not have failed to happen. So, based on Climacus' reasoning, the brute fact view of the world is doubly self-defeating. First, it is irrational, since (a) and (b) cannot be believed at the same time without contradiction. Second, the view oddly results in absolute necessitarianism, since it denies that the world is contingent.

While reference to efficient causation is hardly found outside the "Interlude" of *Philosophical Fragments*, Kierkegaard invokes the notion of final causation and teleology in his journals, as well as in other pseudonymous writings. While the "Interlude" argues that the coming into existence of the world could not have occurred by necessity and thus must be the result of an ultimate free cause, other works suggest that coming into existence is not just efficiently caused but aims and strives toward an ultimate goal or purpose.

Kierkegaard's account of the religious stage of existence, whereby the self exists before God, is particularly relevant here. For example, in *The Sickness unto Death*, Kierkegaard's pseudonym argues that human selves are oriented toward God who is both the goal of human existence and the criterion by which human existence is measured. Anti-Climacus says:

> And what infinite reality [*Realitet*] the self gains by being conscious of existing before God, by becoming a human self whose criterion is God....The criterion for the self is always: that directly before which it is a self, but this in turn is the definition of "criterion." Just as only entities of the same kind can be added, so everything is qualitatively that by which it is measured, and that which is its qualitative criterion [*Maalestok*] is ethically its goal [*Maal*].[15]

In the religious context of Kierkegaard's authorship, the religious self is not only conscious of the divine and eternal standard by which he or she is measured as a self, but he or she also understands that the self is teleologically related to the eternal perfection. In this way, God is the goal for both the existence of the self and the self's ethical projects.

An intriguingly different case of final causation and teleology can be found in Vigilius Haufniensis' *The Concept of Anxiety*. There Haufniensis refers to Romans 8:19 and argues that non-human creation longs, in its imperfect state, and in the form of "objective anxiety," for a more perfect state; that is, nature longs for and desires completeness and wholeness, for unified existence torn asunder by the effect that human sin, through Adam, has had on the world.[16] Consequently, not only is the world the effect of a cause, it also longs for a cause, by desiring a state of goodness intended for it.

Haufniensis' allusion to the teleology of nature is brief, but his discussion benefits from several unstated metaphysical assumptions about perfection and existence. First, he appears to believe in a gradation of goodness or perfection, that some things are more or less perfect than others. He also seems to understand this gradation in

---

[15]   *SKS* 11, 193–4 / *SUD*, 79.
[16]   *SKS* 4, 361–5 / *CA*, 56–60.

causal terms: that is, the relationship between a cause and its effect is that between what is more perfect and what is less perfect. Further, his position is rounded out by the classical notion that existence is good, and that what has more being than another is more perfect. These assumptions result in the position that the cause is not only more perfect but also has more being than its effect.

The argument, then, that the world longs for perfection as its cause rests on the following more foundational reasoning:

1. If X is prior to Y, then X is more perfect than Y.
2. The cause of the world is prior to the world.
3. Therefore, the cause of the world is more perfect than the world.

The conclusion of this argument does not yet justify Haufniensis' claim that all things long for perfection. But it gets us closer to understanding his position. Premise 1 employs a notion of priority that may ring strange to the modern philosophical ear. X is prior to Y, not temporally, but formally, or metaphysically. Indeed, premise 1 wouldn't make much sense if the priority in question were temporal priority, since it is not clear how something's being prior to another thing in time would make it more perfect, much less more real. The notion here is that the cause is greater in being (and thus goodness) than its effect, and, further, that the continued existence of the effect is possible only so long as it strives to be one and unified like its ultimate cause. The continuity of the world, then, is doubly reinforced: first, by its striving to be unified, to exist, and, second, by a cause toward which nature aims. It is apparent, then, that what Kierkegaard understands by cause and effect is not exhausted in modern notions of efficient causation. On the one hand, Kierkegaard accommodates efficient causation, but, on the other hand, he invokes final causation in several areas in his authorship.

See also Contingency/Possibility; Freedom; Leap; Movement; Nature; Necessity.

Certainty

Sara Carvalhais de Oliveira

Certainty (*Vished*—noun; *vis*—adjective)

The Danish word *Vished* ("certainty") derives from the Old Danish *vishiet, weshedh*, and from the Middle Low German *wisheit*, and has the meaning of security, assurance. In Danish the word for "certainty" has maintained this original sense, although within the context of a wider pattern of usage. The Danish term for "certainty" can be used as a synonym for truth, correctness; and it can designate the fact that something is certain or true. Furthermore, the noun "certainty" can be employed to identify the situation or attitude of someone who steadfastly and incontrovertibly holds something to be true, someone who has a conviction that something is certain. In Danish "certainty" can also be used to signify that which serves as proof, documentation, or guarantee.[1]

The term appears most frequently in the *Concluding Unscientific Postscript*, followed by *Practice in Christianity, Christian Discourses, Stages on Life's Way*, and *Philosophical Fragments, or a Fragment of Philosophy*. Of special importance are original discussions around this theme that are found in the *Concluding Unscientific Postscript* and *The Concept of Anxiety*, where "certainty" as "certitude" is essentially linked to the constitution of inwardness and earnestness in the individual. The discourse "At a Graveside," in *Three Discourses on Imagined Occasions*, is also relevant since it exemplifies the existential consistency of a relation of certainty or lack of certainty of the individual who faces the possibility of death.

I. Certitude as Inwardness and as Earnestness

A. Certainty as Inwardness

In the section "Freedom lost pneumatically," in *The Concept of Anxiety*,[2] Haufniensis highlights the fundamental association between "certainty" as "certitude" and the phenomenon of *inwardness*. Firstly, in this section the occurrence of the term "certitude" is often textually accompanied by the determination of inwardness,[3] and this is of great importance for the meaning of "certitude" discussed in this work.

---

[1]   *Ordbog over det danske Sprog*, vols. 1–28, published by the Society for Danish Language and Literature, Copenhagen: Gyldendal 1918–56, vol. 27, columns 269–71.
[2]   *SKS* 4, 438–53 / *CA*, 137–54.
[3]   *SKS* 4, 439, 441, 446, 450 / *CA*, 138, 141, 146, 151.

What is more, in this text what seems to be at stake is that the phenomenon of certainty and the phenomenon of inwardness can be existentially *identified* with each other as *the same* phenomenon, or at least as *different aspects* or shades of meaning of the same life-phenomenon. In this sense, certainty and inwardness are *essentially contemporary* with each other; they cannot be detached or isolated, not even conceptually, without distortion of the profound significance of *certainty*. Secondly, certitude, along with inwardness, constitutes the *subjectivity* of the individual, not in an *"entirely abstract sense"* but, on the contrary, in a completely *concrete* sense.[4] Certainty resides in the interior of one's self. Furthermore, subjective certainty or certitude, as inwardness, is not something immediate, which is already achieved from the beginning, like a kind of personal heritage. Rather, it has to be *posited*, it requires an effort, and it claims to be *produced, generated*.

B. Certitude as Earnestness

"Inwardness, certitude, is earnestness," Haufniensis declares in *The Concept of Anxiety*.[5] This formula seems to become clearer in the discourse "At a Graveside," at least as far the connection between certainty and earnestness is concerned: "The earnest person is the one who through uncertainty is brought up to earnestness by virtue of certainty."[6] From a purely immanent perspective, *there is only one certainty* in this life, which corresponds to the anticipation of its end: death. Nevertheless, at the same time, the certainty of death is not accompanied by the certainty of its meaning; its "content" is and always remains to be fulfilled, since death "is the only thing one cannot with any certainty learn anything about."[7] The certainty of death is not defined by the fact of knowing the "matter" of death. Rather, the relation of the individual to his own death and to the meaning of his life seen as a totality is made certain by his relation to himself from within the comprehension which earnestness inaugurates. Consequently, it is not a question of knowledge that is at stake in the phenomenon of certainty, but rather a question of making a decision within the boundaries of a limited perspective like ours.

II. Certainty versus Proof

In *The Concept of Anxiety*, the pseudonym Haufniensis establishes a distinction between the sphere of intellectual or objective proofs and the sphere of certainty proper. Certainty is in no way made viable by the discovery of a so-called proof, for a "proof" has no traction at all in the domain of subjectivity, of the personality, of the real understanding of one's genuine self, and is no guarantee of the factual connection of one's self with the intimate root of that self. A proof, conceived "intellectually," leaves certainty—certainty as subjectivity, the only possible kind of certainty for an individual human being—untouched. From another point of view, it

---

4   *SKS* 4, 439, 441–2 / *CA*, 138, 141.
5   *SKS* 4, 450 / *CA*, 151. See also *SKS* 4, 446 / *CA*, 146.
6   *SKS* 5, 462 / *TD*, 94.
7   *SKS* 18, 201, JJ:189 / *KJN* 2, 185.

can be said that there is no "objective proof" as a source of existential significance for the life of the individual; it is not produced through and at the end of a process of "objective" reasoning since certainty is not an objective phenomenon. In this sense, the phenomenon of certainty is absolutely indifferent to, and in fact does without, so-called "objective" proofs. This means that there is no "objective certainty." Certainty is, by definition, subjective and personally established. The increase of the magnitude and, partly, the abstract clarity of truth are accompanied by a constant decrease in certainty.[8]

Furthermore, the effort applied in displaying a demonstration is a sign of lack of certainty. This effort is contemporary with a certain absence of certainty; in this process certainty diminishes,[9] as well as inwardness.[10] Interior certainty is due to someone's personal conviction, not about any thesis as such, even if it seems to be thoroughly demonstrated. That is, certainty for the individual human being is essentially lived certainty; it is revealed in actual life-situations as practical proof. The presence of certainty in one's intimate being is "written" with one's life. The relation of the individual to his life reveals whether or not certainty is, after all, available to him as his genuine and profound life-meaning. Certainty is not established by a mode of intellectual reasoning, it is not posited as an intellectual aspect of life; on the contrary, certainty is genuinely established by action and posited in the sphere of freedom within the individual. Any other kind of certainty, fundamentally supported by a course of reasoning taken as proof for the individual, is mere exteriority of one's self in relation to that same self; that is, it is simply an existential hypothesis, an illusion (not at all something "certain" or "a certainty"), as far as the actuality of personal life and as far as the radical significance of the individual to himself is concerned.

A proof requirement denotes a profound lack of certainty. Certainty is lived, concrete sureness, never essentially thought or an abstraction. Objectivity never constitutes certainty; only subjectivity generates certainty. The individual may want to obtain certainty in the sphere of proofs, but nevertheless this undertaking necessarily founders since certainty is not to be sought in the sphere of proofs but rather in that of faith.[11] So-called "absolute certainty" pertains to the domain of specific sciences and not at all to individual existence: there, "thought and being are one, but by the same token these sciences are hypothetical."[12] On the contrary, being in possession of certainty, living one's life in certainty means to be convinced, and this is a sureness that permeates the individual in action, a conviction that is not detachable from action. Only this non-detachment is the validation of certainty, or certainty properly understood.

---

[8]   *SKS* 4, 439 / *CA*, 139.
[9]   *SKS* 4, 439–40 / *CA*, 139.
[10]   *SKS* 4, 442 / *CA*, 142.
[11]   *SKS* 26, 344, NB34:34 / *JP* 2, 1452.
[12]   *SKS* 27, 271, Papir 281 / *JP* 1, 197.

III. Certainty and Action

Certainty is thus attained through the individual's action.[13] Nevertheless, certainty is not the subject of a "once-and-for-all" acquisition. On the contrary, it is only by means of repeated and renewed inward action, through the process of appropriation, that the individual has the possibility of acquiring certainty for himself. It is only through action that he updates his subjectivity with certainty. The one and only possible translation of certainty, for an individual human being, is action. Action or inward action manifests certainty, unequivocally, comprehensively. Action is the mode of acquisition of the self for oneself in certainty. Certainty is not only vitally rooted, but it is also properly acquired through its being vitally rooted. Moreover, certainty is and is not since it is never fully updated; furthermore, there are degrees of certainty. In this sense, certainty is essentially a "gradual phenomenon," never stable, neither stabilized nor "stabilizable" during the lifetime of the individual. It might diminish since it is an open phenomenon.[14] Action is the principle of exclusion, that is, the means whereby certainty regarding existential propositions is posited for the individual by the individual. Certainty not only does not dispense with this mode of expression in action, but, what is more, it is fundamentally and in the strictest sense testimony through action. Consequently, certainty is essentially never an *a priori* factor in action since certainty never exists, in any way, "before" action. The individual commonly adopts a kind of certainty which is compatible with merely immanent cares, a kind of certainty "that endorses our preoccupation with enjoying this life," but which postpones the eternal in him.[15] The individual usually accepts the assurance of another; he accepts the security and certainty apparently given to him by the public, but he does not posit certainty personally by himself.[16] Sensate certainty and historical certainty are simply illusions—they are only forms of approximation, that is, of uncertainty. Moreover, the certainty of numbers is a kind of finite certainty,[17] related to the human individual viewed essentially within the scope of the category of "the herd," the public, that is, the impersonal, in a direction away from inwardness. The certainty of numbers is related to the animal creature in man.[18] The certainty of the mass individual protects him from venturing, that is, puts the individual in a situation where it dominates the absence of certainty. In this sense, to demand finite certainty is to accept deception in one's life.[19] The situation of the individual in life is such that in it there is no certainty whatever about the future, and the individual cannot be absolutely sure of the direction that is being undertaken in life.[20] On the contrary, infinite certainty is impossible to refute; it pertains to the individual's intimate domain. Since the impossible-to-refute kind of certainty is contemporary with objective uncertainty and is contemporary with the absence of

---

[13]   *SKS* 4, 439 / *CA*, 138–9.
[14]   *SKS* 4, 440–1 / *CA*, 140.
[15]   *SKS* 26, 348, NB34:38 / *JP* 3, 2915.
[16]   *SKS* 26, 87, NB31:117 / *JP* 4, 4941.
[17]   *SKS* 26, 125, NB32:14 / *JP* 3, 2980.
[18]   Ibid.
[19]   *Pap.* VI B 38 / *JP* 1, 632.
[20]   *SKS* 23, 191, NB17:40 / *JP* 3, 3709.

contemplative transparency of the individual to himself, its acquisition in action always requires taking an enormous risk, that is, it requires venturing. Being in prior possession of a so-called certainty is the contrary of the idea of venturing, for one does not venture on what one is certain about.[21] Nevertheless, objective uncertainty is precisely the situation of the individual when he strives to obtain certitude in his life. "Existence is so cunning…that the greatest, the utterly, utterly greatest human certainty is precisely what most assuredly cheats us of the eternal—and in the least possible human certainty there is the possibility of the eternal."[22] In this sense, one essential trait of certainty is its objective uncertainty; to gain certainty, the individual risks his whole life on an "if." Paradoxically, the individual abdicates certainty in favor of certainty,[23] the individual takes leave of finite certainty in order to grasp infinite certainty—at this point, objective uncertainty can be transfigured into infinite certainty; certitude is possessed through venturing on what is uncertain from the point of view of probability and of sensate understanding.[24]

IV. Certainty and Faith according to Kierkegaard

Kierkegaard affirms the existence of "*a different kind of certainty*"—the proper expression of certainty here is giving one's life, be it being sacrificed for or, in the extreme possibility, dying for.[25] Kierkegaard holds faith to be the highest and the most passionate certainty.[26] For the individual, there can be no immediate certainty about whether or not one has faith.[27] The certainty of faith is superior to the ambiguity of experience.[28] Experience denotes, in fact, the uncertainty of everything; experience is uncertainty.[29] The direct vision of certainty is not a criterion of inward certainty, for what is at stake in inward certainty is to believe, not direct sight.[30] The certitude of faith (the certitude that relates itself to an eternal happiness) is defined and formed by uncertainty.[31] The certainty of faith does not correspond to the certainty given by physical means; it is not "the kind of certainty related to seeing directly" through the sense organs.[32] This certitude has to be gained always and each time anew with God's help.[33] It is characterized by its firmness, its indifference to or heterogeneity with the outer happenings of life.[34] According to Kierkegaard, one of the elements

---

[21]   *SKS* 7, 386–8 / *CUP1*, 424–6.
[22]   *SKS* 26, 91, NB31:122 / *JP* 4, 4942.
[23]   Ibid.
[24]   *SKS* 5, 364 / *EUD*, 380–1.
[25]   *SKS* 27, 643, Papir 533 / *JP* 1, 256.
[26]   *SKS* 25, 84, NB26:82 / *JP* 2, 1148.
[27]   *SKS* 20, 381–2, NB5:30 / *KJN* 4, 382.
[28]   *SKS* 27, 338, Papir 325 / *JP* 2, 1116.
[29]   *SKS* 18, 282, JJ:429 / *KJN* 2, 261.
[30]   *SKS* 24, 359–60, NB24:61 / *JP* 2, 2302.
[31]   *SKS* 7, 413, 460 / *CUP1*, 455, 507.
[32]   *SKS* 24, 359–60, NB24:61 / *JP* 2, 2302.
[33]   *SKS* 9, 372 / *WL*, 379.
[34]   *Pap.* VII–2 B 235, p. 49 / *BA*, 158.

of Christian life is precisely "an unshakable sureness, an unshakable certainty about one's relationship to God, about God's mercy and love," within a specific understanding of the meaning of this relationship.[35]

Certainty of faith is essentially linked with "certainty of spirit." Qualifications of the spirit, such as immortality, are dialectical, that is, they are at a distance from all immediate certainty. At the same time, they have their proper place in the sphere of faith.[36] "A thinker is literally in hell as long as he has not found certainty of spirit: *hic Rhodus, hic salta*, the sphere of faith, where you must believe even if the world burst into pieces and the elements melted."[37]

"*The only certainty is the ethical-religious.*"[38] Ethical-religious certainty is linked with action, on the one hand, and with faith, on the other, or is constituted by a kind of action subsumed in the comprehension of faith. Certainty has nothing to do with the results of scientific investigations, for these are nothing for the individual; they are not to be appropriated by the individual. There is no certainty to be found in exteriority, but there is certainty only in the inward individual. Immediate certainty is uncertainty—certainty has to be gained; the individual's immediate realm has to be overcome, and this overcoming opens the possibility for the constitution of the only indestructible certainty there is, and this is to be found beyond the "objective," finite, relative, pedestrian and illusory "certainties."

See also Appropriation; Approximation; Choice; Concrete/Abstract; Death; Decision/Resolve; Earnestness; Immediacy/Reflection; Inwardness/Inward Deepening; Objectivity/Subjectivity; Truth.

---

[35]   *SKS* 17, 260, DD:134 / *KJN* 1, 251.
[36]   *SKS* 20, 381–2, NB5:30 / *KJN* 4, 382.
[37]   *SKS* 20, 73, NB:87 / *KJN* 4, 72.
[38]   *SKS* 20, 66, NB:73 / *KJN* 4, 65.

Chatter

Peter Fenves

Chatter (*Snak*—noun, *snakke*—verb)

"Chatter" is the primary word Kierkegaard uses to designate empty and idle speech.[1] Other, less frequently used words with a similar function are "gossip" (*Bysnak*), "prattle" (*Passiar*), and "drivel" (*Vrøvl*). In certain circumstances *Snak* simply means "talk," with the slightly pejorative connotation that generally attaches to the notion of discussion as opposed to action. When Kierkegaard specifically uses *Snak* to describe empty and idle speech, he is not disparaging the intellectual or cultural deficiencies of the speaker. Nor is *Snak* contrasted with straightforwardly serious or important discourse, which would be characterized by its ponderous subject matter and sententious tone. Rather, for Kierkegaard, a tendency toward empty and idle utterance is coextensive with every use of language, since language is based on the generality of its terms, which speakers must resist. Talk of the day's weather is a paradigmatic case of chatter, since speakers are not responsible for, and cannot do anything about, the events of which they speak; but chatter can occur whenever speakers accommodate themselves to linguistic generality and thus fail to involve themselves in their discourse.

"Chatter" and cognate terms appear in a wide variety of Kierkegaard's writings, both early and late, including those published under a pseudonym as well as under his own name. They can also be found throughout his journals and papers. A truncated analysis of chatter emerges in his first book, *From the Papers of One Still Living*, and it appropriately culminates in *A Literary Review of Two Ages*: the former briefly celebrates one of Thomasine Gyllembourg's short stories, and the latter analyzes at length her novel *Two Ages*. The following discussion is divided into two chronologically defined parts: the first charts the emergence of chatter as a theme in the pseudonymous texts, while the second outlines the critique of chatter that Kierkegaard develops in *A Literary Review*.

Kierkegaard uses *Snak* and *snakke* throughout *Either/Or*, usually in the more neutral sense of talking in contrast to action. The aesthete of the first volume draws on this distinction for his discussion of both art and life. Thus, Molière's *Don Juan* is judged to be a less powerful work of art than Mozart's *Don Giovanni* because the music of the opera is seductive, whereas the play includes only talk of seduction.[2]

---

[1]   *Ordbog over det danske Sprog*, vols. 1–28, published by the Society for Danish Language and Literature, Copenhagen: Gyldendal 1918–56, vol. 20, columns 1006–11.

[2]   *SKS* 1, 95 / *EO1*, 115.

According to "The Seducer's Diary," gesture is better than talk at expressing erotic love, because the emptiness of talk is antithetical to the substantial character of love: "Eros gesticulates, does not speak."[3] At the beginning of "The Balance Between Esthetic and Ethical" Judge William begins to elaborate a more exacting characterization of chatter by examining how the phrase "either/or" acquires different functions depending on whether it serves to concretize the situation in which a choice is to be made or, on the contrary, mocks the necessity of such a situation. Only because the Judge notices something beyond "chatter and witticism" in the aesthete's repeated statement, "I simply say Either/Or," does he decide to write him the letters that make up most of the second volume of the work.[4]

Many of the subsequent pseudonymous writings amplify and extend Judge William's reflections on a barely perceptible difference between using a phrase for the purpose of identifying one's own decisive situation and using it for any other purpose. A particularly trenchant version of this critique of the empty phrase, which is phenomenologically indistinguishable from its full counterpart, appears near the end of *The Concept of Anxiety*: "Spiritlessness can say exactly the same thing that the richest spirit has said, but it does not say it by virtue of spirit. Man qualified as spirit has become a talking machine, and there is nothing to prevent him from repeating by rote a philosophical rigmarole, a confession of faith, or a political recitation."[5] Whereas large parts of the *Concluding Unscientific Postscript* are concerned with the "philosophical rigmarole" associated with Hegelianism, *Philosophical Fragments* precisely identifies the condition under which a "confession of faith" turns into chatter. This happens when a believer attempts to communicate what he or she believes without emphasizing that the historical content of the belief "is folly to the understanding and an offense to the human heart."[6] The resulting communication is empty precisely because of its general comprehensibility, and for the same reason its recipients are unprepared to understand that they must make their own movement of faith rather than follow a movement they understand all too readily: the believer "is only talking nonsense and perhaps inveigles the one who comes later to make up his mind in continuity with idle chatter."[7] In a similar vein, but with more attention to the public character of empty speech, the "Letter to the Reader" that concludes *Stages of Life's Way* describes a "reading public" that wants to be assured of only one thing whenever it hears an account of suffering, namely, whether it really happened.[8] As Frater Taciturnus explains, there can and should be no such assurance. Any speaker who successfully persuades the audience that the suffering really occurred robs the audience of the very possibility of belief:

> The more it is emphasized that it is historical and therefore etc., the more he [the speaker] deceives, and if he is paid so little that it is not worth talking [*tale*] about the money he receives, then it is just as certain that he is putting out chitchat [*Snak*], perhaps a good

---

3   *SKS* 1, 385 / *EO1*, 418.
4   *SKS* 2, 145 / *EO2*, 159.
5   *SKS* 4, 365 / *CA*, 95.
6   *SKS* 4, 264 / *PF*, 102.
7   *SKS* 4, 265 / *PF*, 102.
8   *SKS* 6, 410 / *SLW*, 440.

deal of chitchat—alas, for poor pay. A historicizing speaker [*Taler*] such as that merely contributes his share to making the learners devoid of spirit.[9]

The pseudonymous writings thus develop a critique of chatter that indicates why it is so dangerous. Far from remaining isolated to particular utterances, the emptiness of mere talk tends to expand, crowding out, as it were, both silence and full speech. In *A Literary Review* Kierkegaard uses the metaphor of the swamp to capture the character of this situation, which threatens to overwhelm the space of inwardness: "Gossip [*Bysnak*] and rumor and chimeric significance and apathetic envy become a surrogate for each and all....The avenue of the idea is blocked off: individuals mutually thwart and contravene each other; selfish and mutual reflexive opposition is like a swamp—and now they are sitting in it."[10] *A Literary Review* does not directly describe the character of Kierkegaard's age but, rather, identifies its elements by reflecting on Gyllembourg's novel, which contrasts "the present age" with the "age of revolution." For Gyllembourg as well as Kierkegaard, the two ages are not categorically different from each other; rather, "the present age" remains revolutionary, but reflection replaces passion, thus promoting an idle, swamp-like condition in which there is time for talk but no idea as to how one must act: "A passionate, tumultuous age wants to overthrow everything, set aside everything. An age that is revolutionary but also reflecting and devoid of passion changes the expression of power into a *dialectical tour de force: it lets everything remain but subtly drains the meaning out of it....*"[11]

As Kierkegaard proceeds to explain, the process of draining out meaning solicits chatter, which deceptively fills in, and contributes to, the resulting emptiness. Near the end of *A Literary Review* Kierkegaard directly poses the question: "What is it *to chatter?*"[12] And in response he identifies a certain temporal dislocation as the primary characteristic of chatter:

> It is the annulment of the passionate disjunction between being silent and speaking. Only the person who can remain essentially silent can speak essentially, can act essentially. Silence is inwardness. Chattering gets ahead of essential speaking, and giving utterance to reflection has a weakening effect on action by getting ahead of it.[13]

Chatter, in other words, is not simply "mere talk" as opposed to genuine action; rather, it is talk that outpaces action. In this way, Kierkegaard deepens the stereotypical opposition between mere talking and genuine action. Chatter does something to time; indeed, it does something to time by "getting ahead of" action and thus implies, regardless of what chatters themselves may say, that no action is necessary.

See also Communication/Indirect Communication; Edifying Discourses/Deliberations/ Sermons; Language; Press, the/Journalism; Rhetoric; Silence; Writing.

---

[9]   Ibid.
[10]   *SKS* 8, 60 / *TA*, 63.
[11]   *SKS* 8, 73 / *TA*, 77.
[12]   *SKS* 8, 91 / *TA*, 97.
[13]   Ibid.

Childhood

Esben Lindemann

Childhood (*Barndom*—noun)

From the Old Norse *barndómr*, the Danish word refers to the first part of life, the age of being a child.[1] The word "childhood" appears often throughout Kierkegaard's authorship but is most frequently seen in some early journal entries from the beginning of 1837, as well as in *Either/Or* and the *Concluding Unscientific Postscript*. In these texts we find the most thorough treatment of the notion of childhood, although one should add that nowhere in the authorship is it given systematic scrutiny. The notion of childhood is predominantly analyzed as follows: (1) observations on different *stages* in human development; (2) observations on the particular relation between *the poetic* and the childlike; (3) observations on a *Socratic upbringing*; (4) observations on a particular childlike state of being as portal to a wider *critique of the rational*; (5) observations on the connection between *will* and the child's development as part of a more general analysis of the basic existential meaning of will; and (6) observations on childhood as a position between *absolute and relative culture*. These different aspects of childhood will be illustrated and elucidated below.

I. Stages

Kierkegaard's understanding of childhood presupposes a traditional subdivision of life into four stages: child, youth, adult, and old age: "The first is the stage in which the child has not separated himself from his surroundings ('me'). The *I* is not given, but [there is] the possibility of it."[2] At this stage, the child has a fleeting and fragmented perception of the world. It cannot differentiate the manifold impressions from each other and cannot differentiate itself from its surroundings. The child's I-consciousness is yet to be developed, and the child can be said to be one with the rest of the world. Indeed, childhood is characterized by a striving to become an "I." In the child's fragmented perception of life, the I

> is gestalted in vague and fleeting outlines, just like the sea-maidens the waves produce only to form new ones again (see a copper etching). I would like to think that all these profuse and fleeting forms will be formed in a unity by a stroke of magic, these

---

[1] *Ordbog over det danske Sprog*, vols. 1–18, published by the Society for Danish Language and Literature, Copenhagen: Gyldendal 1918–56, vol. 1, columns 1161–2.

[2] *SKS* 17, 117, BB:25 / *JP* 4, 4398.

multitudinous elements standing alongside each other in childhood, crowding each other out in order to enter into the eternal present of the *I*; in childhood there is an atomistic multiplicity, in the *I* there is the one in the many.[3]

Childhood is dominated by coincidence and unpredictability as the child "is immediate and explains nothing...not even to other children, because every child is itself only in an immediate way."[4] Childhood is immediacy and in this immediacy, the child is capable of reflecting neither on itself, nor its surroundings. Childhood as a phenomenon lacks a guiding rational principle. But after the chaos of childhood "comes a peace, an idyllic well-being. It is the youth's satisfaction in family and school (church and state); this is the second stage."[5] So the child stage is followed by the youth stage, and the transition from one to the other is marked by the youth's commencement in school.

However, we observe in Kierkegaard a modification of the template of stages, as he appears to criticize his contemporaries for attributing too much importance to the stages compared to the individual life of each human being: "This is rooted in the haste of the times, which basically misunderstands every age because it believes that each age-level exists merely for the sake of the next."[6] His contemporaries do not have a sufficiently nuanced view of the stages because they believe, erroneously, that the stages automatically follow each other as steps on a ladder, and that one stage is merely a prerequisite for being able to move on to the next. The progression of life and the relation between the different ages is more complicated than that: "let us never forget that even the more mature person always retains some of the child's lack of judgment."[7] The different ages continue to exist and weave into each other: "since no age as such is the absolute, not even what one usually calls one's best years."[8] Hence, the classic subdivision of life into child, youth, adult, and old age should not be seen as an exhaustive description of how a life develops.

"Now comes the question: *what significance* does childhood really have? Is it a stage with significance only because it conditions, in a way, the following stages—or does it have independent value?"[9] Childhood is not just a period of life to be over and done with in order to proceed to the next stage. Kierkegaard criticizes those who feel that a definition of childhood presupposes "the emptiness of childhood."[10] The child is not an empty vessel just to be filled. Childhood carries a reality in itself, and a child should be respected as an individual with intrinsic value.

---

3   Ibid.
4   *SKS* 7, 540 / *CUP1*, 594.
5   *SKS* 17, 118, BB:25 / *JP* 4, 4398.
6   *SKS* 17, 127, BB:37n. / *JP* 1, 265n.
7   *SKS* 5, 380 / *EUD*, 399.
8   *SKS* 1, 41 / *EPW*, 85–6.
9   *SKS* 17, 127, BB:37 / *JP* 1, 265.
10   Ibid.

II. The Poetic

"Children crave fairy stories."[11] Children need the poetic in their lives. The poetic can "simultaneously exercise…an overwhelming and tranquilizing effect"[12] on children, and in that way both stimulate the child's fantasy and create a sense of order in the child's life. If the poetic does not have this effect, it makes "space for an anxiety which, when not moderated by such stories, returns again all the stronger."[13]

The way in which a story is told, however, is significant: "Now the question arises—to what extent *should the storyteller* himself believe these stories? If the storyteller himself believes the stories, then I do not think the question will arise for the children as to whether or not it is true."[14] The sincerity of the storyteller is decisive for the child's experience and empathy. The situation in which the child asks "whether or not it is true"[15] is not desirable, since this means that the spell of fantasy is broken.

"After a story has been told, it is important not to destroy the entire impression by ending with a 'But you do understand, don't you, that it was only a fairy tale?' "[16] This is inappropriate and indicates that the storyteller "has absolutely no sense of the poetic."[17] Similarly, it is inappropriate for both storyteller and listener to "spoil the impression of every anecdote, etc., by probing its factual truth."[18]

"Only when the child himself detects that the teller does not believe stories are the stories damaging—yet not because of the content itself but because of the untruth in regard to the teller—because of the mistrust and suspiciousness which the child gradually develops."[19] What then is harmful to the child is not to be subjected to the inherent fantasy in the stories, but rather to be subjected to a teller who does not believe his tales, as this blocks a dimension of experience in the child's life. The child needs fantasy and the incredible. Adults who do not open the doors of this world to children are perceived with mistrust and suspicion, the reason being that the child already has a finely developed sense of the poetic, and senses when the teller does not believe his own tales. This implies that the child from the outset is capable of differentiating between fantasy and reality.

III. Socratic Upbringing

The child should be included in meaningful conversations with regard to the tales, and one should allow the children themselves to narrate. The adult is not to correct the child's tales strictly, but rather "the child [should be] allowed to read them

---

[11]   *SKS* 17, 130, BB:37n. / *JP* 1, 265n.
[12]   Ibid.
[13]   Ibid.
[14]   Ibid.
[15]   Ibid.
[16]   *SKS* 17, 129, BB:37 / *JP* 1, 265.
[17]   Ibid.
[18]   Ibid.
[19]   *SKS* 17, 123, BB:37 / *JP* 1, 265.

himself and tell them and…then Socratically [be] corrected."[20] The adult should engage the children's own tales through questions and dialogue, "in such a manner that the child is by no means set straight under the coercion of a tutor but seems rather to be correcting others."[21] Using a notion from Kierkegaard's more general didactic program, children should be encouraged to act for themselves and "anyone who otherwise understands how to handle children will certainly not be in danger of encouraging arrogance."[22]

The important thing in narrating to the child is not that the adult's story is heard, but precisely that the child's point of view and manifold questions be taken seriously: "One should arouse in children a desire to ask, instead of fending off a reasonable question, which perhaps goes beyond Uncle Frank's general information or in some other way inconveniences him, with the words: 'Stupid child! Can't he keep still while I am telling the story?'"[23] There is a close connection between a dialogical, questioning approach to the world and the poetic: "One should not schedule the poetic for certain hours and certain days."[24] On the contrary, "[t]he whole point is to bring the poetic into touch with their lives in every way, to exercise a power of enchantment, to let a glimpse appear at the most unexpected moment and then vanish."[25] The questioning approach inherent in the poetic is fundamentally in consonance with how children situate themselves in the world. Hence Kierkegaard concludes: "all general pursuits on behalf of children outside of formal instruction, and this, too, as much as possible, should be Socratic."[26] Further to this, it is not merely the child but also the adult, who should be willing to learn through this dialogical approach. This reciprocal relation is a prerequisite for harvesting knowledge: "We ourselves ought to learn from children, from their marvelous creativity, which…we ought to allow to prevail."[27]

IV. Critique of the Rational

In the introductory "Diapsalmata" to *Either/Or*, Part One, Kierkegaard has the aesthete A write the following: "I prefer to talk with children, for one may still dare to hope that they may become rational beings; but those who have become that— good Lord!"[28] According to A, childhood contains an inherent common sense that should be transferred to adult life. The particular poetic state of being that childhood represents is not irrational but is rather, because of the aesthetic element, a union of the sensuous and the rational. The aesthetic, then, is not an antithesis to the rational, but rather to a state of being where common sense has hegemony, and all things

---

[20]   *SKS* 17, 127, BB:37 / *JP* 1, 265.
[21]   Ibid.
[22]   Ibid.
[23]   *SKS* 17, 124, BB:37 / *JP* 1, 265.
[24]   Ibid.
[25]   Ibid.
[26]   Ibid.
[27]   *SKS* 17, 125, BB:37n. / *JP* 1, 265n.
[28]   *SKS* 2, 27 / *EO1*, 19.

sensuous are repressed. According to A, there exists during childhood a balance between the sensuous and common sense, which would be desirable if it could be transferred to adult life.

This is supported in another aphorism from "Diapsalmata" that describes "a poor wretch"[29] whom A has observed roaming the streets wearing "a somewhat worn pale green coat flecked with yellow."[30] A writes that the color of this coat "so vividly reminded me of my childhood's first productions in the noble art of painting. This particular color was one of my favorite colors."[31] A laments that the playful and experimental mixtures of color typical of childhood are always viewed by others as stark and too strong. A ends his aphorism with the rhetorical question: "Does this not happen with all the color combinations of childhood? The gleam that life had at that time gradually becomes too intense: too crude, for our dull eyes."[32] A postulates that with time we become blind to the subtleties of life, because childlike openness is no longer present. As the common sense of adult life becomes more and more dominating, our understanding of the world becomes more and more limited.

This idea depicted by A shows a life/death dichotomy with life placed in the court of childhood, and death in the court of adulthood. Adulthood lacks the appropriate balance between sensuousness and common sense. The relations between the peculiar and the normal, the living and the dead, the unfamiliar and the familiar are turned on their head. Life is most vivid in the unfamiliar, while the familiar lacks a dimension of life. The peculiar and the incongruous are in accordance with a holistic and balanced state of existence, while normal life and the world are actually lacking something and therefore become unfamiliar. The relation between the child and the adult seems to be comparable: the child is in accordance with itself and existence to a greater extent than normally perceived by the adult.

V. Will

In *Either/Or*, Part Two, Kierkegaard allows Judge William to express his views on childhood. Here we learn that the point of upbringing is not "that the child learns this or that but that the mind is matured, that energy is evoked."[33] Intellectual knowledge is not a goal in itself in bringing up a child. Will is what is essential, and from a strong will follows a strong mind.[34]

When the five-year-old William was given his first homework at school, he attacked it with exemplary passion. The boy did not have an actual understanding of what his duty was.[35] What is paramount is the will to carry out the duty, and only with will comes the notion of duty. There appear to be two fundamental consequences to be derived from William's recollection: (1) that the upbringing of a child should not

---

29   *SKS* 2, 31 / *EO1*, 23.
30   Ibid.
31   Ibid.
32   Ibid.
33   *SKS* 3, 254 / *EO2*, 267.
34   Ibid.
35   Ibid.

have a predefined aim, but should rather awaken a passion and a will in the child, whereby it uncovers and realizes its purpose in and of itself;[36] (2) The goal of the upbringing should not be quantitative but qualitative. To Judge William, the depth of passion is what is important rather than the scope of the knowledge that the child has acquired.[37]

The aesthete A and the ethicist William agree that there are some internal emotional forces that must be awakened in the child, rather than some rational forces that are controlled from without. A advocates greater balance between the sensuous and the rational. William underscores the importance of passion and will as prerequisites for intellect. If we allow will and passion to flourish, the intellect will follow. In passion and will lie an immanent rationality, immanent ethics, just like, according to A, in the aesthetic. Ethics and aesthetics are two sides of the same coin in Kierkegaard's basic notion of childhood.

VI. Absolute and Relative Culture

In the *Concluding Unscientific Postscript*, Kierkegaard has Johannes Climacus write the following about the child's relation to memory and recollection: "a child has much memory (oriented outward) but no recollection, at most the inwardness of the moment."[38] He who achieves the highest degree of existential realization has "recollection, at most the inwardness of the moment"[39]—and here he has something in common with the child. Being present in the moment is an essential characteristic of childhood: "What is it that makes the child's life so easy? It is that so often 'quits' can be called and a new beginning is so frequently made."[40] A child may have a lot of memory, but also has the ability to forget again. It has the ability to forget what happened and get on with life.

A person who has a "recollection, at most the inwardness of the moment"[41] Climacus calls "a fully cultured person."[42] Just like a child, a fully cultured person is present in the moment and does not allow himself to be bogged down by events of the past or the future. But whereas a child forgets to avoid reflecting, the fully cultured person accepts reflection as a condition. He infinitizes his worries and thereby disarms them.[43]

In this connection, Climacus juxtaposes "absolute culture"[44] with "relative culture."[45] The relatively cultured person is unable to infinitize his reflections and

---

36   *SKS* 3, 253–7 / *EO2*, 266–71.
37   Ibid.
38   *SKS* 7, 491 / *CUP1*, 540.
39   Ibid.
40   *SKS* 7, 499 / *CUP1*, 550.
41   *SKS* 7, 491 / *CUP1*, 540.
42   *SKS* 7, 500 / *CUP1*, 551.
43   *SKS* 7, 498–504 / *CUP1*, 549–55.
44   *SKS* 7, 500 / *CUP1*, 550–1.
45   Ibid.

lacks a "recollection, at most the inwardness of the moment."[46] His consciousness is exclusively directed outward toward the events of the outer world. His culture has the aim to master the world, but in his exuberance to master it, he becomes a slave to his own reflections.[47]

"If, therefore, a fully cultured person is placed together with a child, they always jointly discover the humorous: the child says it and does not know it; the humorist knows that it was said. However, a relative culture placed together with a child discovers nothing, because it pays no attention to the child and its foolishness."[48] The industrious, relatively cultured person, who fights to the limit to master the world will—from a fully cultured person's perspective—be perceived as comical. It is this humor that the fully cultured person and the child can discover together. The relatively cultured person takes himself so seriously that he does not perceive the child's perspective of the world, and the particular wisdom inherent in it. The fully cultured person sees everything that the relatively cultured person does not and, together with the child, laughs at the world. He discovers the world with the child. It is, then, not just the child who learns something through this relation, but so also does the fully cultured person.

To summarize, childhood is described as the first part of life, which stretches from birth until the commencement of school. However, childhood should not be viewed as an absolute stage defined exclusively as a time-period. Likewise, childhood cannot be seen as a mere prerequisite for the subsequent developmental steps or as an empty category to be filled. Childhood carries a dignity in itself, on a par with the other life categories. Subsequently, childhood is described as a state of being that is particularly sensitized to the poetic, and in which the world is fundamentally understood and processed through the poetic. In this sense it is not just the adult who can teach the child something, but the adult can also profit endlessly by observing the particular childlike approach to life. This balances an adult's tendency to allow their life to be controlled by rational principles. Many adults may therefore learn from children's ability to unite the sensuous and common sense. Rather than focusing on the child's attainment of intellectual knowledge, one should rather focus on the will as the actual point of departure for bringing up a child. Culture is connected to internal rather than external quantity.

See also Anxiety; Art; Comic/Comedy; Communication/Indirect Communication; Culture/Education; Dialogue; Ethics; Fairytale; Humor; Lyric; Myth; Poetry; Recollection; Stages; Story-Telling; Sympathy/Empathy; Teacher; Will.

---

[46] *SKS* 7, 491 / *CUP1*, 540.
[47] *SKS* 7, 498–504 / *CUP1*, 549–55.
[48] *SKS* 7, 500 / *CUP1*, 551.

Choice

Gerhard Thonhauser

Choice (*Valg*—noun; *vælge*—verb)

From the Old Norse *val*, similar to German *Wahl*. The primary lexical meaning of the Danish term is the act of choosing between at least two options, equivalent to the English "choice" or "selection." *Valg* also signifies the precondition for such an act of choosing: to have a choice, the availability of options. As an application of this general sense it can mean acts of choosing in specific contexts (for example, political ones), including the meanings of English words like vote, election, or poll.[1]

Valg is part of Danish everyday language (signifying all acts of choosing) and can be found in numerous writings by Kierkegaard, though in many instances without terminological significance. At the same time, it is also an important part of Kierkegaard's philosophical and/or theological vocabulary. One could even make the case that Kierkegaard was actually the first one to highlight the status of "choice" as an important philosophical and/or theological category.

The most frequent and best known occurrence of the category "choice" is in Judge William's letter "The Balance Between the Esthetic and the Ethical in the Development of the Personality" in the second part of *Either/Or*. Other important occurrences of the term are in *Upbuilding Discourses in Various Spirits*, *Works of Love*, *Christian Discourses*, *The Lily in the Field and the Bird of the Air*, and, most importantly, *Practice in Christianity*. With the exception of the first edition of *Practice in Christianity*, all these later works were published under the name Søren Kierkegaard. These works develop an understanding of choice that is significantly different from the one presented by Judge William and highlights the relevance of choice for becoming a Christian. In the following, I will start with a critical discussion of the notion of choice in Part Two of *Either/Or*, before proceeding with a presentation of Kierkegaard's later use of the term.

I.

At the beginning of his letter, Judge William stresses the importance of the act of choosing for the development of the personality: "The choice itself is crucial for the content of the personality: through the choice the personality submerges itself in that

---

[1]   *Ordbog over det danske Sprog*, vols. 1–28, published by the Society for Danish Language and Literature, Copenhagen: Gyldendal 1918–56, vol. 26, columns 289–296 (*Valg*), vol. 27, columns 752–7 (*vælge*).

which is being chosen, and when it does not choose, it withers away in atrophy."[2] Closely related to this, he states that there is a certain urgency in making a choice because "when the choice is about an issue of elemental importance to life, the individual must at the same time continue to live, and this is why the longer he puts off the choice, the more easily he comes to alter it."[3] The reason is that during the time in which one postpones a conscious choice, "the personality or the obscure forces within it unconsciously chooses."[4] It is implied that these "obscure forces" choose the aesthetic, and thus, that one already has chosen the aesthetic as long as one has not made a conscious choice.

At the same time, Judge William states that an aesthetic choice, strictly speaking, cannot count as a choice, and that every choice is essentially an ethical one. He tells A: "Your choice is an esthetic choice, but an esthetic choice is no choice. On the whole, to choose is an intrinsic and stringent term for the ethical,"[5] and he underscores, "the ethical, although it modestly places itself on the same level as the esthetic, nevertheless is essentially that which makes the choice a choice."[6]

If we continue to speak of an aesthetic choice, we can do so in two respects: "The esthetic choice is either altogether immediate, and thus no choice, or it loses itself in a great multiplicity."[7] In the first respect it corresponds to the previously discussed circumstance, that one has already unconsciously chosen the aesthetic until one consciously chooses the ethical. This immediate choice of the aesthetic can only figuratively be labeled a choice. In the second respect the aesthetic choice is not on the same level as the ethical choice, since this notion of an aesthetic choice is a matter of a multiplicity of singular decisions within one way of life, and does not concern the fundamental choice between different, competing ways of life. Accordingly, Judge William concludes, "the person who lives esthetically does not choose, and the person who chooses the esthetic after the ethical has become manifest to him is not living esthetically, for he is sinning and is subject to ethical qualifications, even if his life must be termed unethical."[8] One can rightfully be said to be living aesthetically only if one is truly unaware of the ethical. If the ethical has become manifest to someone, he or she can no longer live aesthetically; if he or she nevertheless intends to do so, it must not be considered an aesthetic but an unethical way of life, according to Judge William.

This consideration reveals a fundamental asymmetry between the aesthetic and the ethical, and introduces a lopsidedness into Judge William's argument. For if there were a real choice between the aesthetic and the ethical—if the aesthetic and the ethical represented truly competing ways of life—then it would be an actual option to consciously choose the aesthetic even after the ethical has become manifest. But if the aesthetic and the ethical were equivalent options, then there would be no

---

2   *SKS* 3, 160 / *EO2*, 163.
3   Ibid.
4   *SKS* 3, 161 / *EO2*, 164.
5   *SKS* 3, 163 / *EO2*, 166.
6   *SKS* 3, 165 / *EO2*, 168.
7   *SKS* 3, 163 / *EO2*, 167.
8   *SKS* 3, 165 / *EO2*, 168.

reason to assume that there is any authority of the ethical, and it is no longer evident why a consciously chosen aesthetic way of life should be deemed unethical. The reading of *Either/Or* offered in the *Concluding Unscientific Postscript* supports the interpretation that there is, in fact, no real choice between an aesthetic and an ethical way of life, for the simple reason that there is no such thing as an actual aesthetic way of life. It is stated that the first part of *Either/Or* presents an "existence-possibility oriented toward existence,"[9] "an existence-possibility that cannot attain existence."[10] The ethical remains as the only valid option because the aesthetic is revealed as no option at all in the sphere of existence.

Still, a fundamental ambiguity remains concerning Judge William's argument: Either the choice constitutes the basis for the authority of the ethical—in which case there is no reason why such a choice should not equally be able to serve as the basis for the validity of the aesthetic—or the choice must already be based upon the force of the ethical, an ethical authority which lies beyond the reach of the choice— in which case the question arises why it should be necessary to choose at all. In conclusion, this analysis reveals that there is a tension between Judge William's concept of choice and his concept of the ethical.[11]

There are two additional aspects of Judge William's argument that might arouse criticism. First, it is not clear which choice he is actually referring to. On the one hand he writes: "Rather than designating the choice between good and evil, my Either/Or designates the choice by which one chooses good and evil or rules them out."[12] And later he elucidates: "The Either/Or I have advanced is, therefore, in a certain sense absolute, for it is between choosing and not choosing."[13] On the other hand, he asserts, "the only absolute Either/Or is the choice between good and evil, but this is also absolutely ethical."[14] Is the absolute choice a choice between good and evil, or does the choice first of all constitute this distinction? Another passage directly displays the ambiguity in Judge William's conception concerning this issue: "But since the choice is an absolute choice, the Either/Or is absolute. In another sense, the absolute Either/Or does not make its appearance until the choice, because now the choice between good and evil appears."[15] The second feature that might be a reason for a critical discussion is the claim that if "the ethical is posited by the absolute choice...all the esthetic returns in its relativity."[16] This seems not entirely plausible; the reason is that the aesthetic here means the aesthetic aspects of life, that which makes life pleasant and joyful, not an independent way of life that forms an alternative to the ethical.

---

9   *SKS* 7, 230 / *CUP1*, 253.
10   *SKS* 7, 229 / *CUP1*, 253.
11   A similar interpretation has famously been put forward by Alasdair MacIntyre, who in *Either/Or* detects a "deep internal inconsistency...between its concept of radical choice and its concept of the ethical." Alasdair MacIntyre, *After Virtue: A Study in Moral Theory*, 2nd ed., London: Duckworth 1985, p. 41.
12   *SKS* 3, 165 / *EO2*, 169.
13   *SKS* 3, 173 / *EO2*, 177.
14   *SKS* 3, 163 / *EO2*, 166–7.
15   *SKS* 3, 173 / *EO2*, 178.
16   *SKS* 3, 173 / *EO2*, 177.

As mentioned above, Judge William emphasizes the importance of choice for the personality. He stresses that for the choice, the will is decisive:

> Now, if you are to understand me properly, I may very well say that what is important in choosing is not so much to choose the right thing as the energy, the earnestness, and the pathos with which one chooses. In the choosing the personality declares itself in its inner infinity and in turn the personality is thereby consolidated.[17]

He continues to state that the "person who chooses only esthetically never reaches this transfiguration, this higher dedication."[18] Speaking from the point of view of an ethical person instead, he writes: "I choose the absolute, and what is the absolute? It is myself in my eternal validity."[19] According to Judge William, what one chooses in an absolute sense is the "eternal validity of the personality."[20]

In accordance with this, the only thing that one person can do for another is to help the person to recognize the reality and importance of choice: "This, however, is what is crucial, and it is to this that I shall strive to awaken you. Up to that point, one person can help another; when he has reached that point, the significance the one person can have for the other becomes more subordinate."[21] Accordingly, Judge William advises A to despair. He underscores the central role of the will in despair, and that in choosing despair, the will, which is decisive for the personality, is already present. Already in the choice of despair one chooses himself or herself in his or her eternal validity:

> Choose despair, then, because despair itself is a choice, because one can doubt without choosing it, but one cannot despair without choosing it. And in despairing a person chooses again, and what then does he choose? He chooses himself, not in his immediacy, not as this accidental individual, but he chooses himself in his eternal validity.[22]

This statement stands in conflict with the position in *The Sickness unto Death*, where Anti-Climacus is very clear that choosing despair is not a (final) solution, and moreover, that it is impossible to escape despair by means of one's own power. It could even be argued that the act of choosing oneself that Judge William supports is a mode of despair, a variation of "in despair to will to be oneself."[23] However that may be, it is clear that *Either/Or* does not correspond with the understanding of choice developed in Kierkegaard's later writings.

II.

On very few occasions, later writings refer back to the conception of choice from *Either/Or*. One such instance is in the discourse "On the Occasion of a Wedding"

17   *SKS* 3, 164 / *EO2*, 167.
18   Ibid.
19   *SKS* 3, 205 / *EO2*, 214.
20   *SKS* 3, 206 / *EO2*, 215.
21   *SKS* 3, 172 / *EO2*, 176.
22   *SKS* 3, 203 / *EO2*, 211.
23   *SKS* 11, 129 / *SUD*, 13.

in *Three Discourses on Imagined Occasions* where Kierkegaard underscores the importance of the choice.[24] A similar passage can be found in *Works of Love*.[25]

Much more importantly, several later texts highlight the importance of a radical, absolute choice for becoming a Christian. Interestingly enough, all collections of discourses that are based on the theme of the lily in the field and the bird of the air state at least once that there is a radical choice, an absolute either/or. In the second part of *Upbuilding Discourses in Various Spirits*, Kierkegaard writes that "the glorious thing [is] *that the human being is granted a choice*,"[26] and he specifies what the choice is all about; that it is "a choice between God and the world."[27] In addition, he stresses the necessity of the choice: "The human being must choose *between God and mammon*. This is the eternal, unaltered condition of the choice."[28] One year later in *Christian Discourses*, Kierkegaard writes about the "choice between the two masters,"[29] and states that "to choose God is certainly the most decisive and highest choice."[30] Again one year later, he repeats a similar statement in *The Lily in the Field and the Bird of the Air*:

> There is an either/or: either God—or, well, then the rest is unimportant. Whatever else a person chooses, if he does not choose God, he has missed the either/or, or through his either/or he is in perdition. Therefore: either God; you see, there is no emphasis at all on the second, except by contrast to God, whereby the emphasis falls infinitely upon God. Thus it actually is God who, by being himself the object of the choice, tightens the decision of choice until it in truth becomes an either/or.[31]

In a certain sense, the statements about choosing God are similar to Judge William's elaborations on choosing good and evil; but because they are contextualized within the realm of the religious, they do not cause the same ambiguity between the notion of the ethical and the relevance of choice. They highlight the discovery that "faith is a choice,"[32] a very specific choice where choosing otherwise is irrelevant. In the following, this notion of choice will be explicated in relation to the concepts of imitation, offense, disclosure, indirect communication, and redoubling.

The relation of choice and imitation is only briefly touched upon in *Christian Discourses*, where it is stated that the apostle Peter, in imitation "*left the certain and chose the uncertain*,"[33] and "chose certain downfall."[34] Another brief discussion of this relation, in connection with Christ as the prototype, is found in "The Gospel of Suffering."[35]

---

24   *SKS* 5, 420–1 / *TD*, 44.
25   *SKS* 9, 139 / *WL*, 137–8.
26   *SKS* 8, 301 / *UD*, 205–6.
27   *SKS* 8, 301 / *UD*, 206.
28   *SKS* 8, 302 / *UD*, 207.
29   *SKS* 10, 91 / *CD*, 82.
30   *SKS* 10, 96 / *CD*, 88.
31   *SKS* 11, 26 / *WA*, 21.
32   *SKS* 12, 144 / *PC*, 141.
33   *SKS* 10, 192 / *CD*, 182.
34   *SKS* 10, 193 / *CD*, 182.
35   *SKS* 8, 301 / *UD*, 206.

In *Works of Love* it is stated:

> Christianity must not be defended. It is the people who must see to it whether they are
> able to defend themselves and justify to themselves what they choose when Christianity
> terrifyingly, as it once did, offers them the choice and terrifyingly compels them to
> choose: either to be offended or to accept Christianity.[36]

Here, Kierkegaard emphasizes that there is a radical choice between being offended
and having faith. A similar passage can be found in *Practice in Christianity*:

> That is, he himself makes it clear that in relation to him there can be no question of any
> demonstrating, that we do not come to him by means of demonstrations, that there is no
> *direct* transition to becoming Christian, that demonstrations can at best serve to make a
> person aware, so that made aware he can now come to the point: whether he will believe
> or he will be offended....Only in the choice is the heart disclosed...whether a person
> will believe or be offended.[37]

In another passage from *Practice in Christianity*, the connection of choice with the
disclosure of the personality is further emphasized, when Anti-Climacus writes, "as
he is choosing, together with what he chooses, he himself is disclosed."[38] The idea
that a person becomes disclosed in his or her choices is also well elaborated in *Works
of Love*, although in a different context, namely, that of the theme that love believes
all things:

> Mistrustingly to *believe* nothing at all (which is entirely different from *knowledge* about
> the equilibrium of opposite possibilities) and lovingly to *believe* all things are not a
> cognition, nor a cognitive conclusion, but a choice that occurs when knowledge has
> placed the opposite possibilities in equilibrium; and in this choice, which, to be sure, is
> in the form of a judgment of others, the one judging becomes disclosed.[39]

It is also explained in *Practice in Christianity* that it is the impossibility of direct
communication that constitutes the necessity and importance of choice:

> If someone says directly: I am God; the father and I are one, this is direct communication.
> But if the person who says it, the communicator, is this individual human being, an
> individual human being just like others, then this communication is not quite entirely
> direct, because it is not entirely direct that an individual human being should be God—
> whereas what he says is entirely direct. Because of the communicator the communication
> contains a contradiction, it becomes indirect communication; it confronts you with a
> choice: whether you will believe him or not.[40]

---

[36]   *SKS* 9, 199 / *WL*, 200–1.
[37]   *SKS* 12, 104 / *PC*, 96.
[38]   *SKS* 12, 131 / *PC*, 127.
[39]   *SKS* 9, 236 / *WL*, 234.
[40]   *SKS* 12, 138 / *PC*, 134. A few pages later this connection is affirmed: "There is no
direct communication and no direct reception: there is a choice" (*SKS* 12, 143–4 / *PC*, 140).

In a similar fashion, the relation of choice and redoubling comes into play. In the context of redoubling, Kierkegaard states that a "self can truly draw another self to itself only through a choice."[41] Similarly it is stated, "he [Christ] wants to draw the human being to himself, but in order truly to draw him to himself he wants to draw him only as a free being to himself, that is, through a choice."[42]

III.

To summarize: in the second part of *Either/Or* the pseudonym Judge William offers an extensive account of his understanding of choice. An analysis of this account revealed a fundamental asymmetry between the aesthetic and the ethical, and prompted questions about the consistency of Judge William's emphasis on choice with his conception of the ethical. In several later writings a different understanding of choice is elaborated which stresses the importance of choice for faith. Even though these later works do not include an extensive discussion of the term, they reveal an intriguing understanding of choice that is closely connected with several other important concepts in Kierkegaard's later authorship.

See also Aesthetic/Aesthetics; Anxiety; Communication/Indirect Communication; Despair; Ethical; Faith; Imitation; Offense; Religious; Repentance; Redoubling.

---

[41]   *SKS* 12, 163 / *PC*, 159.
[42]   *SKS* 12, 164 / *PC*, 160.

Christ

Leo Stan

Christ or **Jesus Christ** (*Jesus*—noun; *Christus*—noun)

The name Jesus was imported into English from the Latin *Iesus*, which is a mere transliteration of the Greek Ἰησοῦς. The latter is a cognate of the original Hebrew name, Yeshua, which in its turn represents the contraction of Yehoshua, "Yahweh is salvation." Accordingly, Joseph is told by the angel of the Lord to name Mary's divine child "Jesus, for he will save his people from their sins."[1] As to the appellation "Christ,"[2] it originates from the Latin *Christus* and the Greek Χριστός (the anointed one), which is the title the disciples attributed to Jesus upon the realization that he was the Messiah or the promised liberator.[3] More often than not, in the New Testament Χριστός is used as Jesus' other name.[4]

Kierkegaard embraces Christ as both the redemptive embodied deity and the suffering exemplar, who posits the possibility of deliverance as well as the task of imitation.[5] Thus, while strictly abiding by the letter of the Christian doctrine, he endorses the godly qualities of Christ, but he also insists—this time in step with the Nicene Creed—that Christ's genuine divinity cannot be separated from his humanity. Given the soteriological orientation of his thought, the references to the redeeming exemplar literally pervade Kierkegaard's entire literary *corpus*. However, the works wherein Christ takes center stage are *Philosophical Fragments*, *Upbuilding Discourses in Various Spirits*, *Works of Love*, *Christian Discourses*, *Two Ethical-Religious Essays*, *Three Discourses at the Communion on Fridays*, *Practice in Christianity*, and *Judge for Yourself!*[6]

As a consistently Christian author, Kierkegaard does not hesitate to proclaim Jesus Christ as God incarnate or *the* truth.[7] From a Trinitarian standpoint, this means

---

[1]   Matthew 1:21.

[2]   *Ordbog over det danske Sprog*, vols. 1–28, published by the Society for Danish Language and Literature, Copenhagen: Gyldendal 1918–56, vol. 11, columns 418–19.

[3]   See Mark 8:29 and Acts 5:42.

[4]   See, for instance, Romans 5:6.

[5]   *SKS* 16, 237–8 / *JFY*, 191.

[6]   The theme at hand is tackled to a relatively lesser extent in *The Concept of Irony*, *Eighteen Upbuilding Discourses*, and the *Concluding Unscientific Postscript*.

[7]   See, amongst other instances, *SKS* 10, 110 / *CD*, 98; *SKS* 8, 319–20, 360 / *UD*, 217, 263; *SKS* 11, 65–6, 68, 77 / *WA*, 59–60, 63, 73; *SKS* 12, 163 / *PC*, 159.

that Jesus is consubstantial with the absolute Creator.[8] In a doctrinally correct fashion, Kierkegaard also identifies him with "the Way and the Truth and the Life,"[9] or with the heavenly Son whose will never departed from that of the Father.[10] Thirdly, Christ is the one and only redeemer,[11] the sole hope for the irrevocable annihilation of fallenness. Following the Johannine tradition, Kierkegaard calls Jesus the Word or the highest name of the absolute.[12] As the channel for God's grace,[13] Christ represents the summit of creation[14] or, as Kierkegaard poetically puts it, the immortal sun of mankind.[15] Jesus' divinity can also be glimpsed from his ascension to heaven,[16] which is yet another quintessentially Christian postulate of Kierkegaard's fideism.

To wit, Kierkegaard ascribes to Christ the three absolute qualities of God: omnipresence, omniscience, and all-powerfulness. He points to the Savior's ubiquity when dealing with the ways in which genuine followers can aspire to the celestial realm.[17] Moreover, after the heavenly ascent, Christ becomes contemporary with everything in history; this grants him a perspective on the world that no one else could ever enjoy.[18] Kierkegaard goes further and views Jesus as omniscient as God in the awareness of sin and human evil.[19] Thus, it is by virtue of this absolute comprehension that Jesus prophetically knew his earthly fate.[20] The Redeemer is all-knowing from an additional standpoint since he has full access to the innermost recesses of every single individual.[21]

In view of the third attribute mentioned above, Kierkegaard declares that the Father and the Son share the same absolute authority.[22] Yet, unlike God, Christ, by becoming a historical individual, freely chooses to hide completely his divine fortitude (and therefore become utterly unrecognizable) in order to test one's faith.[23] With that in mind, Kierkegaard unrelentingly underscores the incommensurability between Christ's all-powerfulness and immediacy. His argument is that, were it not so, the struggle of faith would have been severely diluted since it is far easier to

---

[8]   *SKS* 8, 349, 351 / *UD*, 250, 253; *SKS* 11, 61 / *WA*, 55; *SKS* 12, 88, 126, / *PC*, 76, 119; *SKS* 22, 355, NB14:19 / *JP* 6, 6528; *SKS* 20, 234, NB2:249 / *KJN* 4, 234.

[9]   *SKS* 10, 21 / *CD*, 9.

[10]   *SKS* 8, 351, 360 / *UD*, 253, 263; *SKS* 9, 104 / *WL*, 99.

[11]   *SKS* 12, 108 / *PC*, 100; *SKS* 8, 319 / *UD*, 217.

[12]   *SKS* 12, 24 / *PC*, 14; *SKS* 8, 326–7 / *UD*, 225–6.

[13]   *SKS* 11, 279 / *WA*, 143; *SKS* 10, 185 / *CD*, 174. However, this attribute is shared with the Holy Spirit; see *SKS* 23, 80, NB15:114 / *JP* 2, 1654.

[14]   *SKS* 8, 351 / *UD*, 253; *SKS* 17, 222, DD:11 / *KJN* 1, 214.

[15]   *SKS* 10, 291 / *CD*, 272.

[16]   *SKS* 12, 167, 182 / *PC*, 163, 182.

[17]   *SKS* 12, 149–253 / *PC*, 144–262; *SKS* 20, 233–4, NB2:247 / *KJN* 4, 233–4. See also John 12:32.

[18]   *SKS* 12, 169 / *PC*, 166.

[19]   *SKS* 5, 77 / *EUD*, 67.

[20]   *SKS* 10, 84–5, 192, 266 / *CD*, 75–6, 182, 252; *SKS* 13, 83 / *FSE*, 60; *SKS* 20, 226, NB2:222 / *KJN* 4, 225.

[21]   *SKS* 10, 290–1 / *CD*, 271–2; *SKS* 11, 79 / *WA*, 74.

[22]   *SKS* 11, 105–6 / *WA*, 101–2.

[23]   *SKS* 12, 132–7 / *PC*, 127–33.

believe after having physically witnessed the Savior's glory. As it happens, it is immeasurably more difficult to appropriate the absurd faith that the absolute ruler of creation has incarnated himself into a humble servant. So, regardless of the existential difficulties, Christians must believe that the God-man kenotically relinquished his omnipotence[24] and expiated sinfulness through suffering, forsakenness, and death. Be that as it may, by claiming—indeed, pseudonymously—that no one was ever privy to Christ's splendor during his earthly journey,[25] Kierkegaard runs the risk of contradicting the famous episode of transfiguration, to which all synoptic Gospels unambiguously testify.[26]

Inasmuch as Kierkegaard's thought is fundamentally soteriological, the most salient function of the God-man is that of savior. In this regard, Kierkegaard again lacks all trace of skepticism; he is sure that Christ "came into the world out of love *in order* to save the world."[27] Obviously, the savior, while permanently concerned for humanity's reconciliation with God after the advent of sin,[28] is able to effectuate redemption by virtue of his loving divinity.[29] In this precise sense, he represents the selfless giver of mercy,[30] the forgiver *par excellence*,[31] while his disposition to pardon is relentless and thus open to everyone.[32]

The Kierkegaardian redeemer is therefore the suffering deity who atones for all the evil in world,[33] thereby restoring humankind to its original dignity. As holy, the immaculate Christ[34] is the only one able to expunge the maculation of sin. Christ's atonement is a kenotic self-sacrifice,[35] the contradictory crux of which gives added momentum to Kierkegaard's absurdist fideism.[36] As transcendent atoner, Christ exceeds the boundaries of earthly justice and guilt: once faced with the verdict of crucifixion, he refuses to accuse and expects love instead of mere retaliation.[37] After all, the divine *agape* can never be compatible with a vindictive ethos. Still, one has to keep in mind that sinfulness is not completely eradicated by the conciliatory gestures of Jesus. The savior posits the generic *possibility* of redemption, the actualization of

[24]   *SKS* 16, 221 / *JFY*, 172–3. See also *SKS* 13, 83–4 / *FSE*, 61.
[25]   *SKS* 12, 17 / *PC*, 9.
[26]   Matthew 17:1–8; Mark 9:2–8; Luke 9:28–36. See also John 1:14; 2:11; 17:24; 2 Peter 1:16–18.
[27]   *SKS* 22, 355, NB14:19 / *JP* 6, 6528. See also *SKS* 11, 278–9 / *WA*, 142.
[28]   *SKS* 12, 173 / *PC*, 170–1; *SKS* 10, 305 / *CD*, 284–5; *SKS* 12, 295–6 / *WA*, 181.
[29]   *SKS* 12, 141 / *PC*, 137–8; *SKS* 12, 295–6 / *WA*, 181; *SKS* 10, 283 / *CD*, 266; *SKS* 12, 17–8, 29, 155, 161 / *PC*, 9–10, 18, 151, 157; *SKS* 20, 233–4, NB2:247.a / *KJN* 4, 233–4. *SKS* 22, 355, NB14:19 / *JP* 6, 6528.
[30]   *SKS* 10, 304 / *CD*, 283.
[31]   *SKS* 8, 345–6 / *UD*, 246–7.
[32]   *SKS* 10, 306 / *CD*, 285; *SKS* 11, 278–9 / *WA*, 142–3.
[33]   *SKS* 10, 300 / *CD*, 280; *SKS* 11, 258–9 / *WA*, 123; *SKS* 12, 271 / *WA*, 158.
[34]   *SKS* 11, 258 / *WA*, 123; *SKS* 8, 366–7 / *UD*, 269–70.
[35]   For a lyrical illustration of this point see *SKS* 4, 233–40 / *PF*, 26–35.
[36]   *SKS* 11, 212 / *SUD*, 100; *SKS* 7, 186–7 / *CUP1*, 203–4; *Pap*. VI B 45 / *JP* 3, 3085.
[37]   *SKS* 11, 258–9 / *WA*, 123; *SKS* 10, 300 / *CD*, 280.

which requires, however, endless endeavors and struggles on the part of every single individual.[38]

The upbuilding effect of Christ's atonement is rather existential or psychological. That is to say, similarly to the Holy Spirit, the suffering God-man constitutes an indubitable comfort throughout the believer's stormy life and ceaseless tribulations. This comfort can take various forms. For instance, Christ is the only assurance of the individual battling temptations.[39] Likewise, Christ ceaselessly helps the burdened by assuming their misfortunes,[40] and he does so out of unconditional love. Since his ordeals are unmatchable, Christ will always be there in the changes of fortune of the faithful,[41] whereas his death is "the infinite comfort, the infinite headstart with which the striver begins."[42]

The eschatological dimension plays a distinct role in Kierkegaard's overall soteriology. Although Jesus is explicitly recognized as the Messiah,[43] Kierkegaard develops the implications of this quality in a rather idiosyncratic manner. First he puts forward the predictable claim that the certainty of Jesus's second coming is acquired only through faith.[44] Second, he warns the reader that until the final revelation Christ will persist in abasement, and that despite the fact that the savior fervently wishes to erect the city of God in the midst of this world.[45] In the same vein, Kierkegaard observes that any proclamation about the expected kingdom is voiced from the viewpoint of the eternal, not the temporal,[46] and that is why Jesus rebutted the mundane values which the sinful world revered. Thus, the Messiah motif offers Kierkegaard ample opportunity to attack the spiritual decadence of contemporary Christendom.[47]

The messianic resurfaces in relation to the Last Judgment, which is a topic of utmost importance in Kierkegaard's eyes. Christ, according to Kierkegaard, grants an undeniable reality to eternal life and his authority over the latter is equally compelling.[48] Even if Christ gave by his very sufferings and death an initial verdict on the world, his definitive judgment will be brought to completion only in the *parousia*.[49] Until then, every individual is to decide between perdition and salvation,

---

[38]   *SKS* 16, 198 / *JFY*, 147. For this very reason Kierkegaard remarks that, although eternally victorious, Christ will impart the fruits of his triumph only in eternity. *SKS* 12, 182 / *PC*, 182; *SKS* 10, 115 / *CD*, 103.

[39]   *SKS* 11, 256 / *WA*, 120.

[40]   *SKS* 8, 331–46 / *UD*, 230–47.

[41]   *SKS* 11, 254–5 / *WA*, 118–19; *SKS* 18, 131, HH:11 / *KJN* 2, 122–3.

[42]   *SKS* 12, 272 / *WA*, 159.

[43]   *SKS* 8, 319 / *UD*, 217; *SKS* 11, 66 / *WA*, 60.

[44]   *SKS* 12, 39 / *PC*, 24.

[45]   *SKS* 16, 223–4 / *JFY*, 175.

[46]   *SKS* 11, 66 / *WA*, 60.

[47]   See in this regard Kierkegaard's commentary on Luke 18:8, where he argues that, had he returned today, Jesus would have been baffled by the lack of faith and devotion created by collective conformity and the obdurate pursuit of mundane well-being. *SKS* 14, 174 / *M*, 43; *SKS* 14, 198 / *M*, 58.

[48]   *SKS* 8, 319 / *UD*, 217.

[49]   *SKS* 12, 285 / *WA*, 169; *SKS* 12, 181 / *PC*, 181; *SKS* 17, 262, DD:142 / *KJN* 1, 253; *SKS* 20, 395–6, NB5:56 / *KJN* 4, 395–6.

and if one decides to pursue the redemptive path, the urgency of following the religious injunctions is even higher.[50]

Now, concerning the earthly life of Christ, Kierkegaard dwells almost exclusively on its mature side. Nonetheless, he finds time to marvel at the humble circumstances of the savior's birth,[51] which he takes as a sign of exceptional obedience to the only master worth acquiescing to, namely, God. Though it occurred in lowliness and isolation, Jesus's birth is shrouded in superhuman glory, having the full consent of the Father.[52] At the same time, this miraculous event bespeaks Jesus's detachment or alienation from worldliness and, indirectly, his full submissiveness to the will of God.[53]

With regard to Christ's missionary period, Kierkegaard divides it into two phases. The initial one "began with his being idolized by the people, while everything called the established order, everything that had any power and influence, spitefully but cravenly and secretly laid the trap for him."[54] In the second phase, people's enthusiasm faded away, being replaced by disappointment and an ardent desire for revenge.[55]

In general, Kierkegaard's interest orbits around the Golgotha incident and the events immediately related to it. That is probably because of his adamant insistence on the connection between Jesus's sufferings and the dutiful, pathos-filled imitation of the exemplar. This particular aspect surmounts in spiritual and edifying import any other facet of Jesus' humanity. To exemplify, for Kierkegaard, one cannot overemphasize that Christ "relinquished the glory he had before the foundation of the world was laid…in order to suffer."[56] Thus, the physical, psychological, as well as spiritual afflictions endured by Christ seem to be the only truths worthy of remembering vis-à-vis his earthly existence. In Kierkegaard's sobering words, "every day of [Jesus'] life was the burial day for him who was destined to be the sacrifice."[57] Predictably enough, the spectrum and variety of the exemplar's calvary is unbelievably broad. Kierkegaard painstakingly depicts how Christ was misunderstood, laughed at, scorned, spat upon, insulted, frightfully isolated, tortured, scourged, betrayed by his closest friends, and finally put to death.[58] With that in mind, it is no wonder that the Kierkegaardian Christ appears radically heterogeneous to each and every worldly power. In fact, compared to the sinless exemplar, worldliness

---

[50]   *SKS* 10, 304 / *CD*, 283.
[51]   *SKS* 12, 53–4 / *PC*, 40; *SKS* 5, 208–9, 271 / *EUD*, 207–8, 277; *SKS* 27, 108, Papir 78 / *JP* 1, 276; *SKS* 22, 245, NB12:169 / *JP* 1, 344.
[52]   *SKS* 16, 209–10 / *JFY*, 161; *SKS* 27, 281, Papir 285 / *JP* 1, 283.
[53]   *SKS* 16, 209, 212, 216, 227 / *JFY*, 160–1, 163, 167, 179. See also Kierkegaard's brief mention of Jesus' circumcision, which gives him the opportunity to expand upon the patient expectancy of deliverance. *SKS* 5, 208–24 / *EUD*, 207–26.
[54]   *SKS* 12, 67 / *PC*, 55.
[55]   *SKS* 12, 67 / *PC*, 55–6.
[56]   *SKS* 8, 349 / *UD*, 250. See also *SKS* 16, 217 / *JFY*, 167–8.
[57]   *SKS* 12, 172 / *PC*, 169.
[58]   *SKS* 8, 332 / *UD*, 231; *SKS* 12, 88, 89, 112–13, 141–2, 157–8, 178 / *PC*, 75–6, 77–8, 104–5, 138, 153–4, 176; *SKS* 10, 272, 296–7 / *CD*, 259, 276–7; *SKS* 13, 82–3 / *FSE*, 59–60; *SKS* 16, 209 / *JFY*, 160; *SKS* 13, 378 / *M*, 316.

as a whole is sheer ungodliness.[59] And since God is his unique ally, Christ remains more powerful than all the world's powers combined.[60]

To conclude: as savior, forgiver, Messiah, atoner, comforter, and eschatological judge, Christ directly shares in the absolute transcendence or infinite difference of God. He is, in short, "the true Son of God [who] is the true God and one with the Father."[61] However, as the suffering exemplar, the fully human Jesus Christ enters history, agonizes, and submits to his brutal end, thereby establishing the necessity of imitation through abnegation, suffering for the truth, and unconditional obedience to God. As a result, Christ presents us with an essentially paradoxical otherness because he perfectly unites two qualitatively different realms, the human and the divine.[62] In Kierkegaard's words, the fact that Jesus completes "the unity of being God and an individual human being in a historically actual situation,"[63] constitutes "the greatest possible, the infinitely qualitative contradiction."[64]

The fundamental implication here is twofold. On the one hand, as divine the God-man is *eternally* and *qualitatively* different from all humans.[65] On the other hand, although he fully resembles us through his incarnate status, suffering, and pathos, Christ is the *impeccable* exemplar, whom absolutely no follower could equal. Christ's humanity is, therefore, ideal, that is to say, never fully attainable (or repeatable) by any past, present, or future disciple.[66] And yet, even though it reconfirms the creaturely powerlessness in matters of salvation,[67] Christ's human perfection remains momentous in ensuring the endless relationality to the human creature. It is by virtue of Christ's (and the Holy Spirit's) invisible, albeit sustained and all-powerful, guidance, that all religious tasks, no matter how excruciating, become bearable and even wishful, given the ultimate bliss of their promise.

See also Atonement/Reconciliation; Contemporaneity; Defiance; Despair; Dogma/ Doctrine; Faith; Forgiveness; God; Grace; History; Holy Spirit; Humility; Immanence/Transcendence; Immortality; Imitation; Love; Martyrdom/Persecution; Miracles; Offense; Paradox; Passion/Pathos; Salvation/Eternal Happiness/Highest Good; Sin; Striving; Teacher; Witness; World; Worldliness.

[59]   *SKS* 16, 218–9 / *JFY*, 169–70; *SKS* 14, 155–6 / *M*, 31–2; *SKS* 11, 69–70 / *WA*, 64.
[60]   *SKS* 16, 220 / *JFY*, 171.
[61]   *SKS* 18, 353, KK:5 / *KJN* 2, 323 (my translation). See also *SKS* 21, 118, NB7:78 / *KJN* 5, 123.
[62]   *SKS* 18, 83, FF:36 / *KJN* 2, 76; *SKS* 20, 328, NB4:81 / *KJN* 4, 329–30.
[63]   *SKS* 12, 128 / *PC*, 123.
[64]   *SKS* 12, 135 / *PC*, 131. See also *SKS* 21, 301, NB10:85 / *KJN* 5, 311–12.
[65]   *SKS* 8, 197 / *UD*, 92; *SKS* 12, 272 / *WA*, 159; *SKS* 9, 105 / *WL*, 101; *SKS* 10, 324 / *CD*, 299.
[66]   *SKS* 12, 272 / *WA*, 159; *SKS* 9, 104–6 / *WL*, 99–101. For corroboration on this see Hebrews 2:10; 5:9; 7:28.
[67]   *SKS* 10, 324 / *CD*, 300.

Christendom

J. Michael Tilley

Christendom (*Christenhed*—noun)

Christenhed is derived from the title of Jesus, Christ (Χριστός). Χριστός means "anointed one" and is a Greek translation of the transliterated Hebrew term "Messiah." Its lexical meaning in Danish refers to a people or land that calls itself Christian, understands itself as Christian, and is associated with Christian traditions.[1] *Christenhed* is translated by the English term "Christendom," and it should not be confused with the Danish term *Christendom*, which is translated as "Christianity." Although Kierkegaard uses the term too frequently to examine each use of it, his understanding of it is fairly consistent even as his relationship to Christendom changes. He universally disparages Christendom—which he sees as embodied in his own nineteenth-century Denmark—because it is an illusory expression of Christianity, but he treats it differently in the later polemical writings. Throughout most of his authorship Kierkegaard seems modestly optimistic about the prospect of introducing genuine Christianity into Christendom, but this optimism wanes in his later polemical writings.

Christendom (Christianity) means that Christ has authority, and he is that in terms of which other things are understood, whereas *Christenhed* (Christendom) is about self-identification and how Christian people collectively refer to themselves. Kierkegaard expresses disdain for the merely verbal character of Christendom since it abandons what it means to become a Christian. " 'Christendom' is a pack of blather that has fastened itself to Christianity like a cobweb on fruit," and now the cobweb has become confused with the fruit itself.[2] Christendom blathers on "as if this were being a Christian."[3]

The notion that Christendom is merely nominally Christian rather than genuinely so is also part of Kierkegaard's distinction between it and the true church. Christendom, he says, "is by no means Christ's Church."[4] Anti-Climacus distinguishes between the current existing, temporal church—the church militant—and the church triumphant. The church will indeed triumph outside of temporality in

---

[1]   *Ordbog over det danske Sprog*, vols. 1–28, published by the Society for Danish Language and Literature, Copenhagen: Gyldendal 1918–56, vol. 11, columns 413–14.
[2]   *SKS* 13, 268 / *M*, 215.
[3]   *SKS* 13, 267 / *M*, 214.
[4]   *SKS* 13, 268 / *M*, 215.

the *eschaton*,[5] but established Christendom is the ultimate result of thinking of the temporal church as triumphant in this world.[6]

Christendom not only misunderstands the nature of the church, but it also devalues the character of faith and establishes an unhealthy alliance with the world. Because Christianity is thought of as having already achieved its success, established Christendom disdains external show and promotes "hidden inwardness."[7] As a result, it is merely "play[ing] at having faith," whereas New Testament Christianity "understand[s] something very specific by having faith; to have faith is to venture out as decisively as possible for a human being, breaking with everything, with what a human being naturally loves, breaking, in order to save his life...."[8] If Christianity is the same as Christendom, then earnestness and passionate faith are not genuine requirements.

Likewise, Christianity involves a fundamental break with the world—it always entails the possibility of offending the world. "In established Christendom," however, "there is no danger connected with being a Christian."[9] " 'Christendom' is this nauseating dalliance, to want to remain completely and totally in finiteness and then—to make off with the promises of Christianity."[10] Since there is no break with the world, there is, of course, no possibility of offense.[11]

Christendom's purely nominal character also means that it is understood primarily geographically or sociologically rather than religiously. Kierkegaard claimed the spiritual malaise of his society was not "lodged in externalities" but could be addressed by recovering the insight that "Christianity is inwardness, inward deepening."[12] Christendom, by contrast, is known by its externals—what it calls itself and its form of worship—rather than its inward reality.[13] Christianity as inwardness is not indifferent to externals—that is, if "the forms under which one has to live are not the most perfect...they can be improved"[14]—but a person can also be a Christian "under the most imperfect conditions."[15] Christendom is concerned

---

5   *SKS* 12, 206 / *PC*, 209.
6   Anti-Climacus appears to use two terms—the established church and established Christendom—interchangeably in this text.
7   *SKS* 12, 210 / *PC*, 214.
8   *SKS* 13, 267 / *M*, 214.
9   *SKS*, 12, 243 / *PC*, 250.
10   *SKS* 13, 268 / *M*, 215.
11   *SKS*, 12, 120 / *PC*, 112.
12   *SKS*, 14, 112 / *COR*, 53.
13   The idea that Christendom embraces faith as hidden inwardness and that it is also primarily concerned with externals may seem inconsistent, but Kierkegaard seems to have in mind two different ideas here. That Christendom embraces faith as "hidden inwardness" means that faith will be purely private with no impact on the world—it is like a Kantian thing-in-itself that is theoretically implied but impossible to cognize, recognize, or become discursively available. This view is consistent with thinking that Christendom also focuses on the phenomena of Christianity—including calling oneself a Christian and participating in church services—but misses the passion and interest necessary for genuine Christianity.
14   *SKS*, 14, 112 / *COR*, 53.
15   *SKS*, 14, 112 / *COR*, 54.

primarily with its outward condition, whereas Christianity is concerned with the inner religious condition.

Given this characterization, it is possible for entire peoples and nations to be "Christian" in Christendom. They can express the external features of Christianity independently of an inner source. When an inner commitment to Christianity loses its importance and it is only necessary to call oneself "Christian," the result is "Christendom" where "millions upon millions…enter into Christianity all wrong. Instead of entering as an individual, one comes alone with the others. The others are Christians—*ergo*, I am, too, and am a Christian in the same sense as the others are."[16] In Christendom, people do not become Christians by following Christ; rather "we are all Christians by birth."[17] Kierkegaard goes so far as to say that "The kind of existences manifested by the millions in Christendom has absolutely no relation to the New Testament…."[18] Confusing the external appearance of Christianity with the inner reality ultimately results in a situation where, even though "a man's whole life is secularized, his every thought from morning until evening, his waking and dreaming," it still remains the case that "he is, of course, a Christian, for he lives, to be sure, in 'Christendom.' "[19] For this reason, Kierkegaard claims, "Christianity has been abolished in Christendom…."[20]

Kierkegaard recognized that it would be difficult to introduce genuine Christianity into a culture that already considers itself Christian. Thus, he sees a need for a new Socrates who does not have faith just as the original Socrates lacked wisdom.[21] In order to introduce Christianity into Christendom, the missionary must be an outsider to it. "It is the concept of 'Christendom' which must be reformed; what has to be done is the dialectical opposite of introducing Christianity and yet in another sense similar: to introduce *Christianity—into Christendom*."[22] To be a new Socrates is to remove the illusion that Christendom is genuine Christianity, and it requires that the new Socrates use indirect communication.[23]

Kierkegaard applies these themes and categories to his own work, and he believes that it is his task to introduce Christianity into Christendom. He, like Socrates, refuses to *say* that he is a Christian but that is because it involves a category mistake. It treats the God-relationship as "a merely human standard or within the sphere of human comparison."[24] Kierkegaard is not denying that he has a God-relationship, nor that the relation is "Christian." Rather, he is denying any status to externals, to self-identification. Kierkegaard interprets (or perhaps offers a revisionist history of) his own earlier pseudonymous authorship as forms of indirect communication with the implicit aim of uncovering the illusion that all are Christians.[25] Kierkegaard

---

16   *SKS* 23, 82, NB15:116 / *JP* 1, 390.
17   *SKS* 25, 228, NB28:18 / *JP* 1, 402.
18   *SKS*, 13, 268 / *M*, 215.
19   *SKS* 26, 122, NB32:5 / *JP* 1, 407.
20   *SKS* 22, 94, NB11:160 / *JP* 1, 383.
21   *SKS* 20, 318 NB4:65 / *KJN* 4, 318–19.
22   *SKS* 22, 314 NB13:66 / *JP* 1, 388.
23   *SKS* 16, 24–5 / *PV*, 42–3.
24   *Pap.* X–5 B 107, 294–5 / *PV*, 135.
25   *SKS* 16, 24–6 / *PV*, 42–4.

contrasts his own work as the new Socrates with "enthusiasts" who make "an assault on Christendom; [making] a big noise [and denouncing] nearly all as not being Christians."[26] The aim of such "fanatics" is to be polemical and set themselves up as ideal Christians, but Kierkegaard refuses to set himself up as the ideal.

During his late polemic against the Danish People's Church, Kierkegaard's approach to Christendom changes. He offers pointed and explicit critiques of Christendom rather than proceeding indirectly, but he maintains his insistence that he not be called a Christian.[27] Earlier in his authorship he had claimed that a person could be a Christian inwardly despite the influence of Christendom,[28] but in his later polemical writings he no longer sees this as a viable possibility. "To be a Christian in Christendom…is just as impossible as doing gymnastics in a straightjacket."[29] Kierkegaard appears to give up the possibility of a new Socrates, that is, the possibility of introducing Christianity into Christendom. Rather, it must be critiqued and rejected. At the end of the authorship, it appears as if Christianity cannot be redeemed from Christendom. Christendom must be rejected as a simulacrum of genuine New Testament Christianity; it cannot be reformed and genuine Christianity cannot be introduced into it. This shift in attitude is clearly expressed in the final polemical attack against the church, in which Kierkegaard criticizes the entire body of state-appointed clergy,[30] and the politicized character of the Danish State Church itself,[31] seeing no possibility for its reform.[32]

Kierkegaard's criticisms of Christendom are consistent throughout his authorship—it is essentially a geographical and sociological construct that misunderstands the church, faith, and how a Christian ought to relate to the world. Up until his final attack on the Danish State Church, Kierkegaard remained hopeful about the possibility of his own writings serving as an instrument of providence that could once again introduce Christianity into Christendom. At the end, however, Kierkegaard sees no way of becoming a genuine Christian in the cultural context of Christendom.

See also Authority; Christ; Communication/Indirect Communication; Inwardness/ Inward Deepening; Pastor; Spirit; State; Worldliness/Secularism.

---

[26]   *SKS* 16, 24–5 / *PV*, 42.
[27]   *SKS* 13, 266 / *M*, 212.
[28]   *SKS*, 14, 112 / *C*, 54.
[29]   *SKS* 27, 633, Papir 517 / *JP* 1, 409.
[30]   *SKS* 13, 311 / *M*, 255.
[31]   *SKS* 13, 153 / *M*, 111.
[32]   *SKS* 14, 213 / *M*, 69–70.

Church

J. Michael Tilley

Church (*Kirke*—noun)

Kirke is Germanic in origin. Both *Kirke* and "church" are derived from the Koine Greek term κυριακόν, which means "house of the Lord" (probably short for κυριακὸν δῶμα). Its lexical meanings in Danish refer to a place where worship is conducted by Christian believers, a community of religious believers, or an institution that both yields political power and is affiliated with religious believers.[1]

Although the church is discussed in the *Concluding Unscientific Postscript* in reference to Grundtvig,[2] Kierkegaard primarily uses the concept of church in his later writings as he becomes increasingly caustic toward the institution. Kierkegaard rarely distinguishes between the various meanings of the term (for example, the physical building, the community of believers, and the social and political institution), but he develops the concept most fully in *Practice in Christianity* where his explicit characterization of the militant church is the root of his later critiques. In this work, Anti-Climacus compares and discusses the relationship between Christianity and the church. He defends what he describes as the church militant versus both the church triumphant and established Christendom. This section begins with a description of Christ as the victor, who draws people to himself, calls them to struggle, and promises them victory in the struggle. "The place of [Christ's] Church is not here in the world; there is room for it only if it will struggle and by struggling make room for itself to exist."[3] The church is forged in Christ's victory rather than in a teleological goal to which the church must strive. But, "With him it is not as with some other person who once lived, perhaps won some great victory, the results of which we appropriate as a matter of course, whereas nothing is heard from him...."[4] Rather, the life of the church in temporality is book-ended by Christ—his work on the cross and his ascension on the one side and his second coming on the other.[5] It is Christ who constitutes the life of the church—both behind it, as a prototype we are called to emulate, and in front of it in anticipation of the second coming.

---

1   *Ordbog over det danske Sprog*, vols. 1–28, published by the Society for Danish Language and Literature, Copenhagen: Gyldendal 1918–56, vol. 10, columns 358–62.
2   *SKS* 7, 41–52 / *CUP1*, 34–49.
3   *SKS* 12, 198 / *PC*, 201.
4   *SKS* 12, 199 / *PC*, 202.
5   Ibid.

The identification of Christ as a prototype erases the difference between predecessors and subsequent believers, since both enact the very same way of life exemplified by Christ.[6] In this way, the life of the church located in Christ erupts into history in the lives of his followers. The formal and historical unity found in Christ is experienced concretely and given a specific and determinant content in a particular congregational and church setting. This experience is contrasted with "didacticize[d] Christianity" where mere doctrinal statements rather than a holistic, shared way of life forges the truth and life of the church.[7]

The church militant is a normative ideal for the church within temporality to which the nineteenth-century Danish State Church failed to strive, let alone achieve. Anti-Climacus calls Christ's church "the Church militant."[8] He begins to clarify his notion of the church militant by contrasting it with the church triumphant. Treating the temporally existing church as a triumphant church involves three fundamental mistakes: first, it interprets the truth of Christianity as a result rather than as a way.[9] Expressing truth claims and propositions do not express the essence of Christianity. Rather, Christianity is a way of life that emulates the life of Christ. This mistake allows for a second mistake, namely, that in Kierkegaard's Denmark we "are all Christians."[10] This is, perhaps, the chief criticism in the attack literature, and it is informed by a conception of the church militant as well as a critique of the church triumphant. Third, treating the current existing, temporal church as the church triumphant is an attempt to take hold of what can only be achieved through a lengthy process of discipleship, suffering and sacrifice. "[T]his illusion, a Church triumphant, is linked to the human impatience that wants to take in advance that which comes later...."[11] In short, conceiving of the church in temporality as the church triumphant abolishes Christianity because it "assumes that the time of struggling is over, that the Church, although it is still in this world, has nothing more about or for which to struggle."[12] Over time, the idea of the church triumphant manifests itself as "established Christendom." An established church stands on an assumed victory just as the church triumphant does,[13] but in established Christendom, the church disdains external show and promotes "hidden inwardness."[14] According to Anti-Climacus, the church triumphant is appropriate outside of temporality in the *eschaton*,[15] but the established church or established Christendom is the ultimate result of thinking of the temporal church as triumphant in this world.[16] In the church triumphant, the proclamation of one's Christianity is greeted by the world with

---

6   *SKS* 12, 203 / *PC*, 207.
7   *SKS* 12, 200–3 / *PC*, 203–6.
8   *SKS* 12, 205–6, 208 / *PC*, 209, 212.
9   *SKS* 12, 206 / *PC*, 209–10.
10 *SKS* 12, 207 / *PC*, 211.
11 Ibid.
12 *SKS* 12, 208 / *PC*, 211.
13 *SKS* 12, 207 / *PC*, 211.
14 *SKS* 12, 210 / *PC*, 214.
15 *SKS* 12, 206 / *PC*, 209.
16 Anti-Climacus appears to use the two terms—the established church and established Christendom—interchangeably in this text.

enthusiasm and support, whereas in established Christendom, where it is assumed that all are Christians, proclaiming one's Christianity is like making "a special claim that he is a human being; since that, after all, is wanting to bring to consciousness a presupposition that is once and for all and by all assumed and underlies everything."[17]

This notion is precisely the opposite of what the church should be: the church militant. Anti-Climacus contrasts the three mistakes concerning the church triumphant with three characteristics of the church militant. First, the church militant struggles and it *is* only when it struggles. It is always in *becoming* and never *is* on this side of eternity. The church militant, "can truly endure only by struggling—that is, by every moment battling to endure."[18] Second, the church is in the world, but not of the world. The church triumphant and established Christendom mistakenly view Christianity as a kingdom of the world. Denying this notion, however, does not entail that the church militant is not in the world as a community of believers. Rather, it must be in the world, since "[Christianity] is certainly a kingdom in this world, but not of this world, that is, it is militant."[19] Third, being the church militant necessarily involves suffering. It requires that one "express being Christian within an environment that is the opposite of being Christian."[20] As a result, if someone "lived in a Church militant," then "insult and ridicule would assail me…there death would be unavoidable."[21] This notion of the church is intimately connected to Kierkegaard's attack on the church in the polemical literature. Both Kierkegaard's polemics against the notion that everyone is a Christian and his proclamation that Christianity must involve suffering—two of the most prominent themes in the attack literature—are explicitly tied to the concept of the church militant in *Practice in Christianity*.

Between the publication of *Practice in Christianity* and the publication of the polemical literature of 1854–55, it is clear that the tone, method, and framing of these issues fundamentally change. The content of *Practice in Christianity* is presented by a pseudonym as a way to defend the establishment (even in its criticisms of the establishment), but the content of the polemical literature is presented in a shrill tone and as a critique of the establishment. Kierkegaard explicitly articulates this shift in the preface to the second edition of *Practice in Christianity*:

> My earlier thought was: if the established order can be defended, this is the only way to do it: …[Christianity] acknowledges the Christian requirement, confesses its own distance, yet without being able to be called a striving in the direction of coming closer to the requirement, but resorts to grace….Now, however, I have completely made up my mind on two things: both that the established order is Christianly indefensible, that every day it lasts it is Christianly a crime; and that in this way one does not have the right to draw on grace.[22]

---

17   *SKS* 12, 211 / *PC*, 215.
18   *SKS* 12, 208 / *PC*, 212.
19   *SKS* 12, 208 / *PC*, 211.
20   *SKS* 12, 208 / *PC*, 212.
21   *SKS* 12, 209 / *PC*, 213.
22   *SKS* 14, 213 / *M*, 69–70.

This passage shows the continuity and the break between *Practice in Christianity* and the polemical literature. Common themes are developed and advanced, but they are understood in radically different ways. According to the polemical literature, the problem with the People's Church of Denmark is that it is neither consistent with nor seeks to be consistent with New Testament Christianity. "[W]hat is most decisively Christian [is] what is too inconvenient for us human beings, what would make our lives strenuous, prevent us from enjoying life—this about dying to the world, about voluntary renunciation, about hating oneself, about suffering for the doctrine, etc."[23] Christianity involves voluntary suffering[24] and a decisive break with the world.[25] The People's Church fails to embody this form of Christianity for at least three reasons. First, Kierkegaard claims that it confuses church and state. The union of church and state removes the risk of suffering inherent to Christianity by making it difficult, if not dangerous, for non-Christians rather than Christians. "What Christianity needs is not the suffocating protection of the state; no, it needs fresh air, persecution, and—God's protection. That state only does harm; it averts persecution....Above all, rescue Christianity from the state...."[26] Second, the Danish State Church makes it seem as if everyone is a Christian just because one is baptized and a citizen of the state. In short, New Testament Christianity has been abolished because it has become a characteristic of all Danish citizens as a matter of natural birth. Third, since one only needs to be baptized to be a Christian, there is no need to follow Christ's example in one's own life in order to be a Christian.[27]

There is a shift in Kierkegaard's attitude toward the Danish People's Church from *Practice in Christianity*—where he attempts to clarify the true meaning of the concept of church—to the more caustic and critical engagement we find in the polemical literature. In the former, he points to the need to acknowledge the perils of Christendom for the church and Christianity; in the latter, he accuses the Danish People's Church of being complicit in the substitution of Christendom for Christianity.

See also Christendom; State; Pastor.

23   *SKS* 14, 123 / *M*, 4.
24   *SKS* 12, 117 / *PC*, 109; *SKS* 13, 261 / *M*, 206.
25   *SKS* 14, 138 / *M*, 17.
26   *SKS* 13, 206 / *M*, 158.
27   *SKS* 13, 173 / *M*, 129.